Dad,
Happy 50th Birthday! Aren't you impressed, I picked out this book for you!
Lots of love and hugs from your favourite daughter
Claire x x x x

HAPPY 50TH
FATHER FROM
YOUR FAVOURITE
SON
LOVE
Paul x

The coat of arms of the Highland Railway, consisting of the shields of the City of Perth (left) and of the Burgh of Inverness set in front of an eagle, all encircled by a garter

A fine view about 1912 of the Highland shed at Perth with (l. to r.) Glenbarry 2-4-0 35 *Isla Bank*, Small Goods 27, 119 *Loch Insh* (with Drummond chimney), Big Goods 117 (with smokebox wings removed), 146 *Skibo Castle* and 126 *Loch Tummel*.

(*Photo: A.G. Ellis collection*)

HIGHLAND RAILWAY LOCOMOTIVES
BOOK 1

EARLY DAYS TO THE `LOCHS´

J.R.H. CORMACK AND J.L. STEVENSON

THE RAILWAY CORRESPONDENCE AND TRAVEL SOCIETY

1988

ISBN 0 901115 64 9

Published by the Railway Correspondence and Travel Society
21 Winthorpe Road, Lincoln LN6 3PG

COVER DESIGN BY JOHN HOLROYD

Photoset in 9/10 Plantin

Printed by AB Printers Ltd, Leicester

Contents

HIGHLAND RAILWAY LOCOMOTIVES
1855-1957

PREFACE

The Highland Railway has exercised a fascination over many people and much has been written about it. The interest which it has excited can probably be explained in large measure by the romance and beauty of the country which the system traverses and the unique nature of much of its operations. Moreover the courage with which directors, engineers and managers strove to strike east, north, south and finally west of Inverness can hardly fail to arouse admiration.

While much has been written on the locomotives, it quickly became clear to the authors that more information was still available from basic sources. Both of us had the good fortune to be brought up in the north and we have thus been personally acquainted with those engines which survived into the 1920s. We feared that if the locomotive story were not written now in reasonably full detail, the opportunity of doing so might be lost. A rich source of detail has been the minute books, timetables and associated publications which are safely preserved in the Scottish Records Office in Edinburgh and are available for all to study. Moreover many of the LMS boiler record cards are there also and solve many problems (as well as creating new ones by being incomplete!). We are all indebted to Alan G. Dunbar for saving these from destruction and to George Barbour and his staff at the Records Office who do a splendid job in maintaining all the books and documents under ideal conditions and are always ready to give assistance in unearthing details.

Many periodicals and books have been consulted but we have done our best to check from basic sources information so obtained. Two particularly useful books have been *The Highland Railway* by H.A. Vallance and Peter Tatlow's admirably produced *History of Highland Locomotives*. Magazines from early days contain articles and snippets which are valuable, while the Board of Trade Accident Reports provide much of great interest. Mercifully the Highland had a remarkable freedom from serious accidents but the minute books make it clear that minor mishaps were frequent and one must conclude that there were some miraculous escapes from disaster.

Finally we must thank sincerely those who have helped on individual points or took on the tiresome task of reading the text and making comments. Here we should like particularly to thank Graham E. Langmuir, James F. McEwan, Keith Miles, Dr R.A. Read, Montague Smith and David Stirling. We are very grateful also to the many photographers who are individually mentioned elsewhere.

There must be omissions and perhaps also errors. There is certainly conflict and a number of mysteries in available information which are mentioned in the text. If any reader can throw light on these matters we should be delighted to hear from them.

J.R.H.C
J.L.S

1. INTRODUCTION

1.1 Development of the Highland Railway

Throughout the early history of Scotland the high wall of the Grampian Mountains made Northern Scotland extremely difficult for the traveller to penetrate. Indeed it was generally regarded from afar as a dreary and perilous wilderness. Some improvement in communications began to emerge when, following the first Jacobite rising in 1715, the government set in hand the building of roads, although these were mainly for the movement of troops rather than for commercial purposes. They were constructed by the redoubtable General George Wade, and foremost among his works was the first road from Perth to Inverness, completed in 1729. Much of its route was to be closely followed by the Highland Railway main line in the latter half of the next century.

Great changes in the social structure of the Highlands followed the failure in 1746 of the second Jacobite rising and its brutal suppression. The clan system collapsed and the formation of large areas of deer forests caused immense hardship to the crofters, many of whom were forced to emigrate. But it was not until the start of the 19th century that road building on a large scale was initiated and aimed at commercial use. Thomas Telford was responsible for building some 900 miles of road by 1820 and also for the Caledonian Canal which took shape between 1803 and 1823. Stage coaches came to link the principal towns, with Inverness as the natural centre, but these were vulnerable to the snow storms to which the Highlands are subject. Journeys were possible also by sea and much of the merchandise was conveyed thus between Wick, Inverness and the east of Scotland, but for passengers it was a slow way to travel.

The possibility of linking Inverness with the south by rail arose first in 1845 when the Great North of Scotland Railway was formed with the principal intention of building a line from Aberdeen to Inverness. However construction was greatly hampered by lack of money and it was 1856 before Keith, the half-way point, was reached. Earlier Inverness had been more interested in a proposal to build a direct line to the south which had been surveyed by the outstanding civil engineer Joseph Mitchell, but this failed to secure parliamentary sanction. It thus became clear that the most practicable course of action was to compromise and build a railway east from Inverness and meet the Great North at Keith.

As a first step the Inverness & Nairn Railway was formed, receiving its Act in July 1854 and with astonishing speed having the 15 miles of line ready, with the necessary power and stock, for an opening ceremony on 5th November 1855. Further reference to this important event is made under the Raigmore (I) Class.

To push on further east the Inverness & Aberdeen Junction Railway was formed in 1856 and reached Keith, 40 miles beyond Nairn, in August 1858. Now Inverness had a through line to the south, but one with many drawbacks, being circuitous and involving passengers in an inconvenient change of stations at Aberdeen, between Waterloo and Guild Street.

There remained a weight of opinion in Inverness in favour of a direct line to the south in spite of the earlier rejection of Mitchell's plan. Impetus was given by the construction of the Perth & Dunkeld Railway, a branch 8½ miles long from Stanley Junction, 7¼ miles north of Perth, to Dunkeld, this being opened in 1856. Eventually the Inverness & Perth Junction Railway was formed in 1861, again with Joseph Mitchell as the engineer, to build a line from Dunkeld to Forres 25 miles east of Inverness. The Act was obtained later that year, work started in October and the builders achieved the almost incredible feat of introducing through working over the whole route in September 1863, 111¾ miles of line over some of the most difficult and remote country of Britain involving eight viaducts, many smaller structures and two short tunnels.

Meanwhile thoughts had been turning to railway building to the far north, resulting in the formation of the Inverness & Ross-shire Railway which received its Act in 1860. Their line was completed to Invergordon in 1863 and to Bonar Bridge the following year. In the course of these works amalgamations took place, the Inverness & Ross-shire being merged with the Inverness & Aberdeen Junction Railway in 1862 after the latter had absorbed the Inverness & Nairn the previous year. Then in June 1865 the Highland Railway came into existence through the amalgamation of the Inverness & Aberdeen and the Inverness & Perth Junction Railways. Such amalgamations may have been contemplated from early days and certainly the locomotives belonging to the constituent companies had been so numbered as to fall into a coherent series when they came together under Highland ownership.

The advance to the north continued slowly. In 1865 the Sutherland Railway was authorised to run north from Bonar Bridge to Brora but ran out of funds on reaching Golspie in 1868, whereupon the Duke of Sutherland came to the rescue with an offer to finance construction over the following 17½ miles to Helmsdale. As described later under the Special Tank Class, the Duke worked a section of this line for some seven months with his own engine and a coach pending completion of the two mile section between the Highland railhead at Golspie and Dunrobin where the ducal seat is situated. Through working was instituted by the Highland between Inverness and Helmsdale (101¼ miles) in June 1871.

For the final stretch to Wick and Thurso over vast wild moorlands the Sutherland & Caithness Railway came into being, again with financial help from the Duke. The Act of 1871 was followed by opening throughout in July 1874. The Thurso line diverges at Georgemas Junction, a bleak outpost with the layout so arranged as to allow direct working between Wick and Thurso, one or two local trains being operated thus for many years.

The Highland main line was now complete and formed 297¾ miles of route, or 305 operating miles if the Perth-Stanley section, over which the Highland had running powers, is included. In its course it had four principal summits, Druimuachdar 1,484 ft, Dava 1,052 ft, Lairg 488ft and County March (Forsinard) 708 ft. It was single throughout except for the 6¾ miles between Inverness and Dalcross, doubled in 1864, and some further doubling was later effected. In 1898 completion of the Inverness and Aviemore Direct Line, 34¾ miles with extremely heavy engineering works, reduced the Inverness-Perth mileage from 143¾ to 118 but involved the climb to Slochd Summit 1,315 ft.

Before the North line had advanced beyond Bonar Bridge, the Dingwall & Skye Railway was formed to build a line from Dingwall to the west coast at Kyle of Lochalsh, a distance of 63 miles. Strong opposition by landowners caused it to avoid Strathpeffer and make a gruelling climb up the hillside to Raven's Rock, the four miles of 1 in 50 against westbound trains being the hardest of all the Highland's many gradients. The line was opened to Strome Ferry in 1870 but the final 10 mile section to Kyle of Lochalsh, which required much heavy engineering, was not opened until 1897, in this case by the Highland which had taken over the Dingwall & Skye Railway in 1880.

Scottish railways are notable for their short branch lines and the Highland was no exception. It became responsible for working (but not in every case for building) the following branches:

Alves-Burghead, 1862; extended to Hopeman in 1892.
Ballinluig-Aberfeldy, 1865.
Keith-Portessie, 1884.
Dingwall (Fodderty Junction)-Strathpeffer, 1885.
Orbliston Junction-Fochabers Town, 1893.
Muir of Ord-Fortrose, 1894.
Gollanfield Junction-Fort George, 1899.
The Mound-Dornoch, 1902.
Wick-Lybster, 1903.

In addition the I&AJR in 1862 took over the working of the Findhorn Railway from Kinloss until its closure in 1869. There were short goods branches to Inverness Harbour and later to the Caledonian Canal basin at Muirtown. Mention has already been made of the Georgemas Junction-Thurso branch of 1874.

A strange escapade by the Highland, and a financially disastrous one, was their working of the Spean Bridge-Fort Augustus line between its opening in 1903 and 1907. Their main purpose was clearly to block any attempt by the North British to use the line to reach Inverness although by then this had become a very remote possibility.

The openings of the various sections of main and branch lines have of course a close bearing on the construction programmes of the locomotive classes and for that reason have been detailed here.

The Highland branch lines have predictably fared badly over the past fifty years and only the Thurso branch is still open to passenger traffic. Of the others the Alves-Burghead line is still in freight business. In contrast the main lines have, despite various threats, remained intact with the exception of Aviemore to Forres, closed in October 1965. Happily the southern 5¾ miles of this between Aviemore and Boat of Garten are still worked as a preserved line by the Strathspey Railway Company. The net result is that of the 506 route miles of the Highland Railway at its maximum, 402 are still (1988) operated by British Railways.

1.2 Locomotive Superintendents

The Highland Railway and its constituents had the services of seven superintendents covering 68 years. All of them made their mark in different ways.

William Barclay 1855-1865

Born at Montrose in 1824, Barclay was the nephew of Alexander Allan who became Locomotive Super intendent of the Scottish Central Railway and was located at Perth. The designs for all the locomotives built during Barclay's superintendency were actually those of his uncle, the younger man confining his efforts to locomotive maintenance and the other duties of his office under both the Inverness & Nairn and the Inverness & Aberdeen Junction Railways. This work must have been no sinecure with the railway developing steadily over the period, with staff to be trained, works facilities to be built up, and with new engines arriving which were to prove to be of inadequate capacity for the heavier duties.

Within their limits the Allan designs were sound. All had the Allan straight link motion, a feature of Highland design up to the end of the Jones era in 1896, and all were built in the Crewe tradition notably in the design of the fore-end with the smokebox swept downward to embrace the cylinders, this too remaining a Highland characteristic until 1894. Where Allan failed badly was in underestimating the difficulties of working the new Highland main line from Perth to Forres. For this he provided slender 2-2-2 engines for the passenger work and 2-4-0s for the goods, the latter tougher and more capable of being worked to their limits than the singles which were woefully short of adhesion, a fatal failing on this line.

Barclay seems never to have found much favour with the directors and he left the service of the I&AJR in May 1865 under something of a cloud. He secured employment managing a hotel in Liverpool but re-entered railway work later in the locomotive department first of the Great Eastern Railway and then of the Midland between which he was superintendent of the Thetford & Watton Railway.

William Stroudley 1865-1870

Born at Sandford, Oxford in 1833, Stroudley trained as a locomotive engineer at Swindon and after various appointments became manager of the Edinburgh & Glasgow Railway's works at Cowlairs in 1861. He came to the Highland at the time of its formation by amalgamation in June 1865 but was unable to make his mark as a designer because at that period the railway had — at least nominally — sufficient engines for main line work. Although these had many shortcomings, there was insufficient money to provide anything better. Stroudley did however initiate the conversion of the older 2-2-2 class to 2-4-0, although without much success.

The only class which Stroudley did design at Inverness was the Lochgorm 0-6-0 tanks but only one of the three came out during his period of office. These little engines were the forerunners of the celebrated Terrier tanks which Stroudley built when

he moved to the London Brighton & South Coast Railway.

He did however make his mark in a number of other ways, creating as a first priority much needed improvements to Lochgorm Works and doing much to improve the efficiency of train working within the limits of the under-powered engines of his time. He also introduced the distinctive yellow livery to the Highland.

Leaving for Brighton in January 1870, he spent the rest of his distinguished career there until his death in 1889.

David Jones 1870-1896 (Fig 1)

A native of Manchester, born there in 1834, Jones was apprenticed at Longsight in that city and at Crewe. He came to Inverness when the Inverness & Nairn Railway started operations in 1855 and in 1858 became principal assistant to Barclay. When Stroudley moved to Brighton early in 1870 Jones was appointed Locomotive Superintendent from 25th January of that year.

His early years in office were confined to rebuilding and improving existing classes, in particular proving the merits of the 4-4-0 design by converting two 2-4-0s. This led to his Duke class of 1874, an excellent design which was to be enlarged successively into the Clyde Bogie, Strath and Loch 4-4-0s with the Skye Bogies as small-wheeled versions of the Dukes for the Kyle line. At the same time the 2-4-0s were given new boilers and larger cylinders to get the best out of a basically inadequate design. Two classes of tank engine also emerged.

Locomotive history was made in 1894 with the famous Big Goods, the first 4-6-0s to run in Britain. It was indicative of the directors' faith in Jones that they agreed to his wish to build fifteen of this new type in a single order.

Practically all Jones engines had his unique louvred chimney, in essence two concentric tubes with a narrow space between them, the outer tube having louvres on the leading surface so arranged as to create an upward draught. The purpose of this device has never been quite certain but most probably the intention was to lift the exhaust steam well clear of the cab especially while running under light steam. The chimney was surmounted by a thin copper rim and the whole was an unmistakable hallmark of a Jones engine.

The Highland owed a tremendous debt to Jones for transforming the locomotive fleet from struggling inadequacy to sound capability, and doing so with a careful eye to cost by improving existing engines and supplementing these with new designs, each retaining the most effective features of its predecessors.

He would assuredly have brought out a 4-6-0

Fig. 1   David Jones, Locomotive Superintendent of the Highland Railway 1870-1896. Born 25 October 1834, died 2 December 1906.   *(Photo: J.L. Stevenson Collection)*

passenger engine but for his premature retiral, the consequence of an injury sustained on one of his Big Goods engines. On retirement in 1896, as his last design the Lochs were being delivered, he moved to Hampstead where he died in 1906.

Peter Drummond 1896-1912

Born at Polmont, Stirlingshire in 1850, Drummond became an engineering apprentice in Glasgow and thereafter was employed successively on the London Brighton & South Coast, North British and Caledonian Railways before becoming Assistant Locomotive Engineer at St Rollox. He took up the post of Locomotive Superintendent of the Highland Railway in November 1896.

One of his first tasks on arriving at Inverness was to reorganise Lochgorm works, but his first design came out quickly, the Small Ben passenger 4-4-0s primarily intended to replace the old 2-4-0s on secondary work. There soon followed a goods version of these in the form of the Barney class 0-6-0s together

with a passenger design conceived in the first place by Jones, the Castle class 4-6-0s which appeared first in 1900 and were built at intervals up to 1917. They were as valuable a class as the Highland ever possessed.

Drummond's subsequent designs included a small 0-4-4T for branch line work, an 0-6-0T for shunting, eight large 0-6-4 banking tanks and a class of six larger 4-4-0s which were perhaps his least satisfactory design. Some of these bore a resemblance to the engines of his elder brother Dugald on the North British, Caledonian and London & South Western Railways.

In 1912 Peter Drummond left to become Locomotive Superintendent of the Glasgow & South Western Railway. He died at Kilmarnock in 1918.

Frederick George Smith 1912-1915

A controversial figure, Smith came from Newcastle, born in 1872 and apprenticed to the North Eastern Railway at their Gateshead works. After a spell in general engineering he became Works Manager at

Lochgorm under Drummond and succeeded him as Locomotive Superintendent in 1912.

He brought out four more Castles, with some modifications, in 1913 but he was clearly eager to bring out designs of his own. Unfortunately he had uneasy relationships with the Chief Engineer, Alexander Newlands and with the Board who were much concerned at the back-log of locomotive maintenance which had formed at the outbreak of the war. The tragic affair of the River Class 4-6-0s and their rejection as unsuitable for the Highland line in 1915 is covered under that class in Book 2. The sequel was the resignation of Smith under duress and the Highland, already in dire straits at a time of heavy and increasing traffic demands, was thrown into even greater difficulties. In the event the Rivers proved to be one of the best classes which the Highland built, both on the Caledonian Railway, to which they were sold, and in later years when they eventually went into service between Perth and Inverness.

Returning to Newcastle, Smith obtained a post with the Ministry of Munitions and after 1918 he entered the steel business. He died in 1956 leaving several enigmas unsolved.

Christopher Cumming 1915-1922

Joining the Highland when the motive power situation was precarious in the extreme, Cumming was fortunate in having served his apprenticeship with the North British Railway which led to a useful relationship with the Cowlairs drawing office. Moreover his experience as District Locomotive Superintendent at Burntisland must have been valuable also as the Highland had received on loan from other companies a varied collection of locomotives to tide them over the worst period of power shortage. These must have presented many handling and rostering problems.

Cumming had neither the training nor the experience to initiate new designs, nor indeed was there by that time a drawing office at Inverness. The first engines to appear under his superintendency were the pair of superheated 4-4-0s for use on the North line, the design for which was prepared by Hawthorn, Leslie. The Board had in fact requested this before Cumming arrived at Inverness. It has always been a mystery how the Highland obtained authority to build two engines of an entirely new type in wartime. These two were followed by three Lochs and three Castles to existing designs but differing in some details from their predecessors.

Between 1918 and 1921 two new 4-6-0 classes appeared, both again designed and built by Hawthorn, Leslie. These were the Superheated Goods of 1918-19 and the same number of Clan class passenger engines of 1919-21, the last engines to be built by the Highland and upholding to the end their tradition of sound, straightforward, free steaming designs. By the end of Cumming's term of office the Company seems to have had a superfluity of power, and the reluctance to scrap any old engines defies ready explanation.

Cumming was a somewhat shadowy figure and little is known about him. He retired on health grounds in 1922 and died two years later.

David C. Urie April-December 1922

The son of R.W. Urie, Chief Mechanical Engineer of the London & South Western Railway, the young man served his apprenticeship under his father and became Assistant Works Manager at Eastleigh in 1913. At Inverness he had little scope to exercise his talents in new designs during the closing months of the Highland Railway, but plans were prepared for the superheating of the Big Bens. The work was put in hand at the time of the grouping and indeed one of them ran in superheated condition while still bearing the Highland livery.

In 1923 Urie became Assistant Mechanical Engineer to the Northern Division of the LMS and received further advancement in later years.

Lochgorm Works

A repair shop was provided from the start by the Inverness and Nairn Railway on the north side of the line just short of the station platforms. It was situated on the area of what had once been Loch Gorm (the Blue Loch) and at first included a locomotive running shed. Soon it was enclosed in the triangle of lines formed by the North line platforms and the avoiding line.

Each Locomotive Superintendent did his utmost to improve and extend the facilities, despite a general lack of enthusiasm on the part of the Board, and to develop them into a comprehensive locomotive works, capable of all maintenance and rebuilding work as well as a certain amount of new building, a total of 42 engines being built there between 1869 and 1906. An excellent description of the works can be found in the *Railway Magazine* for February 1902. The carriage works at Needlefield, situated on the north side of the avoiding line, are also described. Locomotive running was transferred to the new roundhouse which was opened in 1863 on the south side of the line alongside Eastgate. It eventually comprised 31 roads, all radiating from an open turntable.

While the volume and importance of repair work at Lochgorm was considerably reduced over the years following the grouping of 1923, the works continued in use until towards the end of steam, in anticipation of which they were adapted for diesel locomotive maintenance, mainly in the former erecting shop. Externally the main buildings have undergone suprisingly little change other than by demolitions in 1984-5 at the west end to create space for a new signalling centre.

1.3 Map of the Highland Railway

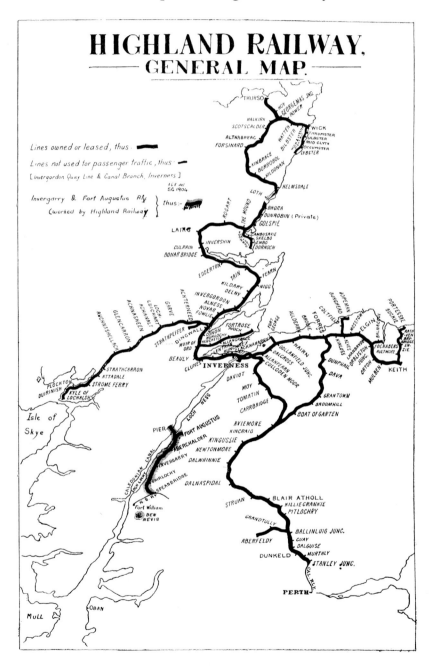

1.4 Principal Features of the Main Highland Railway Routes

Over its maximum route mileage of 506 the Highland had some of the most severe climbs in Britain in terms of a combination of length and gradient. In order to appreciate the haulage problems involved the following is an outline of the characteristics of the main routes.

Perth-Inverness

(a) Northbound. There is a rise, with one two-mile break, for the first 13 miles from Perth to Kingswood Tunnel. This includes two miles at 1 in 75/82 beyond Murthly. From there to Blair Atholl the main gradient is one of three miles on either side of Pitlochry with maxima of 1 in 85/90. From Blair Atholl, 420 ft, there are 18 miles of unbroken climbing largely at 1 in 70 to Druimuachdar Summit, 1,484 ft. The final gradient is from Aviemore, 690 ft, to Slochd Summit at 1,315 ft. This starts gently but steepens to 1 in 75 before Carr Bridge followed by a short descent. From Carr Bridge there are five miles of unbroken climb almost all at 1 in 60/70.

(b) Southbound. From Millburn Junction, Inverness the climb to Slochd starts at 1 in 60 and so continues for 13 miles, although easing for a time to 1 in 70 and with a short drop through Culloden Moor. Some undulations ensue as far as Tomatin from where there are 3½ miles at 1 in 60 to the summit. Climbing begins again at Newtonmore at 1 in 95 for three miles to Etteridge Crossing , then at 1 in 100 with some easier stretches to Dalwhinnie. The remaining five miles to Druimuachdar are mainly at 1 in 80. There follow only 2½ miles at 1 in 80 from Dunkeld to Kingswood Tunnel.

Aviemore-Forres (closed October 1965)

(a) Northbound. Climbing here was confined to some seven miles mainly at 1 in 80 from south of Grantown to Dava Summit, 1,052 ft.

(b) Southbound. There was another severe climb immediately after leaving Forres for 15 miles to Dava principally at 1 in 75. The following three miles to the summit undulated at 1 in 100/200.

Inverness-Keith

(a) Eastbound. As far as Elgin the only significant gradient is two miles of 1 in 103 between Kinloss and Alves. Beyond Elgin there are three miles of 1 in 95/98 through Lhanbryde, but the hardest section is the 2½ miles of 1 in 60 from the Spey viaduct at Orton to Mulben.

(b) Westbound. Apart from the five miles from Elgin to Alves which have stretches as steep as 1 in 105, gradients are generally easy.

Inverness-Wick

(a) Northbound. For the first 61 miles to Invershin the line is relatively level but with some short sharp undulations. From Invershin there is a climb for 7½ miles to Lairg Summit, 488 ft, chiefly at 1 in 70/72 but there are some breaks. There is a short two-mile climb at 1 in 60 from Golspie to Dunrobin, but the principal difficulty is over the 29 miles from Helmsdale to County March Summit, 708 ft. There are constant changes of gradient here with some sections of 1 in 60.

(b) Southbound. The corresponding climb to County March Summit starts at Halkirk and similarly includes some short stretches of 1 in 60. There are 7½ miles of 1 in 80/95 up Strath Fleet to Lairg Summit.

Dingwall-Kyle of Lochalsh

(a) Westbound. The major difficulty is the four-mile gradient at 1 in 50 from Fodderty Junction, two miles from Dingwall, to Raven's Rock Summit, 458 ft. This is followed by 2½ miles of 1 in 50/75 from Garve to Corriemullie Summit, 429 ft. The third climb starts at Lochluichart from where the line climbs with stretches of 1 in 50, but with undulations, to Luib Summit, 646 ft, some three miles west of Achnasheen.

(b) Eastbound. Rising steadily for 5½ miles from Strathcarron to Achnashellach, the line falls briefly and then climbs for seven miles at 1 in 50/95 to Luib Summit. This is followed by three miles of 1 in 50/80 from Lochluichart to Corriemullie Summit and two miles of mainly 1 in 50 from the east end of Loch Garve to Raven's Rock.

Branch Lines

The only branch which calls for particular mention is Keith-Portessie (usually referred to as the Buckie branch). From sea level at Portessie the line rose in some eight miles to a summit of 680 ft between Enzie and Aultmore. There was an easier climb from Keith.

Generally speaking the alignment of the main lines other than Dingwall-Kyle of Lochalsh is excellent, requiring few permanent speed restrictions except for 40 mph (sometimes less) when passing through crossing loops. On the North line a number of restrictions apply between Invershin and Lairg as well as north of Helmsdale.

On the Kyle line many restrictions apply. In Section 3.1 of the Appendix will be found a table dated 1897 of the loads to be taken by the different classes of engine on each section of route.

1.5 Locomotive Depots

The Highland provided locomotive depots at the following 23 locations. The figures in brackets indicate the approximate number of engines allocated at the end of 1922.

Aberfeldy	(1)	Keith	(1)
Aviemore	(15)	Kingussie	(2)
Blair Atholl	(11)	Kinloss	(Closed 1869)
Burghead	(2)	Kyle of Lochalsh	(6)
Dingwall	(4)	Lybster	(1)
Dornoch	(1)	Perth	(35)
Fochabers	(1)	Portessie	(Closed 1907)
Forres	(10)	Strome Ferry	(Closed 1897)
Fort George	(1)	Tain	(2)
Fortrose	(1)	Thurso	(2)
Helmsdale	(3)	Wick	(6)
Inverness	(70)		

In addition the undernoted points are relevant:

(i) The Highland operated the locomotive depot at Fort Augustus while they were working the Invergarry and Fort Augustus Railway between 1903 and 1907. A shed was provided also at Spean Bridge but was never brought into use.

(ii) The Duke of Sutherland kept his engine in a shed first at Brora and from 1896 in one at Golspie.

(iii) During the course of constructing the various sections of line the termporary termini in certain cases had locomotive depots. Known instances include Dunkeld where a shed was built by the Perth and Dunkeld Railway. This was closed when the through line to Inverness was opened in 1863. There were sheds likewise at Bonar Bridge until 1867, at Golspie from 1867 until about 1870 and at Carr Bridge from 1892 until 1897 or 1898.

(iv) It seems probable that some sort of locomotive depot was established at Invergordon when the Highland provided a shunting engine there from about 1905. Facilities would certainly have been necessary during the 1914-18 war.

(v) The roundhouse at Inverness was opened in 1863, before which engines used a building on the north side of the line. This was subsequently absorbed within Lochgorm Works.

1.6 Locomotive Liveries and Number Plates

These are described in some detail under each class and it is necessary here only to summarise the styles adopted during the periods of the various Locomotive Superintendents.

1855-1865 (Barclay)
Livery: Dark Green with black edges or lining. The number was painted on the buffer beam which was red.
Number Plates: See under Stroudley.

1865-1870 (Stroudley)
Livery: Passenger engines were usually dark yellow (officially 'improved engine green') with elaborate double lining (white inner, red outer), ochre border and claret frames. Goods livery was olive green with the same double lining or single white lining and sometimes a darker green border. Some goods engines however carried passenger livery and vice versa.
Number Plates: Brass with flamboyant figures and the Company's name against the brass surround. The

background was at first yellow but was soon changed to blue. Some authorities attribute the introduction of these plates to Barclay a year or so before Stroudley's arrival.

1870-1896 (Jones)
Livery: Until 1883 passenger engines were painted mid-green with triple lining (white inner, black centre, red outer) and a green border. There was no lettering apart from the engine's name. Goods engines were very dark green, almost 'bluebottle', with the same triple lining and again no lettering.

In 1884 a change was made to apple green, generally including the cylinders, with the same triple lining and with a dark green border. Frames were red-brown and there was a vermilion panel, with the triple lining, on the front buffer beam. Again there was no lettering other than the name. This style was applied to passenger and goods engines.
Number Plates: These followed the Stroudley pattern but with a red background.

1896-1912 (Peter Drummond)

Livery: Until 1903 the usual style, although there were variations, was olive green with triple lining (double white, black between) and an olive green border.* Frames, cylinders and steps were in claret. The front buffer beam had a vermilion panel with the same double white and black lining and carrying the engine number prefaced by 'H.R'. The number appeared also on the back of the tender or bunker. The Company was indicated on the tender or tank variably as 'THE HIGHLAND RAILWAY', 'HIGHLAND RAILWAY' or 'H.R'.

In 1903 the Board decided on a more austere livery of unlined olive green of a slightly darker shade than before. The cylinders were painted green, while the buffer beam was either green or vermilion, the panel being discontinued. The three variants of the Company's title were perpetuated.

Number plates: Brass with the number and the Company's name in plain black lettering. From 1905 larger plates were provided, having the number and the Company's name again in plain lettering but now in brass against a dark background.

1912-15 (Smith)

Livery: Light green unlined (but possibly with some red embellishment on the first two Rivers, which were fully painted). The front buffer beam was vermilion and lettered 'H.R' but otherwise the lettering was variable as before. Cylinders were green.

Number Plates: These were removed from some engines after 1914 to be melted down, and instead the number was painted high on the cab side while small metal numerals were usually affixed to the smokebox door in which case only 'H.R' appeared on the buffer beam. On some engines the boiler was painted black.

1915-22 (Cumming)

Livery: Moss green, but from 1920 sometimes light green as on the 1921 series of Clans. The lettering was unchanged except that the number was restored to the front buffer beam and was now prefixed by 'No' instead of 'H.R'. Cylinders were black. During Cumming's superintendency many engines were overhauled by outside firms which, having no stock of the original paint, had to use the closest available. Thus by 1922 quite a variety of greens existed.

*Photographs suggest that several engines painted or repainted at Lochgorm in this style received the Jones apple green, no doubt to use up existing supplies. The engines concerned included Small Goods 21; Glenbarry 46 and 55; Medium Goods 37; Duke 4, 65, 68, 71 and 72; Clyde Bogie 76, 79 and 81; Skye Bogie 33, 70 and 88; Strath 90, 93, 94 and 96; Big Goods 109 and 112; Loch 119, 128 and 131; also Small Ben 9-17 built at Lochgorm in 1899-1901. Of these the darker green was found, in whole or in part, as a border on 10, 15, 37, 68, 76, 93, 96, 112, 128 and 131. But nearly all the rest had the border also in apple green.

Number Plates: These were reintroduced, at first a small style with a black background (on *Snaigow* and *Durn*). Larger plates then appeared, similar to Drummond's second style but from 1917 with a red background. The plates were now made of gun metal and in some cases were fitted to older engines, replacing their original brass plates. Later some of the engines which lost their plates in Smith's time had these refitted, being evidently not needed after all for the war effort!

1922-23 (Urie)

Livery: The only change was that the few engines then repainted were given a green front buffer beam.
Number Plates: No change.

LMS Liveries

These followed closely the LMS practice from 1924, with passenger engines receiving red livery (more exactly crimson lake) with a black border separated from the main colour by a yellow line, while on the cab the new company crest was carried. In this style the Highland engines looked very fine. Goods engines were in unlined black with the usual red panel on the cab carrying 'L M S' in gold. In all cases the number was carried in gold on the tender or tank in 18 in numerals or 14 in on the smaller tank classes.

From 1928 when painting styles were altered no Highland class qualified for red livery, passenger engines becoming black with red lining. But for some odd reason goods engines, hitherto unlined black, also received red lining at Lochgorm for a year or so from 1928. Within the 1928 style there were many individual variations in numerals etc which are noted under the classes. Smokebox number plates were applied to all engines painted in the 1924 style but were generally removed after about 1929 with the new livery. Most if not all of the plates were however retained at the 1928-9 Lochgorm repaintings.

British Railways Liveries

Of the 29 Highland engines which came into British Railways stock only 14 carried their new numbers, the LMS one increased by 40,000, and only one of these, 0-4-4T 55053, received the fully lined out black passenger livery with the first BR emblem. Six simply had the LMS number painted out at Lochgorm and the new number applied in stencilled cream numerals about 12 in high in their place. The other seven were repainted plain black at St Rollox with the number in various styles. Apart from 55053, only Superheated Goods 57955 was given the BR emblem.

Names

It is not entirely clear how the names were applied to the Raigmore (I) engines in their early days while they

Fig. 2   Big Goods 17929, with a small wooden plough fixed to the front coupling hook, at Inverness c.1934.
(Photo: E.E. Smith)

12

Fig. 3   Barney 0-6-0 17699, fitted with a medium plough, in Aviemore shed in 1938. On the right is 14381
Loch Ericht carrying a small plough.   *(Photo: J.L. Stevenson Collection)*

Fig. 4   Big Goods No 108 with the large plough at Inverness, showing special fittings on the smokebox and
the chimney lamp bracket.   *(Photo: Real Photographs)*

had the open type of splashers, but on all other classes throughout the Highland Railway period names were painted in gold without serifs, generally shaded in black on the right or in very light green on the left, and sometimes with both. Shading was however omitted for a few years from 1903. The numbers on the back of the tender or bunker were similarly rendered, as were the numbers on the cab side in the Smith style.

When the LMS liveries were introduced from 1924 the lettering of the names was in gold adorned with serifs, and this style continued until the late 1930s when plain block lettering in yellow was adopted. The only named engines repainted by British Railways, *Ben Alder* and *Ben Wyvis*, had their names painted similarly but in cream and with slightly thinner strokes.

1.7 Special Fittings

Certain fittings and equipment peculiar to Highland Railway practice were carried by all or nearly all classes. Details are given below.

Snow Ploughs

The threat of snow in winter and spring in the Scottish Highlands is seldom far away. On the railway the greatest problem is that of high winds causing drifting which quickly fills the cuttings. While snow fences and in one or two places snow blowers are of value, the regular patrolling of the line with small or medium ploughs is necessary if blockages are to be avoided. Four ploughs were in use by 1864, two more being added in 1870. Thus were evolved three main types which proved very effective and required little change in design over the years.

The first type, the small or nose plough, not unlike a cowcatcher, was attached to the guard irons on engines designed by Jones or earlier, but from Drummond's time some used vertical bars which were bolted to the buffer beam. Another common fitting was the use of links fitted to the coupling hook in place of the screw or three link coupling. Because of the regular attachment of ploughs it was usual for engines in Highland days to have a single link only (and later commonly nothing) on the front coupling hook. The use of the small plough involved no speed restriction and indeed the main line engines usually carried them throughout the danger period. With their regular use, either on train engines or by special patrols, the line could be kept clear of light snow and even small drifts penetrated (Fig 2).

The second or medium plough was over 7 feet in height and thus when attached to an engine came up to about the centre line of the boiler. It could remove drifts up to about 8 feet in depth. Usually particular engines would be fitted with a medium plough and placed at strategic points until the snow risk passed. Speeds of up to 40 mph were allowed when the engine bearing this plough was attached as pilot to a train. Its construction was that of an inclined plane with a large wedge like the bow of a battleship superimposed, a

design to be found also on other railways (Fig 3).

Finally the big plough, some 10 feet high, was a larger version of the medium plough with the cutting edge of iron. This appliance was permanently attached during the snow season to an engine and its main purpose was to do battle with large drifts. In early days as many as four engines might be behind the big plough. Later two Big Goods, 106 and 108 had special fittings on the smokebox to hold it (Fig 4).

In January 1879 the Board had considered an interesting offer from Robert Fairlie the Locomotive Engineer, "to supply bogie engines at a cost of £4,000 each which he thinks would be effective in keeping the lines clear of snowstorms". The Board did not however think that the engines would be suitable.

A statement of the locomotive position dated November 1905 shows that three engines were allocated to snow plough duty, two 2-4-0s, 30 at Aviemore and 37 at Wick — these presumably carrying a medium plough — and Big Goods 108 at Inverness. A snow plough engine was also usually to be found at Forres and at Blair Atholl.

The LMS eventually replaced most of the wooden ploughs with steel ones of similar design and the big plough disappeared. In 1947 eight Caledonian 0-6-0s were sent north in exchange for Barneys, their work to include ploughing for which some improved crew protection was provided, and later some LMS Standard 4F 0-6-0s were fitted with new ploughs and other equipment for use throughout the Scottish Region.

Nowadays all diesel main line locomotives regularly employed on the Highland line carry nose ploughs as permanent fittings, while in 1981 an independent snow blower was supplied to Inverness. Trains on the North line now carry a 'survival kit' for the comfort of passengers who may be stranded on a snow-bound train.

Tablet Catchers

The Highland seldom responded quickly to Board of Trade directives and the introduction of train staff or tablet instruments was achieved only after strong pressure. Installation was complete by 1895 and following this the Manson system of token exchange was adopted on all the main routes. It effected a considerable improvement in train speeds especially on the Inverness-Perth line where some trains were booked to pass stations and there were a number of intermediate crossing loops.

The apparatus was fitted to all tender engines and to those tank engines likely to be involved in main line running. A pivoted arm attached on the left hand cabside carried at its other end heavy brass catching jaws with springs for gripping the received token which was carried in a leather pouch. Behind these jaws was a spring clip which held the pouch to be delivered. As the train approached the signal box the pouch was placed in the clip and the crew swung the arm down to effect the exchange at the ground apparatus, then returning it to the vertical position so that the caught pouch could be retrieved. There was an operating lever extending into the cab (Fig 5).

The ground equipment was very similar, being supported on T-section steel posts, although these were originally of wood. The signalman — pointsman in Highland parlance — extended the slide which held the jaws assembly by pulling on a lever. Normally the apparatus worked well but if a pouch was missed it was liable to fly some distance and a lost token meant delay.

The 0-6-4 Banking Tanks were provided with catchers on either side of the cab to cater for bunker-first running, and the same arrangement applied for a time to one of the Drummond 0-4-4Ts. Another tank to have a catcher was one of the Jones 4-4-0Ts but this was removed quite early. Reference is made to such variations under the individual classes.

After the grouping the LMS and some BR Standard engines allocated to the Highland section received the catcher, as did six Caledonian 4-4-0s and one 0-4-4T. In the case of the Hughes Moguls it had to be fixed to the tender because of the width of the cab.

In the 1950s a lighter type of cab fitting was devised, constructed mainly of steel strip and a similar type was used on the Type 1 and 2 diesels which arrived at Inverness from 1959 as well as on the diesel units operating between Inverness and Aberdeen. However the introduction of tokenless block working between Inverness and Perth made the apparatus unnecessary and elsewhere the operation reverted to hand exchange, the last use of the apparatus being at Forres and Elgin on the diesel units. In their case the exchange was effected by the guard.

Locomotive Lamps

One of a number of practices on the Highland which differed from those on other railways was its lamp code. All trains, passenger and goods, were required to carry three lamps, namely at the base of the chimney, on the left hand edge of the cab roof and on the right hand side of the tender (or bunker or cab). The two last-named lamps showed white to the front

Fig. 5   Tablet catcher of Strath 90, *Grandtully* and ground apparatus, demonstrating the exchange of pouches containing the tokens.
(*Photo: Dr. R. Struan Robertson Collection*)

and red to the rear. All lamp bodies were red.

Lamp brackets were provided on the engines accordingly but on the Rivers and on Cumming's engines the left hand cab bracket was on the cab side rather than on the roof — no doubt because of clearance considerations — with a corresponding bracket on the right hand side of the cab instead of on the tender. On tank engines there were usually two roof brackets, right and left, but on the Banking Tanks the right hand one was on the bunker.

Brackets were provided also at the front on the running board over each buffer, the right hand one being placed 'fore and aft'. Similar brackets were fitted at the rear end of the tender or bunker. Only the Banking Tanks seem to have had a top bracket at the rear but photographic evidence is scarce. Tender-first train working on the main lines was uncommon.

After grouping the standard lamp code was quickly introduced and the brackets were relocated as necessary.

Vacuum Standpipes

When the vacuum brake was fitted to engines by Jones from the mid-1880s he provided them with a swivelling standpipe at the front end. On the 2-4-0s provision had clearly to be made to swing the standpipe aside to allow the smokebox door to be opened, but on the larger tender engines the purpose appears rather to have been to keep the fitting from damage during snow ploughing, the normal running position for the standpipe being lying back flat. Tank classes, other than the Jones 4-4-0Ts, had a fixed vertical fitting.

Drummond in contrast provided fixed standpipes on all his designs except the Castles, but Smith reintroduced the swivelling type and Cumming continued it.

1.8 LMS Power Classifications

The LMS introduced power classifications soon after grouping. These were painted in small gold figures high on the cab sides, but at first appeared on passenger engines only and in certain cases were omitted.

With the change of livery in 1928 classifications were usually shown on both passenger and goods engines, followed by 'P' and 'F' respectively. In a few cases the letter preceded the classification number. For example 14522 showed 'P3' and 14759/62 'P4'. Engines which did not receive the 1928 livery remained unaltered in the showing or otherwise of the power classifications.

The details of the individual classes are as follows:

Class	First LMS Classification	Classification from 1928
Lochgorm Tank	not classified	0F*
Jones Tank	not classified	0P*
Skye Bogie	1	1F*
Clyde Bogie	1	1P*
Strathpeffer Tank	not classified	0P*
Strath	1	1P
Yankee Tank	not classified	0P*

Class	First LMS Classification	Classification from 1928
Big Goods	4*	4F
Loch	2	2P
Small Ben	2	2P
Barney	3*	3F
Castle	3	3P
Shunting Tank	2*	2F
Passenger Tank	not classified	0P*
Big Ben	2	2P
Banking Tank	4	4P
River	4	4P
Snaigow	3	3P
Superheated Goods	5*	4F
Clan	4	4P

*indicates that the classification was not carried on the engine

Of the six classes which came to British Railways, the Lochs, Small Bens and Barneys retained the LMS classifications, but the Clans and Superheated Goods were designated Class 4 being regarded as mixed traffic engines, while the two Passenger Tanks 55051 and 55053 carried '1P' for some time.

1.9 LMS Renumbering

This is fully covered under the classes, but an outline of the principle may be helpful.

After the grouping of 1923 the three Scottish constituents of the LMS, the Caledonian, Glasgow and South Western and Highland, were allocated new numbers between 14000 and 17997, the system being as follows:

14XXX	Passenger Tender Engines
15XXX	Passenger Tank Engines
16XXX	Goods Tank Engines
17XXX	Goods Tender Engines

The numbering in each of these four groups was in order of power classification, with the smaller engines occupying the lower numbers, while the Caledonian and GSW engines were usually numbered in front of the Highland within the power classes.

173 Highland engines were in stock in January 1923, but only 150 were taken into LMS stock and allocated new numbers. Of these four were withdrawn without being actually renumbered.

1.10 LMS Withdrawal Dates

All building, rebuilding etc dates are quoted here in calendar months (where these are known) and the same applies to withdrawal dates.

At the beginning of 1929 the LMS introduced four-weekly accounting and quoted subsequent withdrawals etc in that form, there being of course thirteen such periods in a year. It is generally misleading to convert these to calendar months — for instance Period 6 lies half in May and half in June — but fortunately an official list has been made available to the authors showing the actual day of withdrawal and from this source dates in calendar month form are stated.

In the case of alterations, repainting and suchlike dates, these are almost always taken from observations or from actual days entered on boiler record cards etc and in every case calendar months are stated where such information is available.

2. THE LOCOMOTIVE CLASSES

2.1 Raigmore Class 2-2-2 and 2-4-0 Barclay 6 ft 0 in Engines

This was the first class to run on the first section of Highland metals, the Inverness and Nairn Railway. No photograph or detailed drawing of the class as originally built is known to exist but a sketch is reproduced which depicts No 1 with its essential details. The general design was of the Crewe pattern with inside and outside frames and with the curve of the smokebox swept down over the outside cylinders. The boiler, which was domeless, was fed by pumps and had a raised firebox carrying one spring balance safety valve, the other being on the boiler barrel. The chimney had a brass flare. There were 162 boiler tubes of 1¼ in diameter and the smokebox door was of the lift-up pattern. Allan valve gear, which had just been devised, was employed for steam distribution. Laminated springs were used throughout the engine and tender, the trailing axle having a transverse spring, a type regularly used by the builders. There was no proper cab but only a front weather board, while the splasher had radial slots rather reminiscent of a steamer paddle box. Finally the 4-wheel tender had outside frames, a wheelbase of 8 feet and a tool box at the rear (Fig 6).

While the design is nominally attributed to Barclay, in fact it emanated from Alexander Allan, who was Barclay's uncle, and the same applied to all the engines constructed during Barclay's stay at Inverness. Mention is made of this peculiar situation in Section 1.2 of the Introduction. Allan had left Crewe in 1853 and moved to Perth to become the Locomotive Superintendent of the Scottish Central

Railway which became part of the Caledonian in 1865, whereupon he was dismissed.

Four engines were built by Hawthorns & Co of Leith, Nos 1 and 2 in 1855, 3 in 1856 and 4 in 1857. Nos 1 and 2 were supplied to the Inverness and Nairn Railway, the only engines built for this company, and Nos 3 and 4 to the Inverness and Aberdeen Junction Railway which constructed and operated the line between Nairn and Keith and which absorbed the Inverness and Nairn in 1861. The first two engines are known to have cost £2,375 each. All had to be conveyed to Inverness by sea and it has been stated that they were shipped to the Canal Basin at Muirtown, but this seems unlikely as not only would off-loading facilities be almost non-existent but there could have been problems for a suitably large ship to pass through the entrance locks. It is more probable that they arrived at Inverness Harbour from where the road haul to the station would be quite short. The Board minutes make no reference to the transport of the engines but record many problems with the shipping of the coaches and they state the amounts paid to carters and labourers "for conveyance from the Harbour".

Barclay told the Board on 13th October 1855 that the trial running of No 1 was going well. One of its first duties had been performed on the 24th of the previous month when the directors and chief officers made a journey over the line to inspect progress, a party of about 20 being carried in open wagons fitted with benches. It must have been an interesting

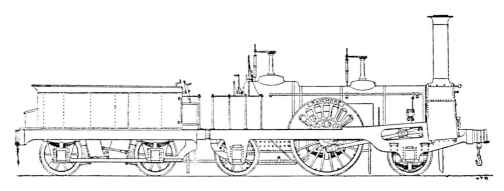

Fig. 6   Line drawing of Inverness and Nairn Railway 2-2-2 No 1 *Raigmore* as built in 1855.

spectacle. According to the *Inverness Courier* the passengers were treated to some quite high speed running as the 15 mile journey to Nairn was accomplished in 35 minutes, leaving Inverness at 2.00 pm. The return from Nairn was made at a more leisurely pace with stops en route in order to inspect the stations.

Dimensions

Not all are known but the following can be given:

Cylinders (2 outside)	15″ × 20″
Boiler	
Maximum outside diameter	3′ 7″
Length of firebox casing	4′ 2¼″
Grate area	12.25 sq ft
Boiler Pressure	100 lbs
Diameter of wheels	
Leading	3′ 6″
Driving	6′ 0″
Trailing	3′ 6″
Tender	3′ 6″
Tractive effort (85%)	5,312 lbs
Wheelbase	
Engine	6′ 10″ + 7′ 4″.
Tender	8′ 0″
Weights (approximate)	
Engine	27 tons
Tender	16 tons
Total	43 tons
Water capacity	1,100 gallons
Coal capacity	2½ tons

Renewal of No 2

As described later, Nos 1 and 2 were converted by Stroudley to 2-4-0s in 1869 (Fig 7). The conversion cannot have been satisfactory as No 2 was turned out of Lochgorm in February 1871 as to all intents and purposes a new engine (Fig 8). It is considered here under the Raigmore class as it did incorporate some parts of the original No 2, almost certainly the wheels and outside frames, also the tender which was rebuilt to increase the capacity from 1,100 to 1,200 gallons. But in other respects the engine was enlarged. A new boiler was provided by Dübs & Co having a barrel slightly shorter than the earlier design but with the raised firebox some 4 inches longer. The boiler had 181 tubes of 1¾″ diameter, a dome on the barrel and Adams safety valves arranged transversely on the firebox. The smokebox door was hinged at the side. New and larger cylinders were provided and Hawthorns supplied new frames, although these would probably be the inner frames only which carried most of the weight, the outer frames being used again. At first there was a chimney with a brass flare, probably taken from the first No 2, but this was soon replaced by a Jones chimney without louvres (Fig 9). The underslung crosshead was likewise shortly afterwards superseded by one with two slide bars. Thicker tyres increased the diameter of the driving wheels from 6 ft to 6 ft 3 in.

The engine was regarded in the books as a 'renewal' of the earlier No 2, a concept which appears frequently in Highland Railway locomotive history and one which could mean anything from a heavy repair to replacement by something entirely new and using no part of the original engine. In this way the cost of providing the new (or rehabilitated) engine could be charged to revenue.

Fig. 7   No 1 *Raigmore* rebuilt as a 2-4-0 in 1869 with Stroudley cab and number plate. Stroudley livery with elaborate white lining and darker border.

(*Photo: J.L. Stevenson Collection*)

Fig. 8   The second No 2 *Aldourie* as turned out in 1871 with domed boiler but with original pattern of chimney (shortened).
(Photo: W.O. Steel per R.N. Essery)

Fig. 9   The 1871 No 2 *Aldourie* at Thurso about the opening of the line in 1874, fitted with Jones chimney.
Green Stroudley livery with dark border outside the double lining.   *(Photo: John B. Russell)*

The dimensions of the new No 2 were as follows:

Cylinders (2 outside)	15½″ × 22″
Boiler	
Maximum outside diameter	3′ 7″
Length of barrel	9′ 7½″
Pitch	5′ 6½″
Length of firebox casing	4′ 6″
Heating surface	
Tubes (181 of 1¾″ diameter)	836 sq ft
Firebox	70 sq ft
Total	906 sq ft
Grate area	13.5 sq ft
Boiler pressure	130 lbs
Diameter of wheels	
Leading	3′ 9″
Coupled	6′ 3″
Tender	3′ 9″
Tractive effort (85%)	7,787 lbs
Wheelbase	
Engine	6′ 10″ + 6′ 11″
Tender	8′ 0″
Total	34′ 3″
Weights	
Adhesion	19 tons 10 cwts
Engine	27 tons 10 cwts
Tender	18 tons
Total	45 tons 10 cwts
Water capacity	1,200 gallons
Coal capacity	2½ tons

Renumbering

The second No 2 became 2A in May 1898 when the number was required for one of the Small Ben class.

Livery

The livery of the Inverness and Nairn Railway was dark green, with edges and boiler bands in black and this would have been applied to Nos 1 and 2. The Inverness and Aberdeen Junction Railway livery was dark green also, the three divisions along the cab side having black-lined panels and the tender side having two panels, all panel corners being concave. The black lagging bands had narrow red edges. Presumably Nos 1 and 2 were finished thus but evidence is scanty. Originally there was no number plate and the number appeared only on the buffer beam.

As converted to a 2-4-0, No 1 was in a very elaborate livery. The colour was again dark green and had a still darker border, the two shades being separated by a narrow white line which traced the outline of the coupled wheels round the splasher and cab side. The sand box and the rest of the cab side were also panelled and the tender was divided into two panels by a white line which formed two side panels with the corners elaborately done. A number plate of Stroudley pattern was latterly on the cab side.

No 2 as converted to a 2-4-0, may well have had this livery also. The new No 2 certainly had it at first but in its case with simpler lining at the corners, and the

21

tender lining was soon modified. See Fig 9. In the course of its long life it must later have had one or both of Jones's shades of green with white, black and red lining and dark green borders.

Names

These were carried from the start and all were to be used again. They were the residences of the directors of the Inverness and Nairn Railway and Inverness and Aberdeen Junction Railway, details being as under:

Raigmore
: The residence close to Inverness of Eneas William MacIntosh who in later years was Chairman of the Highland from 1892 to 1896. A large hospital now occupies the grounds and the house was demolished in the mid-1960s.

Aldourie
: Situated some seven miles from Inverness at the north-east end of Loch Ness, this was the residence of Captain William Fraser-Tytler, a director.

St. Martins
: Residence in Inverness of Colin Lyon Mackenzie, a director and for a time Provost of Inverness.

Ardross
: Near Alness. Residence of Alexander Matheson who was the Chairman of the I&AJR from 1856 until its absorption in 1865 by the Highland of which he became Chairman until 1884.

The directors must have felt honoured to have engines named after their homes (and later after themselves) because the practice continued off and on until 1916.

Rebuilding

For their initial duties between Inverness and Nairn the little singles were reasonably suitable as the gradients are short and do not exceed 1 in 200. However by March 1858 the line had been pushed east to Elgin, involving a two mile climb at 1 in 103 eastbound to Alves, while the further extension to Keith opened in August of that year included a formidable 2½ mile stretch at 1 in 60 where the line climbs east from the Spey valley to Mulben. The opening of the route to Perth presented much greater difficulties and on the long gradients and in stern weather the lack of adhesion and of shelter for the crew showed up the inadequacies of the class only too clearly.

To go some way towards meeting these short-comings, although rather late in the day, Stroudley was given authority by the Board early in 1868 to convert No 1 to a 2-4-0, this being effected in 1869 with the extra driving wheels and axle coming from No 3 which ceased work that year. At the same time the cylinders were enlarged from 15 in by 20 in to 15½ in by 21 in, the extension of the stroke being

achieved by doing some boring fore and aft and by using an eccentric crank pin. A cab in Stroudley's distinctive style was provided, having a straight-top front and half-domed roof. The new coupled wheelbase was 6 ft 11 in. Further authority was given by the Board to convert No 2 to a 2-4-0 in the same year "on the same principle as No. 1" and in this case a wheelset came from No 4. But these conversions cannot have been a success as No 1 lasted only for a further four years and No 2, as already described, was replaced by a virtually new engine little more than a year later. It would appear that, hardly surprisingly, the frames and boilers developed weaknesses.

The new No 2 in contrast survived until 1903 (Fig 10). In October 1894 it was given a reconstructed boiler which had been fitted with a new tube plate, tubes and firebox while the old one did further service on a goods engine, number unknown. Some authorities state that No 2's replacement boiler came from Glenbarry class 32, which is possible although the differing dimensions would have necessitated some structural alteration.

In the Board minutes of 6th December 1870 authority was given to resurrect No 4, by now lacking boiler and driving wheels, and convert it to a 4-4-0 for the Dingwall and Skye line. Nothing more was heard of the matter until Jones reported to the Board on 1st August 1876 that No 4 had been reconstructed to a type similar to the Duke 4-4-0s of 1874. The new (or rather 'renewed') No 4 was in fact the first of the Lochgorm Bogies which formed the second batch of the Dukes and further reference is made under that class. The old No 4 had at least nominally been in stock until then but it is for conjecture whether any of its remains found their way into its successor. The name *Ardross* anyway reappeared.

Work

When new and until the arrival of the Seafield 2-4-0s in 1858-59 the Raigmore singles had to work all trains. Only the first two were in service for the introduction of public services between Inverness and Nairn on 5th November 1855, the pair carrying on unaided until the arrival of No 3 in August 1856 and of No 4 a year later. The opening was preceded by worries about the late delivery of equipment, first of coaches and then of signals and turntables without the installation of which the Board of Trade would not sanction opening.

The inaugural train left Inverness for Nairn at 12.00 noon double-headed by *Raigmore* and *Aldourie*, departing as a press report describes it, "with much éclat", and consisting of 30 "carriages" most of which were wagons fitted with benches. Some 800 passengers were packed into this strange cavalcade and the proceedings appear to have been a complete

Fig. 10   No 2 *Aldourie* in later days at Inverness. Coal rails added to tender.   *(Photo: A.G. Ellis collection)*

success. Speeds of 30-40 mph were reported en route and the 15 mile journey was accomplished in a little over 45 minutes. The inns at Nairn evidently did excellent business so that "on the return journey the outside passengers were not so quiet. There were however no excesses". On the following day a trip was made from Nairn to Inverness and back on which 400-500 passengers were conveyed, speed being stated to have been as high as 50 mph for some two miles. On the special trips on these two days the engines and passenger vehicles were finely decorated and the firemen ('stokers') wore white overalls, the drivers' garb probably being the same.

From 7th November the regular service commenced, in the first week no fewer than 3,200 passengers being carried and slightly more in the second week, while from 1st December goods services, one in each direction, were instituted. Three passenger trains ran each way, being allowed 45 minutes for the 15 mile journey with four intermediate stations, of which one, Cawdor, had the distinction of being opened, renamed (Kildrummie) and closed, all within the space of little more than two years. An omnibus service, connecting with the 9.00 am train from Inverness, was provided from Nairn to Huntly. Here passengers joined the GN of S train to Aberdeen where it was due to arrive at 6.45 pm, a similar service operating in the other direction.

As the line became extended to Elgin and Keith in 1858 and to Dingwall as well as to the south in the early 1860s, the Raigmores travelled further afield. For passenger work they were soon augmented by the Belladrum and Glenbarry classes but, as was to be expected, they were inadequate for the performance required. It is difficult to imagine a class of engine

more unsuited to the Scottish Highlands, the single driving axles providing scant adhesion for the long climbs and the unfortunate crew practically unprotected against the elements. It was in an attempt to overcome these shortcomings that Nos 1 and 2 were rebuilt as 2-4-0s but even then they were unsatisfactory.

However the new No 2 of 1871 was a more robust engine. It was generally on the North line and it appears from a photograph to have worked the first train from Inverness to Wick on 28th July 1874. For many years it worked the Thurso branch and it was photographed derailed in a snow block at Aultnabreac during the great storm of January 1895. It spent its last years shunting at Inverness.

A disastrous accident took place early in the existence of the I&AJR on 4th September 1858 at Mulben, five miles west of Keith and the engine concerned was in all probability one of the Raigmore class. The line had been opened throughout from Inverness to Keith only a couple of weeks previously, on 18th August, but as the Spey bridge at Orton was still incomplete the Board of Trade would not sanction its use for passengers and directed that they be detrained at one side and walk over the adjacent road bridge while the train was hauled across by the engine using a long rope to obviate the need for both it and the coaches to be on the bridge at the same time. Platforms for the passengers were provided at either end of the bridge, that on the east side being very awkwardly placed at the start of the 1 in 60 gradient which rises for 2½ miles to Mulben.

On this day the 4.45 pm train from Inverness, having successfully negotiated the bridge, called at the east bank platform to recouple the engine and to allow the passengers to resume their seats. Fearing problems with restarting, the driver instructed the pointsman to place a wooden block behind one of the wheels of a van, which was the last vehicle, in order, as the Minute Book reads, "that the engine would start more easily to go up the incline of 1 in 60. The engine driver having backed his engine with greater force than expected, the van was thrown off the rails and after trying for 10-15 minutes to get it on the rails again, it was uncoupled and the train proceeded to Keith where it arrived a few minutes after 8.00 pm."

Having disposed of his train, the driver decided to go back to re-rail and retrieve the van. To assist him he took a porter, a pointsman and three cleaners on the footplate before setting out tender first. Unfortunately he seems to have advised no-one in authority of his intentions and indeed the Keith Station Master and other officials had by then left the station. Approaching Mulben the engine ran into what was described as a "blind siding". The tender was derailed and "was lifted upon the footplate by the concussion". Sadly the three cleaners were killed and no doubt considerable damage was sustained by the engine and particularly by the tender.

Some rather less destructive mishaps occurred in the early days of the Inverness and Nairn Railway while the Raigmores were in sole charge. In May 1856 a train arriving at Inverness was inadvertently diverted into the engine shed, then situated on the site of Lochgorm Works. History does not relate whether passengers enjoyed their unexpected shed visit but it is recorded that a pointsman was informed that his services would no longer be required. A few months later the driver and fireman of the Mail Train from Inverness to Nairn "had been guilty of neglect of duty inasmuch as they were partly intoxicated and had quarrelled in discharge of these duties, in consequence of which the Mail Train was stopped between Raigmore and Stoneyfield and delayed beyond the advertised hour". Both men were immediately discharged from the Company's service

and a report on the affair was sent to the Procurator Fiscal for possible legal proceedings.

Such incidents apart, one can say with every justification that the Highland and its antecedents were extremely fortunate in their loyal and responsible staff. The first twenty or so years must have been particularly trying for the locomotive crews with engines constantly underpowered and only latterly providing any real shelter.

Withdrawals

The Raigmore class did not have a long active life, apart from the second No 2 which was nominally in service until 1903, although reported to be dismantled in 1901. One must stress the word 'active' because Nos 1, 3 and 4 remained on the books for several years after they had been dismantled. No 3 came out of service first in 1869 and No 4 was laid aside shortly afterwards, in each case the boiler and driving wheels finding a new owner. No 1 which had been converted to a 2-4-0, was in use until 1873 but was then regarded as "broken down for remaking", a common phrase in Highland records which usually meant that the engine was lying about somewhere in bits and pieces, a description which applied with even greater force to Nos 3 and 4. However all three, as the statistics show, were in stock until their respective 'renewals', Nos 1 and 3 as the two Raigmore II class 2-4-0s in 1877 and No 4 as the second *Ardross*, the Duke class 4-4-0 of 1876. The boilers of Nos 3 and 4 saw further use on Lochgorm Tanks 56 (1869) and 57 (1872) respectively.

Allan, who was almost entirely responsible for the design, seems to have considered little more than the immediate needs of the Inverness to Nairn section for which they were just adequate.

Nevertheless despite their shortcomings the class is of great interest and importance as being the pioneer engines in the Highlands.

Summary of Class

No.	Name	Maker	Works No	Built	Rebuilt as 2-4-0	Withdrawn
1	Raigmore (I)	Hawthorns	129	9/1855	1869	1873*
2 (I)	Aldourie (I)	,,	130	10/1855	1869	2/1871
3	St. Martins (I)	,,	146	8/1856		1869*
4	Ardross (I)	,,	161	9/1857		1870*
2 (II)/2A (5/1898)	Aldourie (II)	Lochgorm	—	2/1871		1903

*These were the dates when Nos 1, 3 and 4 were laid aside. The engines were however regarded as being in stock until the numbers were taken by new engines in 1877 (Nos 1 and 3) and 1876 (No 4). See under 'withdrawals'.

2.2 Seafield Class 2-4-0 (two later 4-4-0)
Barclay 5 ft 0 in Engines

Following the four Raigmore Class 2-2-2 passenger engines, Barclay — once again under Allan's guidance — turned his attention to providing motive power for goods work over the Inverness and Aberdeen Junction Railway. The outcome was the seven 2-4-0s of the Seafield Class, ordered in two lots of three with one additional a year later. They were built by Hawthorns & Co. and delivered in 1858-59. The I&AJR had reached Elgin in March 1858 and it is believed that the engines were brought by sea to Lossiemouth and taken over the Morayshire Railway's branch from there to Elgin. When the I&AJR completed its line to Keith in August 1858 there were 55 route miles to be worked rather than the original 15 from Inverness to Nairn and the need for more power was obvious.

The Seafields were fairly similar to the Raigmores but they were built as 2-4-0s with the driving wheels reduced from 6 ft to 5 ft. Other features were more or less identical, deep outside framing, Allan gear, the smokebox swept over the cylinders, raised firebox, a chimney with a brass flare and a lift-up smokebox door. There were compensating levers between the coupled axles. Once again the boiler was fed by pumps but it now carried a shapely dome over the firebox, while the two spring balance safety valves were located one on the boiler barrel and the other on the dome. It may be noted that on all the classes credited to Barclay the goods engines were provided with domes, whereas the passenger engines were domeless. Possibly the reasoning was that goods working implied a less smooth start and a generally rougher ride for the engine. In these circumstances a dome might be expected to reduce priming.

Once more poor protection was afforded to the crew, a weather board with a slight and almost useless overhang being provided. Here was another difference between the Barclay goods and passenger

Fig. 11   Inverness and Aberdeen Junction Railway 11 in original condition in the early 1860s, showing lift-up smokebox door and weatherboard. Barclay dark green livery with black borders. *(Photo: Wallace, Tain)*

classes in that the former had a longer cab with three vertical divisions on the side, whereas the passenger classes, except the Raigmore Class, had only two. The intention may have been to ensure on goods engines wider visibility for shunting. The Seafield tender was slightly longer than the Raigmore with the wheelbase increased from 8 ft to 8 ft 3 in. (Fig 11).

The seven engines were numbered 5 to 11. Six were delivered in 1858 and the seventh in the following year.

Dimensions

Cylinders (2 outside)	16″ × 22″
Boiler	
Maximum outside diameter	4′ 1″
Length of barrel	10′ 9″
Pitch	5′ 10½″
Length of firebox casing	4′ 2½″
Heating surface	
Tubes (218 of 1¾″ diameter)	1,115 sq ft
Firebox	73.75 sq ft
Total	1,188.75 sq ft
Grate area	12.25 sq ft
Boiler pressure	120 lbs
Diameter of wheels	
Leading	3′ 6″
Coupled	5′ 0″
Tender	3′ 6″
Tractive effort (85%)	9,574 lbs
Wheelbase	
Engine	5′ 11″ + 8′ 4″
Tender	8′ 3″
Weights (approximate)	
Adhesion	18 tons 10 cwts
Engine	28 tons
Tender	16 tons
Total	44 tons
Water capacity	1,200 gallons
Coal capacity	2½ tons

Renumbering

No 7 was transferred to the duplicate list as 7A in 1898, and 11 was renumbered 9 in 11/1893.

Livery

The earliest photograph of the class shows the style of the I&AJR, namely a fairly dark green with black borders and black-lined panels with convex corners, two on the tender side and rear, and three on the cab side. The boiler bands were also black, possibly with thin red edges. A light line matched the wheel outline round the splasher on which the letters 'I.&A.J.Ry.' were painted in gold forming an arc. The number in gold was on the red front buffer beam but there was no number plate. A long narrow maker's plate, with

a bulge in the centre, was on the frame below the splasher.

From 1865 Stroudley introduced the first Highland Railway livery, but it is not known whether any of this class were so painted. All probably carried Jones first shade of very dark green and a colour print by F. Moore shows No 6 in this style. The colour is more blue than green and the triple lining of white, black and red is shown, even the lagging bands being so embellished. The cylinders are lined in red and a red line runs along the lower edge of the frame.

Names

While evidence is scanty, it does appear that the I&AJR applied the names before the formation of the Highland in 1865, this requiring of course the removal of the Company's initials from the splasher. However the first set of names soon disappeared and the engines were nameless for a time. The second group of names referred to towns and estates north of Inverness, but they too disappeared quickly with the exception of *Helmsdale*.

The directors and their residences, as on the Raigmores, provided the first set of names. The individual sources where not obvious, were:

Seafield	The Earl of Seafield, a director.
Bruce	Hon. Thomas Charles Bruce who was Deputy Chairman from 1865 and later Chairman from 1885 to 1891.
Fife	The Earl of Fife, a director.
Altyre	The estate near Forres of Sir Alexander P. Gordon-Cumming, a director.
Aultnaskiah	The residence in Inverness of Alexander Inglis Robertson, a director.
Westhall	There is an estate of this name near Oyne, Aberdeenshire but its connection with the railway is not known.
Stafford	The Earl of Stafford, a director.
Duncraig	This refers to Duncraig Castle on Loch Carron, Ross-shire.
Skibo	The Skibo estate and Castle near Dornoch. This and the foregoing name appeared again on Castle Class engines.

Detail Alterations and Rebuilding

One of the class, 10, was provided with Clark's patent smoke consuming apparatus either at building or soon afterwards, the purpose of this being to save coal rather than to reduce air pollution. It was used extensively for a time on the Great North of Scotland Railway. Other railways like the Highland tried it briefly but found it too costly to maintain. The apparatus consisted of four nozzles, two at the back and two at the front of the firebox through which jets of steam were directed across the surface of the coal. The jets drew in a supply of air, the quantity of which was controlled by the amount of steam being passed. In addition to fitting 10 it was the intention that the two Belladrum Class 2-2-2s should be so equipped but the directors were sceptical of the value and asked for a comparison to be made between 10 and 11, the latter with a conventional brick arch. The result of the test did not favour Clark's apparatus and the directors decided at their meeting of October 1861 to standardise on the brick arch.

Jones was anxious to experiment with a bogie in place of the leading rigid axle, both to make for easier running on the Skye line and to gain knowledge for his projected new passenger class. The Board turned down his first request but in October 1871 he was given authority to convert two of the Seafield Class to 4-4-0s for working the Skye line at a cost of £200 each. 10, which was already awaiting works attention, was taken in hand and appeared in June 1873 with an Adams leading bogie having 2 ft 6 in wheels, together with new frames, a Jones louvred chimney, side-hinged smokebox door and a new 6-wheel tender. Similar changes were made to No 7 and it re-entered traffic in May 1875. 10 may have introduced Jones's well known cab which had, like Stroudley's, a half-domed roof, also round corners and a horizontal joint below the cut-out. No 7 certainly received the Jones cab in 1875, although with a cut-out rather wider than became usual. (Fig 12).

The following altered dimensions now applied to Nos 7 and 10:

Dimensions

Cylinders (2 outside)	17″ × 24″
Diameter of wheels	
Bogie	2′ 6″
Tender	3′ 7½″
Tractive effort (85%)	11,791 lbs
Wheelbase	
Engine	5′ 6″ + 6′ 8″ + 8′ 4″
Tender	5′ 9″ + 5′ 6″
Weights	
Adhesion	20 tons 10 cwts
Engine	32 tons 10 cwts
Tender	24 tons
Total	56 tons 10 cwts
Water capacity	1,800 gallons
Coal capacity	3 tons

Later the vacuum brake was fitted, certainly to No 7 and in all probability also to 10 although this cannot be verified. Neither was reboiled but 10 at least received a new firebox in 2/1891.

The other five, which remained as 2-4-0s, all underwent renovation at the following dates:

5	7/1870	9	12/1876
6	2/1874	11	5/1878
8	2/1886		

The main changes, which greatly improved and updated the appearance of the engines, included the enlargement of the cylinders to 16 in by 24 in (16 in by 23 in in the case of No 6) and the fitting of the Jones

Fig. 12   No 7 converted to a 4-4-0 in 1875 for the Skye line, with Jones chimney and cab also new six wheel tender. The cab is an early pattern with a large cut-out.   *(Photo: Wallace, Tain)*

louvred chimney, side-hinged smokebox door and a cab. The cab was of the Stroudley pattern for the first two altered, Nos 5 and 6, but was probably of Jones style for the others (Fig 13). Tractive effort now became 10,445 lbs and for No 6 10,009 lbs. The chimney and cab alterations on No 8 must have occurred before the fitting of new cylinders. In October 1893 Dübs supplied a new boiler intended for 11 (soon to be renumbered 9) but instead this was stored and the engine was withdrawn four years later.

Tenders

The original tenders were 4 wheel, not unlike those of the Raigmore Class but, as shown in the table of dimensions, having a tank capacity of 1,200 gallons as against 1,100, and a 3 in longer wheelbase. The superstructure was slightly inclined upwards to the rear and a tool box was mounted behind. At their rebuilding Nos 7 and 10 received 6 wheel tenders with unequal wheel spacing of a design similar to those of the Small and Medium Goods, Glenbarry and Raigmore II Classes. Again there was a tool box behind.

Allocation and Work

The class was primarily intended for goods working and they were stated to be 'grand pullers for their size'. They were certainly used on passenger trains as well, particularly on the Skye line where after being rebuilt as 4-4-0s Nos 7 and 10 each spent some 20 years although No 7 in its last years was shunter at Forres. But, willing engines though they were, they were inadequate in size for their tasks on the main line, although not so seriously as the Raigmore Class. The two 4-4-0s had early troubles with the bogies and when working a heavy train in bad weather suffered badly from lack of adhesion. After the arrival of the Small and Medium Goods Classes all were largely displaced from the Perth line as their renamings imply.

The I&AJR lent No 8 for the Board of Trade inspection of the Findhorn Railway on 9th April 1860 while No 6 did some pioneering work in the north when it was on loan to contractors building the Sutherland and Caithness Railway.

Withdrawal

The first to go was No 8 which was withdrawn in 1891, what was left of it being sold for scrap two years later. None of the four remaining 2-4-0s were used after the arrival of the Big Goods in 1894, but the two 4-4-0s lasted a few years longer until finally ousted by the Skye Bogies.

Such were the Highland's first goods engines. Although in much of their work they must have been stretched to capacity, they had quite long lives, a testimonial to the maintenance and improvements which were given to them by Jones. The two 4-4-0s lasted for a surprisingly long time considering their gruelling tasks on the Skye line, and are of particular interest as paving the way for the Duke Class and thus for all the Jones 4-4-0s.

Fig. 13   No 5 *Tain* as rebuilt by Jones with louvred chimney, Stroudley pattern cab and new or modified smokebox. Jones second livery of apple green with triple lining.   *(Photo: Real Photographs)*

Summary of Class

No.	Name	Maker	Works No	Built	Rebuilt as 4-4-0	Withdrawn
5	Seafield (I) /- /Tain (1875) /-	Hawthorns & Co., Leith	163	2/1858	—	5/1897 (Note 1)
6	Bruce (I) /- /Helmsdale (I) (c1874) /-	,,	164	5/1858	—	11/1893
7/7A (1898)	Fife (I) /- /Dingwall (II) (5/1875) /- (c1886)	,,	165	8/1858	5/1875	5/1899
8	Altyre /- /Beauly (II) /-	,,	175	8/1858	—	9/1891 (Note 2)
9	Aultnaskiah (I) /- /Golspie (I) /-	,,	176	8/1858	—	11/1893
10	Westhall /- /Duncraig (6/1873) /-	,,	177	9/1858	6/1873	5/1897
11 /9 (11/1893)	Stafford (I) /- /Skibo /-	,,	209	10/1859	—	6/1897 (Note 3)

Note 1.   Laid aside 10/1894 and not used thereafter.
Note 2.   Sold for scrap 5/1893, but boiler retained and re-used on No.14
Note 3.   Lay idle from 3/1894.

2.3 Belladrum Class 2-2-2 (one later 2-2-2T)
Barclay 6 ft 0 in Engines

The Raigmore and Seafield Classes continued as the passenger and goods engines respectively of the Inverness and Aberdeen Junction Railway until 1862. In that year two more 2-2-2 passenger engines forming the Belladrum Class and two more 2-4-0 goods engines, the 14 Class, were delivered primarily to work the Inverness and Ross-shire Railway which was opened to Dingwall in June 1862 and thereupon merged with the I&AJR.

The Belladrum Class virtually continued the Raigmore design, but with slightly altered dimensions. Framing, gear, boiler and its fittings, chimney, springs, smokebox door etc were unchanged in style but one important development was the welcome provision of a cab. This was of a severely practical design but at least it did have a roof, this being of the half-domed shape. The lower cab side was bisected by a vertical raised seam, above and to the rear of which was the straight-sided cut-out. The latter was identical in area with the upper cab side. The square spectacle window had a vertical division as on the four subsequent designs which came out while Barclay was at Inverness. The two engines of the Belladrum Class were constructed by Hawthorns & Co of Leith in 1862 and were numbered 12 and 13. (Fig 14).

Dimensions

Cylinders (2 outside)	16″×20″
Boiler (158 tubes of 1¾″ diam)	
Maximum outside diameter	3′ 6½″
Grate area	15.5 sq ft
Boiler pressure	120 lbs
Diameter of wheels	
Leading	3′ 6″
Driving	6′ 0″
Trailing	3′ 6″
Tender	3′ 6″
Tractive effort (85%)	7,253 lbs
Wheelbase	
Engine	6′ 10″ + 7′ 4″
Tender	8′ 0″
Weights (approximate)	
Engine	28 tons
Tender	16 tons
Total	44 tons
Water capacity	1,100 gallons
Coal capacity	2½ tons

Fig. 14   2-2-2 12 *Belladrum* at Inverness roundhouse prior to the 1871 conversion to a 2-2-2 tank. Livery appears to be Stroudley's goods style of green with double lining. *(Photo: J.F. McEwan Collection)*

Livery

It is believed that the livery of the Inverness and Ross-shire Railway was the same as that of the Inverness and Aberdeen Junction Railway, namely dark green as has already been described. It is not known whether the engines carried the elaborate Stroudley goods livery of green with a darker green border but 12, from its conversion to a 2-2-2T, is believed to have received his passenger dark yellow with white and red lining and darker ochre border. Lagging bands were in the latter shade, edged with red and white, and the narrow upper cab sides were ochre, painted as extensions of the tank-side and bunker borders. The framing was claret and the name in gold on the tank side with horizontal lettering. It was altogether a work of art, but belied by the engine's indifferent performance.

Later both engines had at least one or other of the Jones styles with the triple lining. 12 certainly had the apple green and the red brown framing of 1885 with the number plate on the bunker.

Names

These were the now usual mixture of place names, directors and their residences.

Belladrum   (Accent on the 'e') This referred to the residence near Beauly of James Merry MP who was a director and large shareholder. The name was used again on 49 of the Glenbarry Class as early as 1864 and it is possible that for a brief period both 12 and 49 carried the name.

Breadalbane   (Accent on the second syllable) This name, subsequently also to reappear, came with the transfer of 12 as a 2-2-2T to the Aberfeldy branch. This terminated not far short of Taymouth Castle, the seat of the Marquis of Breadalbane, a director.

Strathpeffer   This was the branch where 12 later worked.

Lovat   Lord Lovat was another director and large shareholder.

Thurso   This indicated the branch where 13 worked for a time.

12, as will be seen from the summary, was nameless twice between renaming and again in its last days.

Rebuilding

The branch from Ballinluig to Aberfeldy had been opened in 1865 and required a tank engine to work it as there were originally no turntables. 12 was therefore converted to a side tank engine in September 1871. The wheel spacing remained the same but the engine received new frames and a single laminated spring across the trailing axle, later replaced by separate springs set in the usual manner. The Stroudley-style cab with its low domed roof had to be made very short in order to leave room for the rear bunker and tool box. A Jones chimney without louvres was fitted and a side-hinged smokebox door. The weight became 29 tons of which 12 tons were on the driving axle. The water and coal capacities are not known. (Fig 15).

Fig. 15

12 as a 2-2-2 tank, probably when laid aside after 1890. Apparently in apple-green livery with red-brown framing. Number plate on bunker.

(Photo: J.L. Stevenson Collection)

On the Aberfeldy branch 12 was something of a failure and it was eventually laid aside, to be rescucitated however when the Dingwall to Strathpeffer branch was opened in 1885. It acquired a dome on the barrel and a pair of Adams safety valves which were arranged longitudinally rather than transversely on the raised firebox. The original boiler was retained but probably underwent repair.

13 had a less colourful career, remaining a tender engine. In October 1870 the Board authorised alterations which in all probability included the fittings of a Jones chimney and the newer type of smokebox door.

Tenders

The tenders were very similar to those of the Raigmore Class, running on four wheels but somewhat sloped up towards the rear. The capacity was the same as that of the Raigmore tender. With the conversion of 12 in 1871 its tender became spare and was so recorded in the half-yearly stock returns for some years.

Allocation and Work

The two engines at first worked mainly, as intended, north from Inverness and indeed the pair were used to work the first train from Inverness to Golspie on 18th April 1868. However before the line reached Wick in 1874 12 had been converted to a 2-2-2T and sent to Aberfeldy where its poor performance caused it to be relieved of its command in 1880 and replaced by the new Jones 2-4-0 tank, 17. 12 then disappeared from view for a few years before it reappeared, as already mentioned, on the Strathpeffer branch, a much easier task than it had had at Aberfeldy. But even here age and lack of power began to tell and in 1890 the work was taken over by the newly built 0-4-4 tank 13. In its last days it lay idle or performed stand-in duties of the lightest nature.

13 spent much of its time on the Thurso branch between 1874 and 1889 and eventually it found its way to Forres.

Withdrawal

After eight years of partial retirement 12 was taken out of service for repairs in October 1894. However no work was carried out and the engine was at last taken out of stock in September 1898, being recorded as "obsolete tank engine, in pieces" in July 1899 and a year later as dismantled. Once or twice earlier in its life it had been in limbo and had reappeared but this time there was to be no resurrection. 13 was withdrawn in May 1890.

Summary of Class

No.	Name	Maker	Works No	Built	Rebuilt as 2-2-2T	Withdrawn
12	Belladrum (I) /- (c.1865) /Breadalbane (I) (1871) /- (1879) /Strathpeffer (I) (1885) /- (1890)	Hawthorns & Co. Leith	258	5/1862	5/1871	9/1898 (See note)
13	Lovat (I) /Thurso (1874)	,,	259	7/1862	—	5/1890

Note: No 12 was out of use from 10/1894

2.4 14 Class 2-4-0
Barclay 5 ft 0 in Engines

The goods engine equivalent of the Belladrum Class and like them built for the Inverness & Ross-shire Railway, these two 2-4-0s did not greatly differ from the Seafield Class. By the time they had been delivered by the builders, Hawthorns & Co., in late 1862 the Inverness and Ross-shire Railway had been absorbed by the I&AJR.

The cab had its lower side in three divisions in Barclay's goods style, and in other respects the pair were slightly larger than the Seafields, their boiler and firebox in particular having different dimensions. However the framing, running gear, chimney, springs and compensating levers were identical with those features of the Seafields, as were the safety valves, one on the barrel and one cum dome on the raised firebox. A new feature appeared in the form of a mid-feather in the firebox, a device which had been patented by Joseph Beattie of the London and South Western Railway. It consisted of a transverse water tube which divided the firebox into two parts, front and rear, the purpose being to improve combustion and water circulation, although on the Highland it is doubtful if the results justified the extra costs of construction and maintenance.

The two engines were given numbers 14 and 15.

Dimensions

Cylinders	16″ × 22″
Boiler	
Maximum outside diameter	4′ 2″
Length of barrel	5′ 0″
Pitch	5′ 10½″
Length of firebox casing	5′ 10½″
Grate area	15.5 sq ft
Boiler pressure	120 lbs
Diameter of wheels	
Leading	3′ 0″
Coupled	5′ 0″
Tender	3′ 6″
Tractive effort (85%)	9,574 lbs
Wheelbase	
Engine	5′ 11″ + 8′ 4″
Tender	8′ 3″
Weights	
Adhesion	21 tons
Engine	30½ tons
Tender	16 tons
Total	46½ tons
Water capacity	1,200 gallons
Coal capacity	2½ tons

Renumbering

14 was thrice renumbered, becoming 6 in 11/1893, 32 in 11/1897 and 49 in 2/1899. While these are believed to be the official renumbering dates, they are inconsistent with the withdrawal dates of the Glenbarry engines concerned in that 32 of that class is shown as withdrawn in 9/1898 and 49 in 7/1899. Of these the former (the last 2-2-2) was probably laid aside some time prior to the official withdrawal date, and 49 was certainly recorded as "idle" by 7/1899.

Livery

Presumably this was originally the simple green style with black lining as on the Seafield Class. 'I.A. & J.Ry' appeared round the splasher and the number was on the buffer beam. By 1865 the name had superseded the company title on the splasher and it is likely that Stroudley's goods engine green was applied with the white and red lining and claret frames. A number plate was on the middle division of the lower cab side.

Later at least one of the Jones shades with triple lining appeared. Certainly 49 (14) was still in the 1885 shade in 1897 and probably until the end.

Names

Both engines started and ended their lives nameless and it is probable that no name was carried for long. The sources were as follows:

Loch	This referred to George Loch, a member of the original Highland Railway Board of 1865.
Sutherland	This, to be used again twice, was after the Duke of Sutherland, a director and one who did more than anyone else to promote railways in the Highlands.

The other names were taken from places served by the railway. The station for Evanton was at that time called Novar but long afterwards, in 1937, it was renamed Evanton.

Detail Alterations

Jones renovated both engines, 14 in February 1872 and 15 in 1875, each receiving the louvred chimney and having the leading wheels increased to 3 ft 2½ in

Fig. 16   2-4-0 No 6 (formerly 14) at Perth, as fitted in 1872 with Stroudley pattern cab and Jones chimney. Jones apple-green livery.   *(Photo: Real Photographs)*

Fig. 17   2-4-0 No 6, now renumbered 49, at Perth about 1900, shortly before withdrawal.
(Photo: L.G.R. Photographs)

and the driving wheels to 5 ft 2½ in. The smokebox doors were side-hinged by now. 14 was given a Stroudley pattern of cab in place of the Barclay type. If 15 received a new cab at its repair in 1875 it would probably have been of Jones pattern. Both had the mid-feather removed, probably at the dates given above. (Figs 16 and 17).

Later both received new cylinders with dimensions increased to 17 in by 24, 14 in May 1882 and 15 in November 1886. Tractive effort was thereby raised to 11,320 lbs. In July 1894 14 was given the boiler from No 8 of the Seafield Class, and by this time had acquired the vacuum brake.

Tenders

The tender ran on four wheels and was similar to the Seafield pattern. That on 14 later had the tool box taken off and the tank was extended back, the only known instance of this on a 4-wheel tender. This particular one had a straight top and was not sloped up towards the back.

Allocation and Work

It is believed that the engines were sent via Aberdeen to Perth in 1863 to work between there and Pitlochry, a couple of months or so before the through service was inaugurated between Inverness and Perth. After a time 14 seems to have gone to the North line but its later days were spent at Perth. The fact that it had the vacuum brake indicates that it did some passenger work. 15 is believed to have worked for a time between Perth and Blair Atholl and may well have been engaged in banking at the latter point, but it then migrated north and further trace of it seems to have been lost. 14 is reputed to have been kept in immaculate condition when at Perth, suggesting that it was a good engine.

Withdrawal

15 was withdrawn in October 1893 and sold for scrap the following month but the other survived longer. Again there is confusion of dates as 49 (old 14) is shown as withdrawn in 9/1901 but its number was definitely taken by a Lochgorm Tank (ex-16) in 2/1901. One can only conclude that the old 2-4-0 was out of use by the beginning of 1901 but was not actually taken out of stock until later in the year. It was eventually sold for scrap as "Lot 6" in 9/1902.

Summary of Class

No.	Name	Maker	Works No	Built	Withdrawn
14	Loch	Hawthorns & Co.,	264	9/1862	9/1901
/6 (11/93)	/-	Leith			
/32 (11/97)	/Evanton				
/49 (2/1899)	/-				
15	Sutherland (I)	,,	265	10/1862	10/1893
	/-				
	/Dunkeld				
	/Foulis				
	/-				

2.5 Findhorn Railway 0-4-0 Tank
Neilson 3 ft 6 in Engine

This engine stands apart from the line of Highland locomotive development, having been designed by the makers, Neilson & Co. It was acquired in 1862 by the Inverness & Aberdeen Junction Railway when they took over the working of the Findhorn Railway, whose sole engine it had been and where it had been employed in working their three-mile long line from Findhorn, a small port on the Moray Firth, to Kinloss between Forres and Elgin. A request had been made in August 1859 to the directors of the I&AJR to "supply the necessary plant to work the line" but understandably they declined, as they had scarcely enough engines and coaches to work their own expanding system, but they did undertake to supply wagon plant.

The Findhorn Company, intending to open their line early in 1860, had little option but to buy something ready made (and inexpensive). They approached Neilsons who offered them a 4-coupled industrial pug which they had built for stock in 1859. Purchased by the Company in 1860, it was an engine

of very simple design, designated as a Box Tank because of the rectangular saddle tank covering the boiler barrel and firebox. There were inside frames, outside cylinders, laminated springs, a single spring balance safety valve, enclosed in a brass cover, on the raised firebox and a stove-pipe chimney. There were neither dome, running board nor cab, indeed not even a weather board, and altogether the engine could not be described as a thing of beauty. The valves were above the cylinders and were operated by Neilson indirect motion which did not allow cut-off working, while the boiler feed was driven off the crosshead. The footplate had low side sheets, behind which a very limited quantity of coal could be carried and there was a railing across the back. The smokebox door was double, hinged on both sides, and the timber buffers were flat and massive. (Fig 18).

The design was a standard one of Neilson of Glasgow, whose long maker's plate with bulbous centre was on the tank side. On the Findhorn Railway no number was carried. In March 1862 when acquired

Fig. 18   The engine in service on the Findhorn Railway in its original condition prior to 1867.
(Photo: J.F. McEwan Collection)

36

by the I&AJR together with the Findhorn Railway's carriage, brake van and surplus stores the lot was valued at £1,484 15s 6d. Thereafter the I&AJR took over the operation of the line and the engine became their 16, continuing to bear this number when it came into Highland ownership.

Dimensions

Cylinders	12″ × 18″
Heating surface	
Tubes	353 sq ft
Firebox	39 sq ft
Total	392 sq ft
Grate area	12 sq ft
Boiler pressure	120 lbs
Diameter of wheels	3 ft 6 in
Tractive effort (85%)	6,295 lbs
Wheelbase	5 ft 9 in
Length over buffers	21 ft 6 in
Weight	16 tons
Water capacity	530 gallons

Livery

Nothing is known about the livery worn on the Findhorn Railway, but early photographic evidence shows a dark unlined shade, probably black. Presumably some time from 1862 the engine received I&AJR green and certainly after overhaul in 1866 the Stroudley green with white and red lining was carried. At the same time a number plate was mounted on the cab side and the maker's plate removed from the tank. For its last spell of service, with contractors after its sale, the engine does not appear to have been repainted. The cab side still showed faint traces of lining, and in the centre an oval mark was visible where the number plate had been.

Name

No photograph is known which shows the engine with a name, although some authorities state that it bore the name *Findhorn*. From 1860 to 1862 this could equally likely have denoted the owning company. There is a slight possibility that the name was carried after that but much more probably it simply came to be known as 'The Findhorn Engine'. Certainly there was no name after it was sold to contractors.

Detail Alterations

On 8th July 1861 the I&AJR directors considered a letter from the Findhorn Railway asking whether the I&AJR would undertake to repair in their workshops any of the Findhorn plant, also to supply a locomotive during their engine's absence. The I&AJR agreed to meet this request and instructed the Locomotive

Superintendent to expedite the repairs and to "furnish the engine on the most moderate terms". In the following year, as we have seen, it became the property of the I&AJR.

In 1866 Stroudley took it into Lochgorm Works for extensive overhaul. He altered the link motion but retained the indirect drive to the slide valves. The wheelbase was lengthened slightly either to improve stability or to accommodate the modified gear. While it has been stated that new wheels were fitted, it seems unlikely that the Highland would go to such expense but rather that the area of wheel opposite the crank pin was developed into a balance weight extending from the axle boss down to the wheel rim, probably by casting an iron addition. Previously this part of the wheel had carried a 'spare' crank pin hole. The rebalancing, like the lengthening of the wheelbase, would have had the aim of improving the riding of the engine, which after all had never been designed for train working. Stroudley's chimney with a brass flare replaced the stove-pipe and improved the engine's appearance, while a toolbox was set on the tank just behind the chimney. The iron boiler tubes were replaced with brass. (Fig 19).

Allocation and Work

When the Findhorn Railway was inspected on 9th April 1860 by Captain Tyler RE the I&AJR provided for his use No 8, one of the Seafield Class 2-4-0s. He criticised, probably with every justification, the Findhorn engine but sanctioned its use when the Chairman and Secretary attested that speed would not be permitted to exceed 10 miles per hour! As the trains were scheduled to cover the three-mile run in 18 minutes, the timetable was scarcely achievable within such a tight limit. Nevertheless the engine worked the line from 1860 until it closed in 1869, presumably relieved by a 2-2-2 or 2-4-0 when it required attention at the works.

Many of the trains were mixed, and the bulk of such revenue as the line earned came from goods traffic, such as timber, stone, coal, fish, agricultural produce and suchlike, mainly in connection with the harbour which was the main reason for the building of the line. The engine shed was at Kinloss, but coal was stored at the two stations for replenishing supplies as the quantity of coal which could be carried on the engine was extremely limited.

After the I&AJR took over the working in March 1862 their directors were dissatisfied with the remuneration received and they resolved in October 1862 to inform the Findhorn Company that "unless payment is increased it will be necessary to revert (sic) to working by horse power as provided by the agreement". The Findhorn Company agreed to the request, no doubt reluctantly, and 16 remained at

Fig. 19   The Findhorn engine (HR 16) after sale in 1872 to contractors for the Caithness Railway. In use near Thurso. New chimney and other alterations made by Stroudley in 1867. *(Photo: J.F. McEwan Collection)*

work until the line closed in January 1869, after which it was used for shunting at Inverness.

Withdrawal

On 6th August 1872 the Board accepted what seems to have been a handsome offer of £600 for the engine from a Mr John Scott, acting for one of the contractors for the Sutherland and Caithness Railway which was then being built. The engine presumably departed soon afterwards but for some extraordinary reason the Highland continued to show five tank engines in the half-yearly reports, one of which must have been old 16. The figure remained unchanged when the new 16, the third Lochgorm Tank, was put into service in October 1874, this clearly being regarded as a 'renewal' of the absent Findhorn engine now in the ownership of Hector Mackenzie, the contractor for the northernmost section of the Wick line. Later it was similarly employed in the Dunfermline area. Such duties were of course more in line with its original purpose for it was in essence a contractor's engine.

In its early days 16 must have been a fascinating sight with its midget loads on the short-lived Findhorn line. Historically at least it was an enrich-ment to the locomotive history of the Highland Railway.

The Box Tank

This was a variety which originated in the early 1850s and was built over the next two or three decades, many examples surviving into the twentieth century. Several builders made them, and like most tank engines in Scotland they were known as pugs. Such locomotives were intended to work at quarries, collieries and industrial plants of all sorts which were becoming common throughout the land. With a view to cheapness, reliability and ease of maintenance the design and manufacture of the box tank were very simple, stripped as it was to the barest essentials with aesthetic considerations ignored. The engine was generally an 0-4-0T but was sometimes an 0-4-2T, usually with no running board, while the chimney was often not much more than a pipe. The safety valve was over the firebox and frequently there was a lever attached which the driver could hold down when more steam was required for steeper sections, a dangerous practice! (16 was so fitted). The square saddle tank resembled a box. These engines must have been very uncomfortable for the crew.

The Findhorn Company needed something quickly and no doubt this was the best that they could afford. Certainly the power output to haul a single coach, brake van and perhaps one or two wagons over the nearly level three-mile branch would not have been great and speed was in theory at least limited to 10 mph.

Summary of Class

No.	Maker	Works No	Built	Acquired by I&AJR	Sold
— /16 (3/1862)	Neilson & Co.,	422	1859	3/1862	9/1872

2.6 Needlefield Tank 0-4-0T later 0-4-2T
Hawthorns & Co. 4 ft 0 in Engine

Like the last mentioned 0-4-0T 16, this engine also falls outside the continuity of locomotive evolution, the I&AJR acquiring only one example of Hawthorns' decidedly archaic design with the intention of using it on the Burghead branch which opened in December 1862.

The inside cylinders were a novelty for the I&AJR but there were other oddities. The side tanks extended to the front of the smokebox but as they did not reach down to the running board it might be correct to term the engine an early example of a pannier or wing tank. There were inside frames, a raised firebox and laminated springs. The most striking feature was the very tall chimney topped by a brass flare and more than twice the height of the brass dome on the barrel, while a spring balance safety valve in an ornate brass cover surmounted the firebox. There was no proper cab but only a rear platform with a small weatherboard in front, the bunker being between the firebox and the cab side. The smokebox door was hinged at the side. The valve gear is believed to have been an early type, an adaption of Stephenson's motion. (Fig 20).

The design was the maker's who built it in 1863 at a cost of £1,475, one of a number which they had supplied, in some cases differing in details. Other examples were No 3 of the Dalmellington Iron Company, built in 1856, and *Magnus* of the London Chatham and Dover Railway which appeared in 1860.

The I&AJR numbered the engine 17.

Dimensions

Cylinders (2 inside)	13″ × 18″
Heating surface	
Tubes	424.5 sq ft
Firebox	53.5 sq ft
Total	478 sq ft
Boiler pressure	100 lbs
Diameter of wheels	4′ 0″
Tractive effort (85%)	5,387 lbs
Wheelbase	6′ 0″
Weight	16 tons 8 cwts
Water capacity	510 gallons
Coal capacity	15 cwts

Renumbering

The engine was transferred to the duplicate list as 17A in 1879. However from 1880 it ran without a number, no doubt because its duties as carriage works shunter and then as a stationary boiler would have

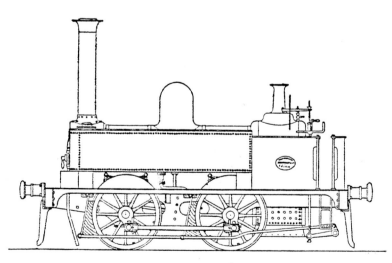

Fig. 20   Line drawing of the 0-4-0 tank as designed and built by Hawthorns, originally for the Burghead branch where it carried the number 17.

made it a departmental engine. In 1898 it was again numbered, now 1A.

Livery

The original style of the Inverness and Aberdeen Junction Railway was green with a black surround on the tank side, cab sides etc. The Stroudley livery applied in this case is said to have had a fine white lining (and, one suspects, also a fine red outer line which photographically would be almost invisible) together with a darker green border. Fig 21 shows the first and rather darker Jones shade with white, black and red lining. The tank side, cab, tool box etc were panelled separately, while the name *Needlefield* was in gold (shaded) on the tank side. A facsimile of a Jones number plate was painted on the cab side/bunker side with the Company's title on the gold surround, and with the centre blank as the engine was, as noted above, without a number at the time. By 1898 the Drummond olive green with black and double white lining was applied, again with meticulous panelling. The dome, previously burnished brass, was now green. The restored number 1A was shown where the imitation plate had been, again painted but within a garter like that encircling the Company's coat of arms. *Needlefield* still appeared on the tank side in gold but with the lettering more closely spaced and some four inches high whereas before it had been about six inches. See Fig 22. It is surprising that such an elaborate style was bestowed upon an engine which was clearly on its last legs.

Name

Hopeman referred to the branch where the engine first worked, although at that time the line reached only as far as Burghead and was not extended to Hopeman until 1892. Needlefield was the site of the carriage works at Inverness, where the engine spent the latter half of its life shunting, the name arising from the pine trees which had once grown there. No name was carried for a year or so between the two namings.

Rebuilding and Alterations

In 1867 Stroudley carried out a rebuild, adding a pair of trailing wheels to improve stability, and at the same time he fitted his standard cab with the domed roof, double spectacle windows and tool box behind.

The chimney was now shorter but the brass flare was retained. (Fig 21). The following dimensions were altered:

Diameter of trailing wheels	3' 1"
Length over buffers	22' 8"
Wheelbase	6' 0" + 6' 0"
Weights:	
Adhesion	14 tons
Total	20 tons

The engine's stability benefited as did also its appearance, the 'Puffing Billy' image having been largely dispelled. The cylinders were 'remade' at Lochgorm in October 1874 and their diameter was increased from 13 in to 13½ in. Jones overhauled it further in 1880 and either then or certainly by 1890

Fig. 21   Unnumbered *Needlefield* rebuilt as an 0-4-2T by Stroudley in 1867. In use as a departmental shunter at Inverness. First Jones livery of mid-green with white, black and red lining. Facsimile of number plate — showing no number!

(Photo: J.F. McEwan Collection)

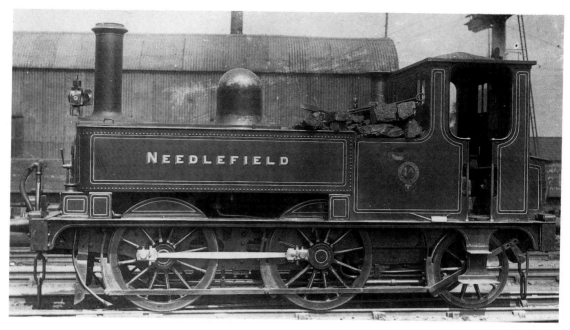

Fig 22   *Needlefield* in its last days as No 1A after receiving a Jones chimney about 1895. Still shunting the carriage works at Inverness. Drummond livery of olive green with black and double white lining. No number plate, but garter enclosing '1A'.   *(Photo: F. Moore (L.P.C.))*

the diameter was increased again, to 14 in. In April 1895 the boiler and outer firebox were patched, while about the same time a Jones chimney without louvres was fitted. Drummond gave the engine a last renovation in 1898 and either then or a little earlier a sandbox appeared below and ahead of the tank on either side. The vacuum brake also was fitted and thus fortified the engine received a number again, 1A, as we have seen. Latterly it was an attractive and smart little engine (Fig 22).

Allocation and Work

Built for the Burghead branch, 17 went there in 1863 the year after its opening. The considerable overhang at the rear caused an unsteadiness even at low speeds and led to the addition of the trailing axle four years later. Despite its limitations it stayed on the branch until it was replaced by Jones Tank 58 in 1879, moving then to Forres as goods yard pilot. In the following year it was taken to Inverness and set to shunting the carriage works there, losing its number.

In 1886 it sank even lower being converted to a stationary boiler for the Lochgorm sawmill. It has also been suggested that it was used actually to turn the machinery. Eventually it was rescued from this ignominy and in 1898, again renovated and numbered, resumed its former duties at Needlefield carriage works. This resurrection was however of fairly short duration as No 1A was reported to be lying derelict in mid-1901.

Withdrawal

In the minutes of the Board meeting of 28th June 1904 the engine was stated to be old and worn, a description applicable to a number of Highland engines around the turn of the century, and the decision was made to take it out of stock. It was sold soon afterwards, together with four 2-4-0s and four spare tenders to John Jackson & Co of Scotstoun, Glasgow, the whole assortment fetching £1,269. So departed one of the Highland's solitary and interesting engines after an unusual career.

Summary of Class

No.	Name	Maker	Works No	Built	Rebuilt	Withdrawn
17	*Hopeman*	Hawthorns & Co.,	275	5/1863	1867	Sold
/17A (12/1879)	/-	Leith				9/1904*
/- (1880)	*Needlefield* (1880)					
/1A (1898)		*Out of use by 1901				

2.7 Small Goods Class 2-4-0
Barclay 5 ft 1½ in Engine

The years 1863 and 1864 saw roughly a trebling of the route mileage operated by the Inverness & Aberdeen Junction Railway with the opening of the Inverness to Perth line throughout in September 1863 and the extension of the North line from Dingwall to Bonar Bridge, effected in stages during 1863 and 1864. Andrew Dougall, who was manager both of the I&AJR and of the Inverness & Perth Junction Railway, met Alexander Allan at Perth on 25th June 1862 to discuss motive power requirements — Barclay's views do not seem to have been sought — and they concluded that the following were the immediate needs, delivery to be given by 1st July 1863:
8 passenger engines "to carry 172 tons up a gradient of 1 in 70"; and 10 goods engines with a similar capability of 200 tons.

The passenger engines were to appear as 2-2-2s, forming the first batch of the Glenbarry Class, which will be dealt with in the next section, while the goods engines were to be 2-4-0s, the Small Goods (or '18') class. The tendering related to both classes and has features of interest which are considered jointly here.

Tenders were sought from five firms, with the proviso that Hawthorns of Leith were to be allowed to build two of the passenger engines as it appears that the agreement of 1855, whereby the firm built two of the Raigmore Class for the I&AJR, provided also for further two engines. It had been agreed in 1859 that the firm would "allow the Company their own time for ordering the balance of engines contained in the contract".

Details of the offers received are as follows:

Builder	Tender Price Each Passenger Engines £	Goods Engines £
Beyer, Peacock & Co.	3,200	3,300
Sharp, Stewart & Co.	2,825	2,825
Robert Stephenson & Co.	2,962	2,988
Neilson & Co.	2,770	2,885
Hawthorns & Co.	2,825	2,925

Neilsons were duly awarded on 9th September 1862 the contract for six passenger engines at £2,770 each and Sharp Stewart that for the ten goods engines at £2,825 each. Hawthorns were asked to build the remaining two passenger engines, but they pointed out that the quotation of £2,825 related to an order for the whole class of eight. After two months of correspondence the price was agreed at £2,900 each. These contracts were to raise the locomotive stock of the I&AJR from 17 to 35 at the end of 1863, the additional 18 engines being specifically to work the Inverness and Perth Junction Railway which in the incredibly short space of little over two years built the 103¾ miles of route from Dunkeld to Forres, authorised in July 1861 and opened throughout in September 1863.

It is perhaps permissible to digress into 1864 and mention that by the end of that year the I&AJR locomotive stock had risen to 55 with the addition of ten more Glenbarry 2-2-2s and of the ten Medium Goods (q.v.). Thus when the Inverness and Aberdeen Junction and the Inverness and Perth Junction Railways amalgamated, leading to the formation of The Highland Railway on 29th July 1865, the new company started life with the undernoted locomotive fleet, which scarcely reflected the gruelling operating conditions:

Class	No. of Engines	Running Numbers
Raigmore 2-2-2	4	1-4
Seafield 2-4-0	7	5-11
Belladrum 2-2-2	2	12-13
14 Class 2-4-0	2	14-15
Neilson 0-4-0 Tank	1	16
Needlefield 0-4-0 Tank	1	17
Small Goods 2-4-0	10	18-27
Glenbarry 2-2-2	18	28-35 and 46-55
Medium Goods 2-4-0	10	36-45
	55	

Apart from the addition of two of the three Lochgorm 0-6-0 Tanks and the changes, earlier recorded, to the Raigmores, these stalwarts carried on the Company's business until mid-1874 when the Duke 4-4-0s started to appear.

In the event the July 1863 date for delivery of the batch of eighteen engines was in no case achieved. As will be seen from the summary below, the first Small Goods arrived in August and delivery was not completed until November, while the eight Glenbarrys were similarly delayed. This placed the Company in a position of the gravest difficulty as the Inverness-Perth through services commenced on 9th September of that year. Consequently engines had to be borrowed from the Scottish Central and Caledonian

Railways, something in the nature of a pool of locomotives being formed to enable the operating requirements of the early months to be met. The I&AJR had lengthy negotiations with Sharp, Stewart and with Neilsons in an endeavour to obtain some recompense for the extra cost of the improvised arrangements, but the minute books do not make clear who won this argument.

Coming now to consider the Small Goods in detail, these engines carried the general Seafield design another step forward. Apart from increased dimensions, the 14 Class was repeated in the framing, chimney, boiler, boiler mountings, gear, springs and cab. The dome was on the raised firebox and carried one safety valve while the other was on the boiler barrel. There was again a transverse midfeather in the firebox on at least two of the engines (this device having been outlined under the 14 Class). The boiler, which was fed by a pair of Giffard injectors, contained 235 tubes of 1¾in diameter, while the smokebox hinges were at the side. The cylinders were inclined at 1 in 8 and a notable feature was the 9 ft coupled wheelbase which was much longer than that of the previous classes. As already mentioned, the Small Goods carried the numbers 18-27. (Figs 23 and 24).

Dimensions

Cylinders	17″×22″
Boiler	
Maximum outside diameter	4′ 1″
Length of barrel	9′ 6″
Pitch	6′ 4½″
Length of firebox casing	5′ 10½″
Heating surface	
Tubes	1,049.5 sq ft
Firebox, including midfeather	114.5 sq ft
Total	1,164 sq ft
Grate area	16 sq ft
Boiler pressure	150 lbs
Diameter of wheels	
Leading	3′ 7½″
Coupled	5′ 1½″
Tender	3′ 7½″
Tractive effort (85%)	13,181 lbs
Length over buffers (approx)	46′ 3″
Wheelbase	
Engine	6′ 0″ + 9′ 0″
Tender	5′ 9″ + 5′ 6″
Total	35′ 3″
Weights	
Adhesion	22 tons
Engine	32 tons
Tender	24 tons
Total	56 tons
Water capacity	1,800 gallons
Coal capacity	3 tons

Renumbering

In order to make their numbers available for Barney 0-6-0s, three Small Goods were in 8/1902 given numbers previously occupied by Medium Goods which were sold for scrap in the following month viz:

18 renumbered		36
20	”	38
21	”	39

27, which long outlived the rest of the class, was transferred to duplicate stock as 27A in 1913, its capital number then being occupied by a Castle. Between 1916 and 4/1918 it ran as 27B, indicating that it was regarded as a departmental, i.e. non-revenue-earning, engine presumably on snow plough and/or ballast working.

Livery

This was originally the I&AJR lined green already described when dealing with the Seafield Class. The initials of the Company followed by the number were on the splasher and the maker's plate was on the middle panel of the lower cab side. From 1865 a start was probably made in applying the Stroudley goods livery, but 20 and, it is believed, 24 had the Stroudley passenger livery of dark yellow with the appropriate lining. In all cases a number plate of Stroudley pattern was fixed to the cab side and displaced the maker's plate. The name was painted on the splasher in place of the initials.

From the early 1870s Jones colours were introduced, usually when engines of the class received his new cab, and the very dark blue-green may well have been given to the whole class. Later the apple green of 1885 certainly graced 20 and 22 also probably others. The Drummond olive green, with black and double white lining and with H.R on the tender was applied at least to 21, a variant being found on this engine in the shape of a black border on and between splasher and sandbox, with single inner white lining. Elsewhere it was normal. Probably 27, the last survivor, was the only one to have the later unlined olive green. This engine's splasher in the early 1900s still had faint traces of lining as on 21, while its tender was unlettered and the front buffer beam was green with 'H.R 27'. Latterly its tender was lettered and the dark wheel outline border on the splasher was visible to the end.

Names

These could not have been on at the start nor could they have lasted for long as photographs showing them are almost non-existent. They were entirely geographical to remind the public of the Company's expanding system.

Fig 23   A line of four 2-4-0s engaged in bridge testing on the Aberfeldy branch at Ballinluig in 1865. The classes are apparently (l. to r.) Small Goods, Medium Goods, Small Goods and Seafield, the last still without cab.

(Photo: W.O. Steel per R.J. Essery)

Fig 24   21 with the big plough prior to its boiler explosion in 1872 and subsequent rebuilding. Barclay dark green livery.

(Photo: F. Moore (L.P.C.))

Tenders

The tender ran on six wheels with asymmetrical spacing as shown in the table of dimensions. There was a tool box on the rear platform. At the rebuilding of the class from 1876 the tender capacity was increased from 3 to 4 tons.

Rebuilding and Alterations

Jones did a great deal to get the best out of the Small Goods by enlarging the cylinders and fitting new boilers, cabs and chimneys.

The first step was the enlargement of the cylinders from 17in by 22in to 17in by 24in on 18 to 23, this involving the fitting of eccentric crank pins. The dates of this work were as follows:

18	1/1872	21	4/1874
19	11/1871	22	11/1873
20	6/1872	23	9/1873

At the same time 21 received a new and more modern boiler to replace the original which had "blown apart" in 1872 (Fig 25). Then between 1876 and 1893 all except 21 had the cylinders enlarged to 18 in by 24 in and were given new boilers which had a dome on the barrel and safety valves arranged transversely over the firebox. In the first rebuilds, i.e. 21 and 24, also possibly one or two more, Adams type safety valves were fitted, but most received the lock-up type. The Jones cab replaced the original in the whole class and all were given a louvred chimney either at rebuilding or before. Wheel diameter was increased from 5 ft 1½ in to 5 ft 3 in by the substitution of steel tyres for the original iron ones. In their rebuilt form the Small Goods presented a much more substantial appearance and tractive effort was increased by some 20% except on 21 which retained the 17 in by 24 in cylinders. The boiler pressure on this engine appears to have been reduced to 150 lbs latterly. (Figs 26 and 27).

The dimensions where changed from the original were as follows:

Dimensions

Cylinders (2 outside)	18″ × 24″
Boiler	
Maximum outside diameter	4′ 0″
Length of barrel	10′ 3″
Pitch	6′ 6″
Heating surface	
Tubes (223 of 1¾″ diam.)	985 sq ft
Firebox	93 sq ft
Total	1,078 sq ft
Grate area	16.2 sq ft
Diameter of wheels	
Leading	3′ 9″
Coupled	5′ 3″
Tender	3′ 9″

Tractive effort (85%)	15,737 lbs
	(14,037 lbs on No.21)
Length over buffers	47′ 4½″
Weights	
Adhesion	25 tons 0 cwts
Engine	35 tons 10 cwts
Total	59 tons 10 cwts
Coal Capacity	4 tons

After 1883 the whole class with the exception of 24 received the vacuum brake, the ejector exhaust pipe being carried inside the boiler.

The dates of fitting the new boilers are shown in the Summary of the Class. Subsequently various firebox renewals and boiler exchanges took place. For example 21 was given a new firebox in July 1885, but retained the Adams safety valves. 22 received a new boiler in February 1892 and its 1878 boiler was then overhauled and fitted to 20 in the following November. 24 was given a new firebox and tubes in October 1895.

Allocation and Work

The Small Goods were engaged on goods work throughout the system, and the fact that all except one received the vacuum brake indicates that they were employed on passenger work at times also. They probably did most of their work on the Perth line and it is known that 26 was stationed at Perth for almost all of its life, being a firm favourite for a time of the foreman Tom Jagger who saw that the paintwork and mechanical condition was kept in tip-top order. 27 was also a Perth engine for some years.

One task in which all the 2-4-0 classes participated was the piloting of trains, from Forres and Blair Atholl mainly but also from other points. Rear end assistance was not permitted by the Board of Trade for a long time but it was common practice to detach the pilot on the move — the fireman of the train engine having this hazardous task — so allowing it to run ahead and clear the train which could thus proceed without stopping. Indeed at Dalnaspidal a signal was provided at the south end for the specific purpose of letting the pilot into the wrong (i.e. Up)side of the loop, this being before the doubling of the 1900s. This operation did on at least one occasion go wrong as will be described under the Clyde Bogie Class. The Working Timetables of the early 1890s lays down the undernoted pattern of assistance which seems to have been typical also of the previous decade:

Blair Atholl: 9 assisting trips, 6 to Dalnaspidal and 3 to Newtonmore.

Forres: 8 assisting trips, 6 to Dava and 2 to Grantown.

When assistance was given to Newtonmore or Grantown the engine was turned there and was

Fig 25   21 after the boiler explosion, showing position of the mid-feather in the firebox.
(Photo: W.O. Steel per R.J. Essery)

Fig 26   21 in 1902, as rebuilt in 1874 with new boiler having Adams safety valves, Jones cab and louvred chimney.
(Photo: LCGB Ken Nunn Collection)

Fig 27　　　27 at Perth in its final form with lock-up safety-valves. Unlined olive green livery of 1903.

(Photo: A.G. Ellis Collection)

booked to pilot a train on the return journey. Otherwise it returned light.

The arrival of the later engines of the Duke Class and of the Clyde Bogies in the 1880s eventually displaced the 2-4-0s largely from this work but another task which they undertook until the end was the snowplough working for which some were given special fittings. This was the last duty of the long-lived 27A which was snowplough engine at Forres between 1919 and 1921.

From the middle 1890s the Small Goods were relieved of main line goods work on the Perth line by the Big Goods, and elsewhere the Barneys of 1900 confined the active survivors to local goods and shunting duties. 19 ceased to be mobile as early as 1896 when it succeeded *Needlefield* as a stationary boiler for the works sawmill and indeed the twilight of the class was by now setting in.

The major catastrophe which befell the Small Goods occurred on 4th January 1872 to 21. It was working the 6.00 am Inverness to Keith Goods consisting of eleven wagons and brake van when the boiler exploded about ¾-mile east of Fochabers station (later named Orbliston Junction). The outer shell of the firebox was blown off and disintegrated into three pieces, one of which landed 200 yards away while the dome finished up 70 yards beyond this. The engine was not derailed and, separated from its tender, ran on for some 600 yards, the tender however

and most of the train coming to a stand off the rails. The enginemen were thrown out onto the side of the cutting but both survived although with fairly severe injuries. A "breaksman" travelling on the engine was trapped by the tender and killed.

The Board of Trade report as usual gives much interesting background information, for example that the engine had run 96,866 miles over the 8½ years since it had been delivered, "this comparatively small mileage being due to the fact that the engine was generally kept in winter with a snow plough fixed on it, and so only went out occasionally." It was concluded that the main cause of the explosion was the defective condition of the stays on the left side of the copper firebox, but other factors had contributed. Twenty stays had been renewed two months previously and it was suggested that a hydraulic test ought to have been carried out which would in all probability have indicated the presence of further defective stays. In any event lessons were no doubt learned from the affair and mercifully no other boiler explosion was reported on the Highland before or since which is to the credit of all concerned.

21 was in trouble again on 2nd August 1894 when it was working the 10.40 am Inverness to Perth goods, consisting of 26 wagons and two brake vans. Having attached sister engine 23 as pilot engine at Kingussie, the train was waiting at Newtonmore to cross the 11.50 am Perth to Inverness passenger when the latter

48

ran through the Down home signal and collided at some 8-10 mph head-on with the goods train, the south loop points being set for the Up line. The engines of the passenger train, made up of 16 vehicles, were Strath 96 piloted by Medium Goods 44. All four engines received superficial damage but some vehicles on both trains were badly smashed, including a North British Railway horse box into which a passenger, an Edinburth professor, had moved at Blair Atholl in order to feed his horse. He thereby lost his life, the only passenger to be killed in a Highland Railway accident apart from the victims of the Baddengorm Burn bridge collapse of 1914 which could fairly be considered as an Act of God. The Company's record of passenger safety was indeed remarkably good.

The accident was primarily due to the Down distant signal which for some unexplained reason was lying in the off position, but the passenger train crews seem to have reacted slowly to the fact that the home signal was at danger. The other factor was the position of the south loop points. Ironically new instructions were about to be issued which required such points to be set always for the left-hand road except when a train was leaving the loop.

Among the interesting detail to be found in the report of the Inspecting Officer, Major Marindin, is that the Newtonmore Station Master ("station agent") came on duty daily at 7.30 am and remained on until 12.00 midnight.

Withdrawal

Years of hard service caused much wear and tear so that latterly the class was long overdue for replacement on their heavier duties. Their gradual demise began after the arrival of the Big Goods in 1894 but like old soldiers they never seemed to die but rather to fade away. The half-yearly returns give an interesting insight into the condition of the older engines at this time. At the end of August 1896 there were 26 engines under or awaiting repair out of a total fleet of 128, while on 28th February 1897 the respective figures were 36 and 133 (ie 27% out of action). Withdrawals and the arrival of the Bens had roughly halved the repair figure by the end of 1899.

As might be expected in such a situation, it is usually very hard to state a definite date when engines at this period actually ceased work, this applying particularly to all the 2-4-0 classes. Most of them were sold for scrap and the dates of sale are almost always stated in the relevant Board or Committee minute and such dates are quoted in the Summary as denoting the ultimate fate of the engines. In many cases however they were out of service, often with parts removed, for months or years beforehand. For example, a visitor to Lochgorm in 1901 reported the following as lying out of use: Small Goods 18 and 20; Medium Goods 40, 41

and 43; Glenbarry 47 and 55. In another part of the yard could be found old boilers, wheels, cylinders, motion etc of Raigmore (II) No 2A; Small Goods 22, 23 and 24; Glenbarry 29. Yet there seems to have been enough left of 23 and 24 for them to be sold for scrap, together with 25, to P. & W. MacLellan, Glasgow in September/October 1902. 22 had been laid off as early as 1896 but was not written off until 1901. 19 was officially recorded as "lying in pieces" in 1901 but was evidently not written off until 1902.

Later offerings to MacLellans were 36 (ex-18) and 38 (ex-20) in September 1906, the former having been laid off in 1901 but later reinstated. Both were to be taken to Glasgow on their wheels for breaking up, together with Glenbarry 55 and five tenders. 39 (ex-21) was sold in 1909, but to whom is not known. Mystery surrounds 26. It has been stated that it was withdrawn in 1903 and this is borne out by a Return of Rolling Stock dated November 1905 in which it does not figure. However it is believed to have remained in use (or was perhaps brought back into use) as a snowplough engine until about 1910 when it was laid aside at Perth. Its withdrawal in 1913 is clearly recorded.

Further reference is made under the Glenbarry Class which follows to the difficulty of distinguishing between the dates when these old engines ceased to work and when they actually were taken out of stock.

27, albeit on the duplicate list from 1913, far outlived the rest. Its tender had been sold to MacLellans in 1906 and it must have acquired one from a scrapped engine. As 27A it witnessed the arrival of the LMS as a sexagenarian in 1923, being latterly designated as "only used on a snowplough" for which work it was seen, apparently usable, at Forres on 5th August 1921. It was not taken into LMS stock and by August 1923 the end was near as it lay derelict in the locomotive cemetery at Culloden Moor awaiting disposal. (Fig 28).

A proposal was made to the Board in May 1900 that tenders should be sought for rebuilding Small Goods 19 and 26, also Medium Goods 43 as 0-6-0 tank engines. No decision was made at that time but by the middle of the following year a start had been made in constructing the tanks which eventually appeared in 1903-4 as 22, 23 and 24. These will be described in Book 2. With so many half-dismantled engines lying about one cannot be positive but it seems likely that the wheels and motion of 19 and of one other Small Goods, most probably 22, also those of 43 were used to construct the Shunting Tanks in conjunction with three virtually new Glenbarry boilers. Another three pairs of coupled wheels and axles would also have been needed.

The Small Goods became increasingly under-powered for the work which they were required to do, but they were tough little engines and within their limits gave good service under difficult conditions for over thirty years.

Summary of Class

No.	Name	Maker	Works No	Built	Rebuilt	Withdrawn
18 /36 (8/1902)	Inverness (I) /-	Sharp, Stewart, Manchester	1416	8/1863	2/1887	Sold 9/1906 (Note 1)
19	Dingwall (I) /- /Golspie (II) /- (c.1886)	”	1417	”	8/1879	1902 (Note 2)
20 /38 (8/1902)	Birnam (I) /-	”	1426	”	1/1882	Sold 9/1906
21 /39 (8/1902)	Forres (I) /-	”	1427	”	4/1874	Sold 9/1909
22	Aviemore (I) /-	”	1436	9/1863	10/1878	1901 (Note 3)
23	Murthly /- Dalcross (II) /-	”	1437	10/1863	12/1890	Sold 9/1902
24	Invergordon (I) /- /Lairg /-	”	1438	”	12/1876	Sold 10/1902
25	Novar /-	”	1439	”	2/1890	Sold 10/1902
26	Beauly (I) /-	”	1440	11/1863	5/1893	1913
27 /27A (1913) /27B (1916) /27A (4/1918)	Conon /-	”	1441	”	2/1891	8/1923

Note 1 Laid aside in 1901 but later reinstated
Note 2 Stationary boiler from 1896
Note 3 Laid aside in 1896. Recorded as 'idle for remaking' in 7/1899 and as 'lying in pieces' in 1901.

2.8 Glenbarry Class 2-2-2 (later 2-4-0)
Barclay 6 ft 1½ in Engine

The background of increased operating mileage leading to the building of the eighteen Glenbarry Class 2-2-2s for passenger work has been covered in the introduction to the Small Goods Class, mention being made of the contract for six of the first batch of Glenbarry Class engines to Neilson & Co. at £2,770 each and that for the other two to Hawthorns & Co at £2,900 each. Delivery was made between September and November 1863 to the I&AJR. It was then decided to build a further batch of ten for which the contract was quickly let to Neilsons who made delivery in the latter half of 1864. The eighteen engines became 28-35 and 46-55.

Allan's persistence in providing still more single engines is indeed hard to follow as by mid-1861 the remaining sections of the Inverness to Perth main line had been authorised and it must have been obvious that to work the passenger services efficiently something more robust than these little engines would be needed. Possibly his thinking may have been influenced by the Civil Engineer. Certainly the Glenbarry Class had enlarged cylinders and boilers as compared with the Raigmore and Belladrum 2-2-2s, but there was little other basic difference. The frames, motion, Allan gear, chimney, safety valves and other features were as on the earlier classes and the cab resembled that of the Belladrum Class. Two Giffard injectors were provided in preference to the two pumps on the Raigmores and to the one injector and one pump on the Belladrum pair. The Glenbarry domeless boiler contained 204 brass tubes of 1¾ in diameter and there was a raised firebox. Despite the provision of a side-hinged smokebox door on the Small Goods shortly before, that on the Glenbarrys reverted to the lift-up variety. The tender ran on six wheels and was similar to the Small Goods type except that it had 5 cwts of extra coal capacity (Fig 29).

With a view to comparison, the firebox arrangements differed somewhat and most included a mid-feather (for a description of which see the 14 Class). It is generally stated that the first eight, 28-35, had a longitudinal mid-feather, two fire doors presumably

Fig 29   31 *Princess* in original condition as a 2-2-2, apparently in workshop grey paint. Lift-up smokebox door and shallow cab. (Compare the latter with the Small Goods cab).   (Photo: F. Moore (L.P.C.))

being provided side by side, and that nine of the second batch of ten, 46-54 had the Beattie firebox with the transverse mid-feather, while the final engine, 55, had a conventional firebox. However photographic evidence suggests that 29 and 35 at least had the Beattie firebox, the latter probably when new. There were differences also in cylinder dimensions. 28 and 29 had cylinders 17 in by 22 in but on the rest of the 1863 batch, 30-35, they were 16½ in by 22 in. Barclay, once more on Allan's advice, returned to 17 in cylinders in the engines built in 1864, 46-55.

Dimensions

Cylinders (2 outside)	(on 28, 29, 46-55)	17″×22″
	(on 30-35)	16½″×22″
Boiler		
Maximum outside diameter		3′ 11″
Length of barrel		9′ 9½″
Pitch		5′ 11¾″
Length of firebox casing		6′ 1⅔″
Heating surface		
Tubes		964 sq ft
Firebox (inc mid-feather)		115.2 sq ft
Total		1,079.2 sq ft
Grate area		20.33 sq ft
Boiler pressure		120 lbs
Diameter of wheels		
Leading and trailing		3′ 7½″
Coupled		6′ 1½″
Tender		3′ 7½″
Tractive effort (85%)	(of 28, 29, 46-55)	8,823 lbs
	(of 30-35)	8,312 lbs
Wheelbase		
Engine		6′ 9″ + 7′ 9″
Tender		5′ 9″ + 5′ 6″
Weights		
Adhesion		14 tons
Engine		31 tons
Tender		24 tons
Total		55 tons
Water capacity		1,800 gallons
Coal capacity		3¼ tons

In the case of 55, which had no mid-feather, the firebox heating surface was somewhat less than on the rest.

Renumbering

The only engine to be renumbered and to appear thus in service was the long-living 35 which was transferred to the duplicate list as 35A in 2/1911. A list dated 31st July 1899 shows 29, 30, 31 and 53 as 29A, 30A, 31A and 53A respectively, but the engines appear to have been out of service by that date. This is one of a number of instances of the confusion and conflictions which surround the Glenbarry class.

The notes to the Summary of the Class on page 59 indicate only too clearly the chaotic situation at this period, particularly evident with the Glenbarrys, relating to withdrawals. There were, it seems, two withdrawal dates, firstly the date when the Locomotive Superintendent stopped the engine from further use, and secondly the date when the Accountant took it out of the books. Normally these dates would be more or less identical but with many of the Glenbarrys they differed widely. In the latter half of the 1890s new engines were coming into service in some numbers making the retention and maintenance of the 2-4-0s of increasingly doubtful value. Yet a fair amount of money had been spent on them in the last Jones' years and the Accountant was no doubt reluctant to write this off, although the engines concerned were probably partly dismantled. Terms like "broken down for remaking" recur, usually meaning that the engine was awaiting a possible reboiling or heavy repair, while "standing idle" is a term also used which seems to have indicated that the Accountant was about to ask the Board to authorise the coup de grace. The modern term 'stored unserviceable' might be a rough parallel. Another Highland peculiarity was that an engine like 48, which was used as a works boiler from 1894, was still apparently regarded as being in capital stock until 1901 when the stationary duties finished.

While the reasons for these complexities are far from clear, they were evidently related more to book-keeping than to traffic operation. In an account such as this greater importance is attached to the date when the engine ceased to be used, but this is often not known.

Livery

The first livery in service was the dark shade of green with black panelling on the splasher, cab, tender etc, the name painted round the splasher and the Barclay number plate, all as described for the Seafield Class. Early photographs of 31 and 35 appear to show them in workshop grey and are therefore misleading.

After the Stroudley liveries were introduced one would have expected this class to receive the passenger version of dark yellow with double lining. While some of them may have been so painted, the few surviving photographs of Glenbarrys in Stroudley style show them in his goods livery of dark green with the appropriate panelling and double lining.

Most of them would no doubt have received the first Jones livery of 1870. Later, when the lighter green of 1885 came along 29, 30, 32, 48, 50, 51 and 53 certainly had this with the triple lining, darker border and red brown frames and steps. But the triple lining of this style tended to be simplified in that the

Stroudley double lining of white and red with the darker green border was still applied to engines with the Stroudley cab, ie 28 and 29, also to the solitary remaining single, 32 which still retained the Barclay cab.

Of the engines which survived into the Drummond era, 35, 46 and 55 at least received the olive green with black and double white lining and the lettering 'H.R' on the tender. Later 35 acquired the unlined olive green, losing the lettering on the tender for a time but recovering it before the end. After being reboilered by Sharp, Stewart in 1896 28 and 29 had red coupling rods.

Names

A number of these were geographical and thus do not require explanation but the following are the origins of the others which were appearing for the first time. The class shared a total of 34 names of which 18 had already been used.

Glenbarry	The Banffshire home of William James Taylor, a director. It was situated near the station of that name on the GNSR.
Highlander	A general name of no specific significance.
Prince and Princess	These names were bestowed in honour of the Prince and Princess of Wales who were married in 1863. In contrast to almost all the other names these were never altered and they remained together until death did them part. 30 *Prince* apparently had the honour of being the first to enter the newly opened roundhouse at Inverness in 1863.
Atholl	As with *Sutherland* which was appearing for the second time, the Duke was signified. Both were directors.
Kingsmills	The residence in Inverness of Colonel Hugh Inglis, a director.
Isla Bank	The residence at Keith of George Kynoch, a director.
Clachnacuddin	This denoted the famous stone beside the River Ness upon which women rested their tubs while washing clothes, the Gaelic meaning 'Stone of the Tubs'. The stone is now outside Inverness Town House.
Cadboll	The residence near Invergordon of R.B.A. Macleod, a director.
Badenoch	A large district of Upper Speyside, roughly centred on Kingussie.
Caithness	This referred to the Earl of Caithness, a director.
Dunphail	Dunphail House, near the station of that name, was the residence of Major L. Cumming-Bruce, a director.
Macduff	Viscount Macduff, a director.
Cluny	Cluny Castle, near Newtonmore, was the seat of Euan Macpherson of Cluny Macpherson, a director.

Of the other non-geographical names, *Seafield*, *Bruce*, *Aultnaskiah* and *Stafford* have been explained under the Seafield Class, and *Lovat* under the Belladrum Class.

Moving ahead to modern times, it is good to record the naming of British Railways diesel locomotive No 37 261 as *Caithness* at a ceremony at Wick on 14th June 1985. In this case the name refers to the District.

Detail Alterations and Rebuilding

30-35, which had been built with cylinders of 16½ in diameter, soon had these increased to 17 in, so bringing them into line with the rest of the class.

From 1871 Jones undertook the alteration of the class — with the exception of 32 — to 2-4-0s with the object of improving adhesion, and it was on the Glenbarry Class that he first fitted his well known louvred chimney, the whole class receiving this from 1871 onwards. He also fitted new cabs, those on 28 and 29 being after the Stroudley pattern as Jones had not yet evolved his own but the rest (or nearly all the rest) receiving the Jones cab with the horizontal joint and the rounded corners. A side-hinged smokebox door replaced the original and compensating levers were provided between the laminated springs of the coupled wheels. This work of conversion, in which the original boiler was retained, was carried out on 28, 29, 31, 33, 34 and 46-55 between 1871 and 1884 (Fig 30). Individual dates are shown in the Summary of the Class.

The dimensions where they were changed became as follows:

Wheelbase	
Engine	6' 9" + 8' 9"
Total	35' 9"
Weights	
Adhesion	25 tons
Engine	35 tons
Total	59 tons

Jones also began to fit new and larger cylinders to some of the class. 28, 29, 31, 33, 34 and 46-49 received 18 in by 24 in and 50-55 17 in by 24 in. This work almost certainly coincided with these engines' conversion to 2-4-0s.

From 1891 Jones began a more thorough renovation on very much the same lines as on the Small Goods. Several of the class were provided with a new and more up-to-date boiler having a dome on the barrel and lock-up safety valves arranged transversely over

Fig 30   50 *Badenoch*, rebuilt as a 2-4-0 in 1878 and with Jones cab but retaining the original boiler now with louvred chimney. At Forres c1890.   *(Photo: W.O. Steel per R.J. Essery)*

Fig 31   55 *Invergordon*, converted to a 2-4-0 in 1874 and with new boiler fitted in 1895.

(Photo: A.G. Ellis Collection)

the firebox. There were 223 tubes of 1¾ in diameter. Jones also increased wheel diameters by 1½ in by fitting thicker tyres. The first to be so treated were 30 and 35, which were still 2-2-2s, and at the same time they were at last altered to 2-4-0s and were given larger cylinders, 17 in by 24 in and 18 in by 24 in respectively. The others to be reboiled were 28, 29, 46, 47, 51, 54 and 55, the work usually being carried out at Lochgorm but 28 and 29 were dealt with by Sharp, Stewart in Glasgow. However the frames of these two appear to have been weak as the pair soon suffered frame failure and had to be laid aside, a similar situation arising with 51, and others later. Indeed provision of new boilers to these old engines seems to have been ill-advised, especially as new engines were coming in some numbers (Fig 31).

The dimensions of the reboiled engines now became as follows:

Cylinders (2 outside)	18″×24″ or 17″×24″
Boiler	
Maximum outside diameter	4′ 0″
Length of barrel	10′ 8¾″
Pitch	6′ 5½″
Length of firebox casing	5′ 5½″
Heating surface	
Tubes	1,093 sq ft
Firebox	93 sq ft
Total	1,186 sq ft
Grate area	16.2 sq ft
Boiler pressure	150 lbs★
Diameter of wheels	
Leading	3′ 9″
Coupled	6′ 3″
Tender	3′ 9″
Tractive effort (85%) (with 18″ cylinders)	13,219 lbs
(with 17″ cylinders)	10,809 lbs
Weights	
Adhesion	26 tons 10 cwts
Engine	37 tons 10 cwts
Total	61 tons 10 cwts
Coal capacity	4 tons

★Some authorities maintain that in certain engines, e.g. 28 and 29, the boiler pressure was 160 lbs. This cannot be confirmed.

By 1900 the condition of the frames of the reboiled engines was causing great concern, a report being submitted to the Board in May stating that "the frames of several engines rebuilt a few years ago are now completely worn out". This must have referred to the Glenbarrys. At the same meeting the strange proposal was discussed to convert 28 to a 4-4-0, but as its frames had by then collapsed the idea would have involved complete reconstruction. Nothing further was heard on the matter and 28 was written off in 1903. In contrast 35 was given a new firebox in

1904 which no doubt contributed to the engine's survival until 1923.

In 1895 Jones intended to rebuild 31, 33, 48 and probably three others to become similar to the Raigmore II Class for use on branch lines. New frames and boilers had been ordered from Sharp, Stewart but on Jones's retiral Drummond cancelled the order.

To the alterations and rebuilding there was one exception, 32 which as earlier mentioned, remained a single to the end, keeping also the Barclay cab (Fig 32). But it underwent some change as it acquired 18 in by 24 in cylinders in 1889 also the louvred chimney and a side-hinged smokebox door. It had been the intention to convert the whole class but Lochgorm never got round to dealing with 32. The minute of January 1882 reaffirming the conversion of the last six states that the cost would be £300 each.

The vacuum brake was fitted later to the whole class with the possible exception of 32. The ejector exhaust pipe was carried inside the boiler.

Attention must be drawn to the very early example of Jones louvred chimney which he fitted to 29 at its rebuilding in August 1871. This had the four vertical tiers of louvres, as later became standard, but they were arranged in six horizontal layers instead of the usual four and the rim was slightly narrower than later practice. This was doubtless an early trial of a chimney which was intended to create an upward draught of air to lift steam and smoke high. Whether any more 'six-bands' were made is not known, but this is the only one of which a photograph is known (Fig 33). Jones must have decided that four bands of louvres were sufficient for the purpose. Later 29's unique chimney was replaced by the conventional louvred pattern.

The following table shows the dates of the fitting of new cylinders and new boilers to the Glenbarry Class. The dates of conversion to 2-4-0 can be found in the Summary of the Class.

No	New Cylinders		Fitted with new boiler and larger wheels
	17″×24″	18″×24″	
28	—	8/1872	2/1896
29	—	8/1871	5/1896
30	9/1891	—	9/1891
31	—	5/1884	—
32	—	2/1889	—
33	—	3/1883★	—
34	—	12/1883	—
35	—	7/1892	7/1892
46	—	6/1880	12/1895
47	—	7/1880	6/1895
48	—	1/1881	—
49	—	4/1879	—
50	4/1878	—	—

Fig 32   32 *Cluny* which was never rebuilt as a 2-4-0 but received a louvred chimney, new cylinders etc. At Dingwall.   (*Photo: J.F. McEwan Collection*)

Fig 33   29 *Highlander* fitted with an early type of chimney having six horizontal layers of louvres instead of the usual four. c1874.   (*Photo: F. Moore (L.P.C.)*)

51	7/1875	—	c.1896
52	2/1876	—	—
53	11/1873	—	—
54	8/1873	—	8/1896
55	9/1874	—	1/1895

*The date of 11/1881 is also quoted

35A is believed to have had a flared chimney for a few years and to have retained this until 1923. Yet it undoubtedly had a pure Jones chimney before it ceased work in August 1923.

Tenders

These were the same as those of the Small Goods class but the coal capacity at 3¼ tons was 5 cwts more. The wheels were not quite evenly spaced, as will be seen from the table of dimensions. There was a tool box on the rear platform. The coal capacity was increased to 4 tons at rebuilding, although it is not clear how this was achieved. Certainly coal rails were added in some cases, the last survivor 35A being so provided, while at some stage a new and stronger tender was built for 30.

Allocation and Work

While it seems scarcely credible, these 2-2-2s when new worked the chief passenger trains on the main Inverness-Perth line. As would be expected, with loads of any size and on the long gradients their adhesion proved inadequate. Their rebuilding as 2-4-0s improved their performance but by then the Duke Class had appeared and taken over the principal trains, although the Glenbarrys could still be seen on main line piloting work. They also began to find their way to the North line — the line to Wick was opened throughout in 1874 — and to Keith, the names giving a clue as to their spheres of action. 30 and 31 are recorded as having worked the Royal Train north of Inverness. The longer survivors ended their days on shunting or on branches, 55 being on the Thurso branch at the turn of the century. 35, the sole survivor after 1906, was for a time kept at Perth for use with the snow plough and had special fittings for the purpose. Latterly, as 35A, it was ballast engine at Aviemore, being seen so employed there as late as July 1923.

51 was involved in a serious accident on 27th February 1879. It had assisted the 9.30 am passenger train from Perth between Blair Atholl and Kingussie and was returning piloting Duke 64 on the 10.18 am Up Mail from Inverness when its leading axle broke near Inchlea between Newtonmore and Dalwhinnie. As the Board of Trade report reads "The leading engine ran over the bank into a river and was much damaged, and the tender of this engine, which was thrown bottom upwards into the river, 50 yards from the engine, will have to be entirely rebuilt. The train engine and tender were upset on the top of the bank and the four leading fish vans were also upset. The other vehicles in the train remained in an upright position, but were all off the rails". By one of the miracles apparently present at most Highland Railway mishaps, no passengers nor servants of the Company were injured, the four enginemen remaining on their footplates. One odd feature which came to light was that eleven days before the accident, while piloting the 9.30 am Down train, 51's axle had similarly broken but no derailment had occurred. The axle had been quickly replaced at Lochgorm with a second-hand one which had apparently run some 250,000 miles, and the engine was returned to traffic within two or three days.

In his report, produced as quickly as 2½ weeks after the accident, Major Mandarin expressed the view that the exceptionally hard winter which had frozen the ground to a depth of two feet had contributed to the failure making the track less resilient and so harder on the rolling stock. Incidentally it is stated that 51 had run 339,876½ miles from construction in 1864 up to the time of the accident.

55 was another of the class which caused a near disaster when a broken spring resulted in its derailment 1½ miles north of Helmsdale while working the 12 noon Wick to Inverness passenger train on 14th September 1875. The engine ran down a bank and overturned, the chimney being severed. The fireman was killed and the driver badly hurt but no passenger complained of injury. The engine had run no less than 41,400 miles since being altered to a 2-4-0 exactly a year previously. In a rather less spectacular mishap in January 1893 53 was derailed at trap points at Forres during shunting operations with the result that two enginemen were fined a day's pay for passing a signal at danger.

Withdrawals

Mention has already been made of the difficulty of putting firm dates against the early classes and of the particular problems with the Glenbarrys, due in part to the fact that the frames started to fracture under the weight of the new boilers fitted from 1891, causing engines to be laid aside but not immediately taken out of stock.

The first of the class to cease work were those which were not reboilered, 33 being laid aside in 1893, followed by 34 in 1895, but these were not taken out of stock for some years. Likewise 52, dismantled in 1896, was not written off until 1899. 50 left the active ranks in 1897 and there was a considerable reduction in 1898 when 28-32 were laid aside, 32 being the last single on the Highland. Withdrawal of 28-30 from stock was not immediate. The Summary shows the position as far as it can be established but information is often conflicting.

Of the later withdrawals a number were sold for breaking up, 48 and 54 to P.& W. MacLellan, Glasgow in 10/1902 and 11/1903 respectively, and 55 to the same firm in 1906 (minus its boiler which went to Medium Goods 37). The Board Minutes of 28th June 1904 record that 46 and 47 were "aged and should be sold", following which an offer of £1,269 was accepted from John Jackson of Scotstoun, Glasgow for these two together with a further three engines and four spare tenders.

The frame fractures must have been a source of great embarrassment in view of the large expenditure on new boilers, especially on the two engines sent out to Sharp, Stewart. The Locomotive Committee at their meeting in May 1900 recommended that four engines should be fitted with heavier frames to work out their boilers and that 28 should be rebuilt to a four-coupled bogie engine, but nothing was done on these lines. Later three of the Glenbarry boilers were used on the 0-6-0 Shunting Tanks of 1903-4, probably those of 28 and 29 and perhaps that of 30. The last survivor by far was 35A which, together with one Small Goods and one Medium Goods saw the grouping in 1923, although none were taken into LMS stock.

The Glenbarrys were the first passenger class to run in numbers on the Highland. Old fashioned and inadequate at the start, the subsequent rebuildings improved their performance as well as their appearance, but the 2-4-0 rigid wheel arrangement scarcely put them into the ranks of express engines. The waste of money on reboilering was regrettable but the early loss of the engines was not too serious as by then new and much more capable motive power was becoming available.

Summary of Class

No.	Name	Maker	Works No	Built	Altered to 2-4-0	Withdrawn
28	Glenbarry /Grantown (5/1896)	Hawthorns & Co Leith	299	9/1863	8/1872	1898 (Note 1)
29	Highlander (I) /Forres (II) (5/1879) /-(c.1898)	,,	300	10/1863	8/1871	1898 (Note 1)
30	Prince	Neilson	966	,,	9/1891	1898 (Note 2)
31	Princess	,,	967	,,	5/1884	1898 (Note 3)
32	Sutherland (II) /Cluny (II) (1874)	,,	968	,,	—	9/1898
33	Atholl (I) /Birnam (II) (8/1886)	,,	969	,,	3/1883	4/1899 (Note 4)
34	Seafield (II) /Perthshire (II) (c.1889)	,,	970	,,	12/1883	4/1897 (Note 5)
35 /35A (2/1911)	Kingsmills /Isla Bank (1888)	,,	971	11/1863	7/1892	8/1923
46	Clachnacuddin (I) /Kingussie (II) (1883)	,,	1055	6/1864	5/1880	Sold 6/1904
47	Bruce (II) /Lovat (II) /Beauly (III) (1886)	,,	1057	,,	7/1880	Sold 6/1904
48	Cadboll (I) /Dingwall (III) (1886)	,,	1056	,,	1/1881	Sold 10/1902 (Note 6)
49	Belladrum (II) /Helmsdale (II)	,,	1058	7/1864	4/1879	Sold 7/1899 (Note 7)

No.	Name	Maker	Works No	Built	Altered to 2-4-0	Withdrawn
50	Aultnaskiah (II) /Badenoch	,,	1059	,,	4/1878	4/1897 (Note 8)
51	Caithness (I) /Blair Atholl (1874)	,,	1054	5/1864	7/1875	1900 (Note 9)
52	Dunphail	,,	1060	9/1864	2/1876	1899 (Note 10)
53	Stafford (II) /Golspie (III) (1886)	,,	1061	,,	11/1873	1901 (Note 11)
54	Macduff	,,	1062	10/1864	8/1873	Sold 11/1903 (Note 12)
55	Cluny (I) /Sutherland (III) (1874) /Invergordon (II) (1884)	,,	1063	,,	9/1874	Sold 9/1906

Note 1   28 and 29 were laid aside in 1898 due to frame breakage following the fitting of new boilers, but they were evidently not written off until 7/1903. 29 must have appeared in the books as 29A because its capital number was re-occupied from 7/1898. The wheels, cylinders, motion and other parts of 'No 29A' were to be seen lying about in Lochgorm Works yard in 1901.

Note 2.   30 seems to have been in existence still in 7/1899 when recorded — see above — as 30A.

Note 3.   Recorded as sold to a colliery in 1899, but this may refer to the boiler only, the rest of the engine being scrapped (nominally as 31A).

Note 4.   Had been standing since 9/1893 minus boiler which had been sold to the Rose Street Foundry, Inverness.

Note 5.   Engine out of use since 2/1895. Boiler put onto 31 in 1896. It is also recorded as being still in stock in 7/1899 but 'idle since 1897'.

Note 6.   Stationary boiler in Lochgorm Works from 1894 following boiler repairs.

Note 7.   Sold to a colliery.

Note 8.   Also recorded as being still in stock in 7/1899 but 'standing idle'.

Note 9.   Standing idle by 7/1899.

Note 10.   Dismantled 8/1896. Last in traffic 4/1893.

Note 11.   Shown in 7/1899 (probably dismantled) as 53A.

Note 12.   Out of use by 1901 due to frame fracture.

2.9 Medium Goods Class 2-4-0
Barclay 5 ft 1½ in Engine

The section dealing with the Small Goods class made brief reference also to the Medium Goods class which the directors of the Inverness and Aberdeen Junction Railway authorised on 24th September 1863 while the Small Goods and the first eight Glenbarrys were being delivered. Relations were becoming strained with Sharp, Stewart because of the late delivery of the earlier order but nevertheless they were awarded the contract for the ten Medium Goods which they delivered quickly between April and June 1864. They were given the numbers 36 to 45, thus splitting the continuity of the Glenbarrys which when completed carried the numbers 28 to 35 and 46 to 55.

The Medium Goods, also known as the '36' class, were similar to the Small Goods in most respects but had the cylinder stroke increased from 22in to 24in and the boiler barrel lengthened by 9 in to 10 ft 3 in, so extending the already long coupled wheelbase from 9 ft to 9 ft 3 in. Outwardly the two classes were practically identical, and the general description of the Small Goods can serve for both classes. The number of boiler tubes in the Medium Goods is not known for certain and may have varied, but it is known that in some engines at least there were 252 tubes of 1¾ in diameter, whereas the Small Goods had 235 (Fig 34).

Dimensions

Cylinders (2 outside)	17″×24″
Boiler	
Maximum outside diameter	4′ 1″
Length of barrel	10′ 3″
Pitch	6′ 4½″
Length of firebox casing	5′ 8⅞″
Heating surface	
Tubes	1,220 sq ft
Firebox	93 sq ft
Mid-feather	29 sq ft
Total	1,342 sq ft
Grate Area	15.5 sq ft
Boiler pressure	150 lbs
Diameter of wheels	
Leading	3′ 7½″
Coupled	5′ 1½″
Tender	3′ 7½″
Tractive effort (85%)	14,380 lbs

Fig 34   38 at Inverness roundhouse prior to 1882. Fitted with Jones chimney but still with original boiler and cab. Stroudley goods livery of green with double lining.   *(Photo: Real Photographs)*

Length over buffers	47' 7½"
Wheelbase	
Engine	6' 3" + 9' 3"
Tender	5' 9" + 5' 6"
Total	35' 6"
Weights	
Adhesion	23 tons
Engine	33 tons
Tender	24 tons
Total	57 tons
Water capacity	1,800 gallons
Coal capacity	3 tons

Renumbering

The following renumbering took place:
    41 to 41A (1905)
    42 to 42A (1/1912); 37 (10/1915); 37A (4/1918)
    44 to 44A (2/1912)

Livery

Originally the class was in dark green with black lining as in the earlier goods classes. Later one or two, including 38, appeared in the Stroudley goods style of dark green with the double lining, while from the mid-seventies several must have received the very dark green of the first Jones livery with triple lining and black border. From 1885 the apple green with triple lining, darker border and red brown frames was applied to 37, 38, 40 and 42 at least. The Drummond lined style with 'H .R' on the tender appeared on 37, first in a hybrid form in which the colour was still Jones's apple green but the cab had Drummond's black and double white lining with the darker green border, while the splasher had only a single white line along with the black. Soon afterwards this engine was given Drummond's standard olive green and full lining. 42 ran for a time in the Jones lined apple green, attached to a tender with Drummond lining, and latterly, then renumbered 37, it was in unlined olive green with 'H .R' on the tender. 44 was similar but with an unlettered tender. Both retained to the last the darker border on the splasher and sandbox also the arc marking the division between these.

Names

These were applied only from about 1867 or even later and they were not retained for long. All were geographical as with the Small Goods. After this it became the Company's practice not to name goods engines.

Rebuilding and Alterations

Between 1876 and 1889 Jones rebuilt the class in much the same way as he had dealt with the Small Goods, enlarging the cylinders to 18 in by 24 in and increasing the wheel diameter by 1½ in. He fitted a more modern boiler with a slightly larger heating surface than the new Small Goods boiler. It had a dome on the barrel and safety valves arranged transversely over the firebox, generally of the lock-up type but one engine at least, 36, had the Adams type. There were 223 tubes of 1¾ in diameter and the firebox was flush with the barrel. At the same time the Jones cab was fitted, the cab side being slightly narrower than on the Small Goods. The Jones louvred chimney took the place of the original and in the case of 38 at least the

Fig 35   38 at Perth in its final form with Jones boiler and cab fitted in 1885. Jones second livery. At Perth c1900.

(Photo: Real Photographs)

Fig 36   44 in unlined green livery. It can be seen that the vacuum standpipe must be swung aside to allow the
          smokebox door to be opened.   (Photo: F. Moore (L.P.C.))

new chimney was fitted before rebuilding, which was usually done at Lochgorm but 42 was rebuilt by Neilson in Glasgow (Figs 35 and 36).

The dimensions where different were as follows:

Cylinders (2 outside)	18″ × 24″
Boiler	
Maximum outside diameter	4′ 1″
Length of barrel	not known
Pitch	6′ 6″
Length of firebox casing	5′ 6″
Heating surface	
Tubes	1,045 sq ft
Firebox	93 sq ft
Total	1,138 sq ft
Grate area	16.2 sq ft
Boiler pressure	160 lbs
Wheels	
Leading	3′ 9″
Coupled	5′ 3″
Tender	3′ 9″
Tractive effort (85%)	16,786 lbs
Weights	
Adhesion	25 tons 10 cwts
Engine	36 tons 10 cwts
Total	60 tons 10 cwts
Coal capacity	4 tons

After rebuilding a number of further repairs to boilers and fireboxes have been recorded and it may be of interest to quote these:

36 New firebox and front tubeplate 1/1891; new tubes 7/1895.

37 Tubeplate repairs and new firebox 11/1896.

38 Received 1887 boiler 9/1891.

39 New tubes (red metal) 4/1895.

40 New tubes (red metal) 1/1895.

41 New firebox, tubeplates and tubes (red metal) 6/1894.

42 Repaired by Neilson 4/1896. Received new firebox, tubeplate and tubes.

43 New tubes (red metal) and tubeplate 4/1890.

44 New tubes (red metal) and tubeplate 11/1890.

45 New tubes (copper) 12/1894.

The later history of 42 (42A from 1/1912) is complex and information is at times conflicting. It appears that it exchanged numbers with 37 and the latter was then offered (as 42A) for sale as scrap in 9/1915, there being a Stores Committee minute to this effect. However its boiler, which had earlier come off Glenbarry 55, was recovered and after repair at Lochgorm was fitted in 1/1916 to the former 42A which was then returned to capital stock, renumbered 37. All this was necessary because its former capital number 42 was

Fig 37   42A fitted with a Drummond flare on the louvred chimney. Shortly afterwards renovated in 1915 and
returned to capital stock renumbered 37. Wooden cab doors.   *(Photo: A.G. Ellis Collection)*

Fig 38   The last Medium Goods, 37 now 37A, at Inverness in August 1923, fitted with a plain Drummond
pattern chimney.   *(Photo: A.W. Croughton)*

now occupied by a Drummond 0-6-4T. Some authorities maintain that parts of other engines were used in restoring 42A/37 and this is not unlikely. The Highland was particularly hard pressed at this juncture and would have used any such methods to produce a reasonably serviceable engine. Its stay in capital stock was brief as it was back in the duplicate list in 4/1918 as 37A and about that time received an unlouvred chimney with a flared top (Fig 38).

The whole class, except 36, was given the vacuum brake, the vacuum ejector exhaust pipe being carried inside the boiler.

Tenders

The tenders were the same as those of the Small Goods and Glenbarry Classes. The original coal capacity of 3 tons was increased to 4 tons later. At the time of its withdrawal 37A (ex-42) had an outside-framed tender, taken from the Duke Class, Bruce Series.

Allocation and Work

The class was put to work goods trains on all the main lines and they also assisted with passenger traffic at times of need. They did very good work within their limits and this tribute is paid in *The Construction and Works of the Highland Railway* by Joseph Mitchell: "An ordinary goods train of 20 wagons of 200 tons gross load is drawn up the steepest inclines by one engine, having 17-inch cylinders and 24-inch stroke". This statement is confirmed in the H.R. Appendix of 1897 which shows that the Medium Goods as well as the Small Goods were permitted to take 20 loaded wagons from Blair Atholl to Dalnaspidal (the Big Goods were allowed 28). On the Skye line the 2-4-0s' limit was 17, while on another difficult section, from Orton to Mulben, the figure was 18.

A latter-day allocation of the class shows 38, 39 and 44 at Inverness, 37 and 42 at Perth and 36 at Forres. "Spare, out of traffic" were 40, 41, 43 and 45.

In November 1905 37 was snowplough engine at Wick and reported to be in good working order, and indeed several of the class appear in photographs of snowplough operation including 43. 44 was latterly spare engine at Forres while 37 (ex-42) was spare at Wick between 1915 and 1919. In 1922 the latter, now 37A, was at Perth shed, used mainly by the civil engineering department, and in August 1923 just before withdrawal it was on a ballast train at Millburn Junction, Inverness.

Withdrawal

As with the Small Goods class, several of the Medium Goods were laid aside, in some instances for a year or more, before being sold or otherwise liquidated. The date of sale has in most cases been taken in the summary as the ultimate fate of the engine.

39 and 40 were laid aside about the end of 1901, the former being sold for scrap in September 1902 to P.& W. MacLellan of Glasgow together with 36, 38 (minus tender) and 41. All were broken up at Inverness. 43 had been laid aside as early as 1898 but was still lying at Lochgorm in 1901 in company with a number of others including Medium Goods 40, 41 and 45. As has already been mentioned, 43 was one of the three 2-4-0s — the others being 19 and 26 of the Small Goods class — which were proposed for rebuilding as 0-6-0 tanks. The proposal was not immediately adopted but it appears that the wheels and motion of 43 did indeed go towards the construction of 24, the last of the Shunting Tanks of 1903-4. 43 was written off in 1903. In June of the following year 40 and 45, which had been out of action for at least three years, were included in a consignment of five old engines and four tenders sold to John Jackson of Scotstoun, Glasgow for scrap. There was then a respite until July 1912 when 44 was sold. 37 was withdrawn in 1915 and sold in October of that year, presumably without its boiler as this was transferred, as we have seen, to 42A. Tenders had in fact been invited for the sale of 42A but as 37 and later 37A it outlasted the rest until August 1923. Thus one example of each of the three 2-4-0 classes, the Small Goods, Glenbarry and Medium Goods outlived the rest and survived until grouping, although none were taken into LMS stock.

The Medium Goods served their owners well, although their power became increasingly inadequate in dealing with the steadily increasing traffic and train loads. With the arrival of the Big Goods they were quickly taken out of the front line. It is strange that the Highland with its gradients relied for so long upon four-coupled engines for working its goods trains and was so late, in comparison with other railways, in introducing 0-6-0 goods engines which Drummond started to build as late as 1900, six years after the fifteen Big Goods arrived on the scene.

Summary of Class

No.	Name	Maker	Works No	Built	Rebuilt	Withdrawn
36	Nairn /-	Sharp, Stewart	1506	4/1864	9/1876	Sold 9/1902
37	Struan /-	,,	1507	,,	12/1885	Sold 10/1915
38	Kincraig /-	,,	1508	,,	8/1882	Sold 9/1902
39	Aviemore(II) /-	,,	1509	5/1864	4/1884	Sold 9/1902 (Note 1)
40	Keith /-	,,	1510	,,	5/1885	Sold 6/1904 (Note 1)
41 /41A (1905)	Kingussie (I) /-	,,	1511	,,	4/1887	Sold 9/1902 (Note 1)
42 /42A (1/1912) /37 (10/1915) /37A (4/1918)	Lentran /-	,,	1512	,,	12/1882	8/1923
43	Dava /-	,,	1513	6/1864	5/1880	1903 (Note 2)
44 /44A (2/1912)	Brodie /-	,,	1519	,,	2/1879	Sold 7/1912
45	Dalcross (I) /-	,,	1520	,,	2/1889	Sold 6/1904 (Note 1)

Note 1. 39, 40, 41 and 45 were laid aside c.1901.
Note 2. Date written off. Out of use from c.1898. Parts believed to have been incorporated in 0-6-0T 24 of 1904.

2.10 Lochgorm Tank 0-6-0T
Stroudley 3 ft 7 in Engines

The lack of shunting tanks had early become apparent. The I & AJR directors at their meeting on 26th May 1865 were informed by the manager that the Company was being charged £800 per annum for engine shunting in the goods department of the Scottish North Eastern Railway at Perth and it was then resolved to purchase two second-hand tank engines. By performing the work with their own power the directors hoped to save some £400/500 per annum. Earlier, in November 1864 they had studied drawings of a tank engine to work the Aberfeldy branch which was to open in 1865. There must also have been need for shunting engines at Inverness.

However no immediate action resulted from these deliberations. Eventually in June 1868 the Highland Board authorised the construction of a small 0-6-0 tank, designed by Stroudley specifically for shunting at Inverness. The engine appeared the following February from Lochgorm, the first to be built there, but there was a gap of four years before a second came out, this one being for similar work at Perth. By this time Jones had taken over as Locomotive Superintendent. Two years later, in 1874 the last of the trio

appeared, nominally as a replacement for the 0-4-0 tank 16 which came from the Findhorn Railway and which, as we have seen, had been sold in 1872 for £600. Jones seems to have built this third engine on his own initiative because he informed the Board on 3rd May of what he had done, indicating that he had fixed the price at £1,400.

These three little tanks have a particular interest in being the only class designed for the Highland Railway by Stroudley. They have been variously described as side tanks and as saddle tanks and indeed the design was truly a combination of the two as their side tanks, mounted on the running board, met over the boiler barrel in arch form. The size and shape of the class must have been largely dictated by the fact that for the first two it was planned to use the boilers off the two Raigmores, now laid aside, Nos 3 and 4. New tube plates were so fitted as to reduce the length of the barrel by a few inches. New cylinders and frames were purchased from outside — from what firm is not known — but otherwise the engines were built at Lochgorm.

Frames and cylinders, the latter inclined at 1 in 9,

Fig 39   57 *Lochgorm* in the early 1880s with original boiler but with Jones chimney. Sandboxes integral with smokebox. The Stroudley livery and number plate are well shown. *(Photo: W.O. Steel per R.J. Essery)*

were inside and steam distribution was by Stephenson's link motion. A dome was provided over the firebox and was surmounted by a pair of spring balance safety valves arranged transversely. There was a new smokebox which had the unusual feature that the forward sandboxes were integral with its base, each forming a bulge, while the smokebox front was slightly inclined backward from the base. The boiler, pitched at 5 ft 5 in above rail level, contained 162 tubes of 1¾ in diameter. The wheels were spokeless, possibly of cast iron with iron tyres, and the axles had laminated springs.

The three engines carried numbers 56, 57 and 16 in order of construction. The first, 56, had a Barclay-Stroudley chimney with a brass flare and a lift-up smokebox door, but in both of these respects the original condition of the other two is not certain. It is more likely than not that, being built during Jones superintendency, they received the Jones chimney without louvres, and 57 certainly had that before rebuilding in 1897. The cab, termed 'house', had a low-domed roof and there was space between the forward extension of the lower cab and the firebox which on the right side served as a coal bunker. A tool box was placed outside the rear sheeting of the cab (Fig 39).

Dimensions

Cylinders	14″ × 20″
Boiler	
Maximum outside diameter	3′ 7″
Length of barrel	7′ 9½″
Pitch	5′ 5″
Length of firebox casing	4′ 2¼″
Heating surface	
Tubes	608 sq ft
Firebox	63 sq ft
Total	671 sq ft
Grate area	12.25 sq ft
Boiler pressure	120 lbs
Diameter of wheels	3′ 7″
Tractive effort (85%)	9,299 lbs
Length over buffers	25′ 3″
Wheelbase	6′ 0″ + 6′ 0″
Weight	23 tons 10 cwts
Water capacity	750 gallons
Coal capacity	¾ tons

16 received a new boiler when built and its dimensions may have been slightly different.

H.R. Renumbering

The following renumberings occurred:
56 to 56A (7/1919), 56 (9/1919), 56A (7/1921); 56B (5/1922)
57 to 57A (7/1921), 57B (5/1922)
16 to 49 (2/1901), 49A (7/1912)

No 16 took the number of a withdrawn 2-4-0 and so enabled the first series of Small Bens to occupy the numbers 1-17.

LMS Renumbering

All three Lochgorm tanks were taken over by the LMS and were given numbers 16118, 16119 and 16383. It has never been clear why 49 was numbered at the end of the Drummond 0-6-0 Tanks rather than being allocated 16120 but it is believed to have been in poor order in 1923 and narrowly escaped being withdrawn. Having been repaired and thus requiring an LMS number, presumably it was wrongly thought by someone unfamiliar with the Highland Classes to be similar to 16380-2 series. 56B was the oldest Highland engine to be taken into LMS stock.

Names

Balnain referred to Balnain House still extant as the earliest Georgian house in Inverness. It was used as a hospital for Cumberland's army after the battle of Culloden, and later passed into the possession of the Fraser family. Its association with the railway is not so clear but Captain Fraser-Tytler is referred to as "of Balnain" when listed as one of the promoters of the Inverness & Nairn Railway. The family later resided at Aldourie, another engine name.

Lochgorm is of course the title of the Highland Railway workshops which occupy the site of a former Loch Gorm or Blue Loch.

St. Martins was appearing for the second time. It was the Inverness residence of Colin Lyon Mackenzie. (See the Raigmore (I) Class).

Dornoch and *Fort George* related to the branches to which 56 and 16 were sent to work in 1902 and 1899 respectively. Both these names were removed after a few years while the engines were still in Highland livery, probably when they ceased regular work on these branches.

57B *Lochgorm* however retained the name until it was given LMS livery in 1929.

Livery

The original livery was that used by Stroudley for goods engines, green with white and red lining and darker border. Presumably the edge of the running board was in claret. The name appeared on the tank and the Stroudley style of number plate was on the forward extension of the lower cab sides. The first two had later — and the third probably from the beginning — the mid-green introduced in 1874 and all could have had the apple green of ten years later, both of these styles having the Jones triple lining, but the dearth of photographs makes proper identification of liveries impossible.

All three went on to carry the Drummond olive

green with double white lining and claret frame edges and steps, this probably coinciding in the case of 16 and 56 with their renaming, and in this form they must have presented a particularly trim appearance. In due course all were repainted in unlined olive green. In 1917 when 56's tank was enlarged the number plate was moved to the rear bunker.

They all came into LMS stock and by 1926 16118 (56) and 16383 (16/49) had appeared in the LMS first goods style, unlined black with the number in 14 in numerals on the tank and with the red panel lettered 'L M S.' on the rear bunker of 16118 but in the case of 16383 on the forward extension of the lower cab side. Each had a smokebox number plate.

57 retained its Highland livery, or at least traces of it, until 1929 when it was repainted in the LMS second goods style of black with red lining, having 'L M S' on the tank side and the number 16119 in 10″ numerals on the extension of the lower cab side. No smokebox number plate was ever provided.

Detail Alterations

As no original photographs or drawings of the class can be traced, it can only be conjectured whether certain details were original or were added later. This particularly applies to 16 and 57 which were completed under Jones. The earliest photographs, dating from the 1880s or 1890s, show all three with the Jones unlouvred chimney and side-hinged smokebox door, both details which, in the case of 56 at least, must have been acquired later. An early change found in all cases was the removal of the lower bulge on the smokebox sides which contained the sandboxes. In their place square sandboxes were fitted.

In 1896-97 the old boilers on 56 and 57 were replaced by new ones of almost identical dimensions, the engines being recorded as having been 'renewed'. It will be recalled that these old boilers dated from the first days of the Inverness and Nairn Railway in 1855-56. At the same time the wheel diameter was slightly increased by the fitting of new tyres.

The following were the slightly altered dimensions after this work:

Boiler pitch	5′ 4½″
Heating surface	
Tubes (158 of 1¾″ diameter)	578 sq ft
Firebox	63.6 sq ft
Total	641.6 sq ft
Grate area	12.5 sq ft
Diameter of wheels	3′ 8″
Tractive effort (85%)	9.087 lbs
Weight	26 tons

In considering further alterations it will be simpler to describe the engines individually.

No 56 was rebuilt as above in February 1896 and from that rebuild, if not earlier, it had a Jones

chimney without louvres. In 1902, by which time it had received the vacuum brake, boiler pressure was raised to 130 lbs, making the tractive effort 9,845 lbs. About 1910 a rear bunker of 1¼ tons capacity was provided, and in 1917 the tank, still of the same form and over-arching the boiler, was extended back to the cab thereby increasing the water capacity to 900 gallons. Finally around 1920 a modified chimney was fitted, having a wide flare in the Drummond style. The wheels remained spokeless to the last (Figs 40 and 41).

No 57 at an early date had the front and rear pair of wheels partly spoked, only the middle pair remaining spokeless. Rebuilding was in August 1897 as already described. A rear bunker of 1¼ tons capacity was fitted by 1910 but the old coal space was retained. Around 1925 Ross pop safety valves, arranged transversely on the dome, replaced the spring balance valves. An overhaul was carried out late in 1927 from which the engine emerged with the flare-reduced Stroudley chimney from 16383 and the boiler from 16118 (now withdrawn), but retaining the Ross safety valves and still in Highland livery. A final visit to the works took place in 1929. As this engine was never called upon to perform any passenger working, vacuum brake was not fitted. (Figs 42 and 43).

No 16, unlike the other two, received a new boiler when built and retained this until withdrawn in 1927. It had the Jones chimney without louvres at the turn of the century, but later for most of its life it had the Stroudley chimney, which probably came from 56 with the top of the flare removed. No 16 received heavy repairs in June 1896 and by 1899 had the vacuum brake. By 1910 there was a rear bunker of 1 ton capacity, the former coal space being kept. The wheels did not remain spokeless, as a triangular opening between one pair of spokes was formed on both sides of each wheel. On its withdrawal the Stroudley chimney went to 57, so apparently completing the round of all three engines! (Figs 44 and 45).

Other changes which have not been recorded may well have been made in the course of the long lives of this fascinating trio.

The LMS allocated classification N3 to the boilers of the Lochgorm Tanks. That of 16383 received number 10, indicating its date of 1874 which made it one of the oldest in the Northern Division, whereas the 1896/7 boilers of 16118/9 were given numbers 453 and 520 respectively.

Allocation and Work

The class were very largely used for shunting, for which they had been built, for a time at Perth but mainly at Inverness where they were well suited to the Harbour and Canal Basin branches. But their

Fig 40   56 *Dornoch*, vacuum fitted, outside Dornoch shed at the opening of the branch in 1902. Separate sandboxes. Drummond olive green livery with white lining and claret frames.

(Photo: J.L. Stevenson Collection)

Fig 41   56 as LMS 16118 with extended tanks and having a chimney with an enlarged flare. At Dingwall in 1926.

(Photo: Major S. Forbes)

Fig 42   57B *Lochgorm* shunting at Dingwall in 1926. Rear bunker fitted in 1910. Jones chimney and pop valves on dome.   *(Photo: A.G. Ellis Collection)*

Fig 43   57A as LMS 16119 about 1930 in lined black livery and incorrectly bearing classification 2F.   *(Photo: A.G. Ellis Collection)*

Fig 44　　16 *Fort-George* on the branch train at Gollanfield Junction about 1899. *(Photo: J.F. McEwan Collection)*

Fig 45　　16/49 as LMS 16383 employed as shed shunter at Inverness. Stroudley chimney (later on 57B), vacuum brake and bunker extension.　　　　　　　　　　*(Photo: J.L. Stevenson Collection)*

71

maximum axle load of 10 tons made them ideal also for light railways, in particular the Dornoch branch which was opened on 2nd June 1902 with 56 working the inaugural train. It remained there, on and off, for a number of years and could be found shedded at Dornoch as late as the summer of 1919. From the 1920s it was mostly about Inverness and was to be seen on the Harbour branch in August 1921. But it was also available to relieve on branches and was on the Strathpeffer branch in Autumn 1926 in LMS livery as 16118.

Although it was specifically built for shunting at Perth, 57 seems to have spent most of its life at Inverness. However in 1926 it was at Dingwall and on one occasion replaced a failed engine on a ballast train on the main North line. Like 56 it was noted on the Inverness Harbour branch in 1921 and it spent most of its last years on light shunting work of this nature. It was to be found also shunting in and about the roundhouse.

No 16 was on the Fort George branch for some years about 1899, but does not seem to have been recorded again until 1919 when, as 49A, it was at Wick, possibly as spare for the Lybster branch in addition to shunting. As orphan of the LMS renumbering storm, it spent its last days shunting at Inverness which at this time seems to have been able to provide a number of light jobs suitable for engines on their last legs.

The Terrier Tanks

As is well known, these little engines were the forerunners of the famous Terrier Tanks, built by Stroudley from 1872 onwards for the London Brighton and South Coast Railway which he joined in February 1870 after leaving the Highland. The boilers of the Terriers were very similar in dimensions to the old 1855 boilers which Stroudley had used for the Lochgorm Tanks but with a higher working pressure, 140 lbs as compared with 120, while the Terrier

cylinders were 1 in smaller in diameter. The wheelbase of the two classes were identical but the Terriers' 3 ft 11 in wheels were larger than the Highland engines' 3 ft 7 in. Here comparisons end because there is no similiarity between the remarkable performances of the Terriers on heavy passenger trains and the gentle stroll of 56 from Dornoch to The Mound!

By an extraordinary turn of events the two classes, closely related but designed and built over 600 miles apart, must have worked for a year or so side by side when early in 1918 the Admiralty bought five Terriers (LBSCR 637/8/73/81/3) and sent them to work at their sidings at Inverness and Invergordon. The two classes must have mixed freely at Inverness and it is not impossible that one of the Lochgorm Tanks was around Invergordon at this time working in the extensive sidings which existed from the late war years until lifted between 1922 and 1924. These had occupied much of the land lying to the seaward side of the railway between Invergordon and Alness.

Withdrawals

The Lochgorm Tanks were remarkable for their longevity, a tribute to their good design, sound construction and usefulness. 16383 (16/49) was the first to go, in January 1927, having lasted 52 years. 16118 (56), withdrawn a year later, saw 58 years, while 16119 (57) made the 60 mark.

It is a matter for regret that Stroudley was not required to design a main line engine for the Highland. The passenger engines in his time undoubtedly left a great deal to be desired but in theory at least they were sufficient in numbers. There certainly was an insufficiency of money to build anything better and Stroudley at least did much to get the maximum out of what there was. Certainly from his only design there emerged three delightful engines, each with an individuality of its own.

Summary of the Class

HR Nos Original	1922	LMS No.	Name	Maker	Built	Rebuilt	Withdrawn
56	56B	16118	Balnain /Dornoch (1902)	Lochgorm	2/1869	2/1896	1/1928
57	57B	16119	Lochgorm	,,	11/1872	8/1897	12/1932
16	49A	16383	St Martins (II) /Fort-George (1899)	,,	10/1874	—	1/1927

LMS Power Classification OF was allotted in 1928, but 16119 was wrongly painted as '2F'.

2.11 Duke Class 4-4-0
Jones 6 ft 3½ in Engines

We have already seen how the Highland locomotive stock in 1864 comprised 55 engines, namely 24 2-2-2s, 29 2-4-0s and a couple of tanks of dubious parentage. These numbers remained much the same for the next ten years and indeed the only additions up to mid-1874 were the first two of the Lochgorm Tanks. The new No 2 of the Raigmore Class was also added, in 1871, but was regarded as a 'renewal' of the old No 2. The figure shown in the half-yearly report dated 28th February 1874 was 57 which is misleading as it must have included Raigmores Nos 1, 3 and 4, all of which had been laid aside well before 1874. The last two had been bereft of driving wheels since 1869!

Traffic requirements had increased considerably over the same decade with the North line reaching Helmsdale in June 1871 and the Dingwall and Skye Railway being opened to Strome Ferry in the previous August. Even so, the Board was in no position to authorise new main line passenger engines until these works were completed, but they did allow Jones to convert Seafield 2-4-0 No 10 to a 4-4-0 in 1873, primarily for use on the Skye line but also clearly with a view to experimenting with it before completing his design for a new passenger engine for which there was a sore need.

The start of the 1870s had seen the gradual development of the 4-4-0 engine, chiefly in Scotland at first, but Jones deliberated for a long time between a leading bogie and a pony truck — the Highland 2-4-0s had a rigid leading axle — eventually deciding that a William Adams bogie with a central pivot was the most suitable for his purpose. This was what he applied to the Seafield before committing himself fully on his new design.

The Board's original proposal, expressed at their meeting on 1st October 1872, was to build six of the 4-4-0s, these to be ready for the opening of the North line through to Wick in 1874, the new engines going

Fig 46   67 *Cromartie* at Perth in 1891 waiting to go to the General station to work north. Note the meticulous trimming of the tender which has no coal rails.   *(Photo: Real Photographs)*

73

Fig 47   31 (ex-4) *Auchtertyre* at Inverness, the nominal reconstruction of Raigmore Class No 4 and the first
of the Lochgorm Bogie series. Adams safety valves. Drummond 1903 unlined livery.

(Photo: F. Moore (L.P.C.))

to work on the Perth line so releasing engines to move north. An offer by Dübs & Co of £3,485 each was accepted on 26th April 1873, whereupon the firm went on to offer a reduction of £15 per engine if ten were ordered and the Board on 3rd June accepted this not over-generous concession. Delivery was stipulated for April 1874 and Dübs did reasonably well, delivering all ten between June and August. In the event the line to Wick was opened on 28th July.

The design differed from the great majority of British 4-4-0s in having outside cylinders. It was indeed a distinctive style and one which with gradual enlargements and improvements was to continue throughout Jones's superintendency, the main characteristics being the massive outside framing sloping upwards over the slide bars, the cylinders being inclined at 1 in 12, the louvred chimney appearing on a new class for the first time and Adams safety valves set transversely over the firebox. The cab, once more known as a 'house', provided splendid protection and was based on Stroudley's design which first appeared on the rebuilt Raigmore No 1 in 1869. The cab front was horizontal along the top with windows which were rectangular apart from a rounded inside corner to fit the boiler. Its roof was formed in a low ellipse and Jones designed rounded front vertical corners. There was a horizontal joint along from the foot of the cut-out.

The frames, a weak feature in the earlier classes, were of wrought iron with horn blocks of cast steel, the connecting and coupling rods were of Yorkshire iron and the ends of the coupling rods were case hardened obviating the need for bushes. The valve gear was Allan's straight link motion. Compensating levers were fitted between the laminated springs of the coupled wheels. An interesting feature was the provision of Le Chatelier counter-pressure brake, a description of which is in a later paragraph. Finally the tender was of a new design with outside frames which enclosed the springs (Fig 46).

The ten 1874 engines carried the numbers 60 to 69 and they were followed by a further seven, numbered 4, 71 to 75 and 84, built at Lochgorm between 1876 and 1888 and having some slight differences mainly in the boiler and tender. The first ten are referred to here as the Bruce Series after the first name of 60 — they were often called the 60 Class also — while the last seven are generally known as the Lochgorm Bogies (Fig 47).

Dimensions

Cylinders	18″×24″
Boiler	
Maximum outside diameter	4′ 2″
Length of barrel	10′ 8½″
Pitch	6′ 6″
Length of firebox casing	5′ 5½″
Heating surface	
Tubes (223 of 1¾″)	1,132 sq ft
Firebox	96 sq ft
Total	1,228 sq ft

Boiler pressure	140 lbs
Diameter of wheels	
Bogie	3' 9½"
Coupled	6' 3½"
Tender	3' 9½"
Tractive effort (85%)	12,338 lbs
Length over buffers	51' 3"
Wheelbase	
Engine	6' 0" + 6' 9" + 8' 9"
Tender	5' 6" + 5' 6"
Total	41' 6"
Weights	
Adhesion	26 tons 10 cwts
Engine	41 tons
Tender	30 tons
Total	71 tons
Water capacity	1,800 gallons
Coal capacity	4 tons

Lochgorm Bogie Series

The first of these, No 4 of 1876, was identical with the Bruce Series 60-69. Authorities differ on its background but it is a fact that Jones reported to the Board in August 1876 that "No 4 engine and tender [of the Raigmore Class] had been reconstructed to the large powerful bogie type recently made by Dübs & Co., Glasgow for the Company at a price of £3,480 each, whereas No 4 stands in the Company's books at £2,580, revenue account having been debited with the whole cost of construction". Capital account was then debited with the difference, ie £900, a confusing piece of figure-work. The idea of reconstructing No 4 was first mentioned to the Board in December 1870 when it was resolved to convert it to a bogie passenger engine at a cost of £120! In fact very little of what remained of old No 4 could have been used for the new engine, but at least it kept capital expenditure to a minimum, which was an important factor at that time.

The other six Lochgorm Bogies had a slightly different boiler from that of the Bruce Series. The pressure was raised to 150 lbs and in the case of 84 to 160 lbs. Lock-up safety valves were fitted in tall brass columns, again placed transversely, while the tenders had the normal arrangement of frames with the springs visible. Many of the parts used for the Lochgorm Bogie series were bought in. The last to be built, 84, which came out in 1888 after the Clyde Bogies had been delivered, seems to have been something of a spare time job. Jones told the Board in December of that year that he had been "gradually building a new engine and tender of the ordinary bogie type out of revenue". The price in this case was £2,300 which, as in the case of No 4, was considerably less than the Company had had to pay Dübs. This engine differed from the rest also in that it had a Clyde Bogie tender

having greater water capacity.

The dimensions of the Lochgorm Bogie Series where different from the Bruce Series were as follows:

Heating surface		
Tubes (210 of 1¾" diam)		1,058 sq ft
Firebox		93 sq ft
Total		1,151 sq ft
Boiler pressure		150 lbs (on 84 160 lbs)
Tractive effort (85%)		13,219 lbs (on 84 14,100 lbs)
Weights		
Adhesion		27 tons
Engine		42 tons
Tender	30 tons (on 84 31 tons 10 cwt)	
Total	72 tons (on 84 73 tons 10 cwt)	
Water capacity	(on 84) 2,100 gallons	

The longer tender on 84 increased its wheelbase by about a foot while the length over buffers was 53ft 3 in. See also under 'Tenders'.

Renumbering

67 exchanged numbers with Skye Bogie 70A in 2/1923 but was then laid aside and did not appear in traffic as 70A. No 4 was renumbered 31 in 2/1899 to clear the number for a Small Ben. It was transferred to the duplicate list as 31A 9/1911 as were 71 (7/1912), 72 (7/1913), 73 (12/1916), 74 (12/1916), 75 (3/1917) and 84 (4/1917).

Names

The seventeen Dukes shared a total of 34 names which must constitute something of a record. Some of the names had already been used and have been explained with the class first bearing them, while others are of geographical locations which are obvious, but the origins of the rest are as follows:

The Duke /Duke	The Duke of Sutherland, a director and the major force in initiating railway development in the north.
Stemster	The residence of Alexander Henderson, director, near the village of Duncansby in Caithness.
Huntingtower	An earlier residence of William Whitelaw, director and later from 1902 Chairman. It is situated some three miles west of Perth.
Ault Wharrie	The residence at Dunblane of J.G. Stewart, director.
Dalraddy	The residence near Aviemore of Donald Grant, director, (also the name of a crossing loop nearby).
Ardvuela	The residence at Helensburgh of Robert M. Wilson, a director. He became Chairman from 1913 to 1915.
Muirtown	The residence just outside Inverness of Francis Darwin, director.

The Lord Provost /Sir James	Both names referred to Sir James Falshaw who was a public works contractor with wide interests and who had played a large part in the building of the Inverness and Nairn Railway, as well as building some of the Scottish Central. From 1865 he was a director of the Highland and around 1874 he became Lord Provost of Edinburgh, for which service he was knighted.
Auchtertyre	The residence at Elgin of Thomas Yool, director.
Grange	The residence at Forres of James Grant-Peterkin, director.
Thurlow	Lord Thurlow of Dunphail, director.
Rosehaugh	The residence near Avoch, Ross-shire of James D. Fletcher, director.
Beaufort	This presumably referred to Beaufort Castle, the seat of Lord Lovat near Beauly, he being a director. Surprisingly the name was retained despite the arrival in 1902 of No 147 *Beaufort Castle*.
Dochfour	The residence at the north-east end of Loch Ness of James R. Baillie, director.

It is interesting to note that three of the names of counties reappeared many years later, again on outside cylinder 4-4-0s, the LNER Class D49 Shires, while Class 47/7 Diesel 47709 is named *The Lord Provost*, as was a North British Atlantic.

Tenders

As originally built, the tenders of the Bruce Series and of No 4 had outside framing with the springs concealed behind it, whereas those of the next five Lochgorm Bogies 71-75 had inside frames with the springs visible. 84 differed from them all in having a Clyde Bogie tender, again with the springs visible. Later there were some exchanges of tenders, not only between the two series of Dukes but also with the Skye Bogies' tenders, which were slightly larger, and with those of the Clyde Bogies which were larger still. It is however almost impossible to distinguish in a photograph between a Skye Bogie tender and the Lochgorm type. Certainly 62, 64, 65, 67 and 31 (ex-4) received inside-framed tenders and those behind 64 and 65 looked like the Skye Bogie type. 75 also appears to have had a Skye Bogie tender and 71 a Clyde Bogie one. The 1900 Diagram Book adds further perplexity by stating that 74, 75 and 84 had water capacity of 2,200 gallons, being provided (presumably on the tender) with a well tank, possibly a latter addition.

It is not clear what purpose was served by locating the springs behind the framing in this way as inspection and replacement must have been made very difficult. One possibility is that the intention was to protect the springs from damage while passing through a newly ploughed snow drift.

Counter Pressure Brake

A brief description of Le Chatelier's system is necessary, especially as the Highland was the chief exponent of it in Britain. The original practice on the long downhill stretches had been to put the valve gear into reverse and keep the regulator slightly open. This had the effect of working against and thus slowing down the movement of the pistons. But there could be quite serious consequences. An inwards draught of hot air from the smokebox through the exhaust pipe, frequently along with ashes, caused considerable wear to the cylinders, while the hot gases and ash passing into the boiler did further damage. It was to remedy these ill-effects that Le Chatelier introduced his system. A control cock was provided to inject a mixture of steam and hot water into the cylinders and exhaust pipe so as to prevent hot ashes and gas from entering the cylinders. The lubrication was cut off just before the counter-braking was applied, so preventing oil from being carried into the boiler. In the Dukes the control cock which combined the steam blower and he counter-pressure hot water injection was placed on the face of the firebox at the right hand side of the cab. On the Highland the system worked quite satisfactorily but the only other British railway to adopt it was the Great Southern and Western of Ireland. Two of the English railways experimented with it. In the 1870s some Midland 2-4-0s of the 890 Class, designed by Kirtley, were so fitted but the apparatus was soon removed. On the London and North Western Ramsbottom tried it on engines working coal trains on steeply graded lines in the Abergavenny district but with little success, the cylinders being badly scored. E.L.Ahrons attributed the partial failure of the system in Britain to want of care and attention on the part of the drivers. It certainly appears to have worked well on several French railways.

Apart from the Highland 4-4-0s which were given the Chatelier brake when new, several of the old 2-4-0s were so equipped in later years. The exact number is not known but Medium Goods 42 and 44, also Glenbarry 55 are stated to have had this 'water break' according to the Board of Trade report on an accident at Dava on 10th February 1886.

Livery

An early photograph of 67 appears to show the Jones lining out but with the tender side divided half way into two panels, in the manner of the Raigmore and Belladrum Classes. There is no information as to whether this style of painting the tender was normal on the Dukes, the photograph concerned being a works view of the engine in light shop grey, and temporarily bearing the name *The Duke*. Most of the engines were finished in mid-green with white, black and red lining and with a green border. But deliveries of the last three or four were overtaken by the 1885 change to apple green with the usual lining, dark green border and red-brown frames and steps. They were thus finished accordingly. Later the apple green with the usual accompaniments was applied at least to 64, 65, 67 and 69 also in all probability to others. The Jones number plate was fitted from the start.

From 1896 the Drummond style was introduced, olive green with black and double white lining together with an olive green border, the frames and steps being claret. This style was applied at least to 62, 65, 68, 69, 4, 71 and 72. Of these 65 and 71 had 'The Highland Railway' on the tender and the other five had 'H . R' Most of them seem to have survived long enough to receive the unlined olive green all-over which was introduced in August 1902. For some time 31 (ex-4) 68 and 75 had no lettering on the tender but 75 at least had 'H . R' restored.

Continuous Brakes

It was with the Dukes that trials were carried out with a view to adopting the one form of continuous brake. In 1882 two experimental trains were fitted up,

one having the vacuum brake and the other the Westinghouse. Each was worked by a Duke, No 4 and 64 respectively being the selected engines. The minutes are unfortunately silent on the reasons why the vacuum was chosen at the end of the day but record the setting up of a committee to enquire into the various forms of brake, the Chairman being the Duke of Sutherland who appears to have been in close touch with the Midland and the Great Northern Railways. Those of the Dukes built from 1883, that is those numbered from 71 onwards, received the vacuum brake when built and it was fitted at the same time to the earlier members of the class. Westinghouse equipment was fitted additionally to 62, 71 and 72 for working stock from the Caledonian, North British and Great North of Scotland, all of which were Westinghouse railways. This brake was soon removed from 64 and later from 62 and 71, both around 1900 (Fig 48).

Detail Alterations

The Dukes as a whole underwent few changes. Contrary to what has been stated by a number of authorities, nine of the Bruce Series, 60-66 68 and 69 finished their lives with the original boilers but new fireboxes were fitted from 1887 onwards. Probably coinciding with this, lock-up safety valves replaced the Adams pattern on five of these engines at least, 61, 62, 63, 65 and 69. However 68 definitely retained the

Fig 48   62 *Huntingtower* in original condition but with Westinghouse pump (removed c1900).

(*Photo: A.G. Ellis Collection*)

Adams valves. Another change was the raising of the boiler pressure to 150 lbs on all these with the exception of 65. 67 *Cromartie* also received a new firebox in 1898, had the pressure raised and was given a change of safety valves. It went on to receive the boiler off one of the Lochgorm Bogies, 74 which was withdrawn in 1913. Following this 67 was sent for overhaul to the North Eastern Railway works at Gateshead (see below), where it was given a steel firebox in 1916. The boiler was evidently still in fair shape because it was taken off in 1922, given a copper firebox and fitted to Skye Bogie 70A which was reinstated to capital stock in 2/1923 by assuming *Cromartie's* number 67, the number 70 now being occupied by *Loch Ashie*. One of the many mysteries of the closing years of the Highland is why *Cromartie* was given another boiler — presumably the old one off the Skye Bogie — only to be sent up to the locomotive cemetery at Culloden Moor now renumbered 70A. There was clearly no prospect of returning it to service but the Highland, as we shall see again later, evidently considered that there would be an advantage in having as many nominally complete engines as possible when the take over by the LMS was to be negotiated.

One new Lochgorm Bogie boiler is understood to have been obtained in 1898, possibly from Sharp, Stewart. It seems likely that this was fitted first to 74,

then to 67 and so on as stated above. This is consistent with the LMS boiler list of September 1923 which shows the 1882 Skye Bogie 14277 (67) as carrying boiler 543 on 1898. Although 74 was withdrawn after giving up its boiler to 67, it received another to enable it to be returned to service during the war years 1914-18. The boiler in question may have been that off 67 after attention at the Rose Street Foundry, Inverness which is known to have repaired a boiler in 1914.

During and just after the First World War four of the Dukes were repaired in England, as follows:

67	NER Gateshead Works	1916
73	R. Stephenson & Co	1916(?)
75A	Yorkshire Engine Co	1921
84	NER Gateshead Works	1915 or 1916

Several of the class received a Drummond flare on the louvred chimney, namely 67 (c.1916), 71 (by 1915), 72 (by 1923), 75 (after 7/1922) and 84 (by 1916). See Fig 49. On the last two mentioned the height of the chimney was slightly reduced in the process. 84 had undergone a further change by 1923, receiving a louvreless chimney of Drummond style (Fig 50). By 1922 67 had reverted to having a chimney of the normal Jones pattern.

The LMS appear to have allocated classification N.46 to the Duke boiler, but the only such boiler which entered LMS service was that on Skye Bogie 67

Fig 49   71A *Clachnacuddin* awaiting scrapping at Lochgorm in July 1915. Jones chimney with Drummond flare.
(Photo: LCGB Ken Nunn Collection)

(14277) and this was put into Class N.22 in common with the boilers on the rest of the Skye Bogies.

Allocation and Work

The Dukes were immediately put onto the principal passenger services between Inverness and Perth where they proved their reliability and power. There was certainly no comparison between their performance and that of the little 2-2-2s and 2-4-0s. They remained unchallenged on these duties until the arrival of the Clyde Bogies in 1886 and of the Straths in 1892 enabled some of the Dukes to be sent to the North line or sometimes to the Skye line. On the latter 63 was recorded working a construction train at the extension of the line forward to Kyle of Lochalsh in 1897.

They had their share of mishaps, notably an incident which occurred when 74 was heading the 4.20 pm mixed train from Dingwall to Strome Ferry on 14th October 1892, as recounted by John Thomas in *The Skye Railway*. The passenger portion was as usual marshalled in the rear and thus was not provided with the continuous brake. In the course of the journey it was discovered that the guard's brake had failed but it was considered that it was safe to proceed. At Achnashellach, where there is a falling gradient at each end of the station, the first two wagons were to be detached, the procedure being that the engine would run forward clear of the siding points, after which the wagons would be rope-hauled into the siding. However when the engine eased back to slacken the coupling prior to being uncoupled, the train began slowly to move back on the falling gradient. The fireman, who was on the footplate, backed further to try to catch the train but the driver in the dangerous position between the engine and the train could not manage to secure the coupling in the darkness. Then 74 and its crew set off backwards down the gradient in search of the runaway which gathered speed on the 1 in 60, only to be halted by the succeeding uphill gradient of 1 in 75, whereupon it ran forward again and collided with the engine. Surprisingly little damage was done and only minor injuries to passengers, but the Board of Trade, who had for years been quite rightly pressing the Company to marshal their mixed trains with the passenger portion next to the engine, increased their pressure, but this was countered by prolonged correspondence and similar delaying tactics. It was not until a further such accident was only narrowly averted in 1897 — reference is made under the Skye Bogie Class — that the Highland was at last prevailed upon to comply with the order.

On the Perth line 67 piloted by Clyde Bogie 76 was derailed at Ballinluig on 7th July 1891, while 71 piloting 68 on a goods crashed into a fallen tree at Killiecrankie on 17th November 1893, both engines finishing well down the embankment. 71 showed marks of the accident on its tender for the rest of its life.

By the middle of the 1890s the work of the Dukes remaining on the Perth line had become mainly that of assisting the later 4-4-0s. An account of a journey on the afternoon train from Inverness to Perth shortly before the opening of the direct line in 1898 shows that *Loch Tay*, then almost new, was the train engine. At Forres a Duke was attached as pilot as far as Kingussie where, whilst the passengers were partaking of much needed refreshments, it was transferred to the rear of the train and proceeded to bank up to Druimuachdar.

The 1901 allocation of the class shows that they had become dispersed:

Inverness: 31 (ex-4), 64-69, 72, 74, 84.
Blair Atholl: 60, 61.
Forres: 62, 75.
Perth: 71.
Thurso: 73.
Idle at Lochgorm: 63.

The Perth and Blair Atholl engines were probably employed on the local trains between these two points and on banking to Dalnaspidal. Others began to appear on branches, 65 for example being the Fortrose engine in 1904. A more distinguished role was played by 61 when it was selected late in life as a Royal Train pilot on 8th September 1902, running the regulation 20 minutes ahead of the Royal Train in its progress from Invergordon to Elgin at which stage the GN of S took over for Ballater.

With the withdrawal of all but one of the Bruce Series by 1909 the Dukes had become rare south of Aviemore, but 72 and 73 appeared on Perth-Blair Atholl locals for a period prior to 1914. Probably the last working of a Duke at the south end was that of 84A *Dochfour* which turned up on a ballast train at Pitlochry about 1919.

In the summer of 1919 only five remained in service. 73A and 75A were at Inverness, 67 and 84A at Forres and 72A at Aviemore. The last to be in use was 75A.

Withdrawal

The condition of the Bruce Series was causing concern by 1907, Drummond reporting to the Locomotive Committee in April on the position of the "ten engines of the Sixty class". He pointed out that the boilers were then 33 years old and he recommended that engines of a more modern type should be built to replace them. At their June meeting the Committee accepted the offer of the North British Locomotive Co. to build four of the "Ben class of engine with larger boiler" to be delivered in 1908, and on the strength of this it was agreed at the September meeting that four of the Bruce Series, 61, 63, 66 and 68, all of which had been laid aside for breaking up, should be sold to P.& W. MacLellan, Glasgow for £1,352. Their numbers were reoccupied by the new engines, four of the Big Bens which cost £3,900 each (see book 2). Thus the sale of the old engines gave the Company a useful cash start.

On 1st September 1908 the Locomotive Committee recommended that five more of the Bruce Series should be sold, namely 60, 62, 64, 65 and 69. Of these 60 and 62 had been withdrawn in August and 65 and 69 followed in September and in January 1909 respectively, the Stores Committee resolving that "old engines 65 and 69 should be taken into [stores] stock as 'engines, locomotive, old' and credit allowed to the Locomotive Department". The credit appears to have been a meagre £231 each. A similar book-keeping entry for 60 and 62 is recorded but not until June 1909, some ten months after their withdrawal.

Finally the story ends with the Stores Committee minute of 28th September 1909 which reported that old engines with tenders 60, 62, 65 and 69, also 2-4-0 39, had been sold for scrap together with 64 which had been laid aside earlier that year. In the case of 64 however the boiler and firebox were excluded from the sale while the tender tank was bought back from the scrap dealer. These items were then put together

as an installation to provide water for washing-out purposes at Inverness shed.

Thus the only Bruce to survive this holocaust was 67 which, as we have seen, later received 74's boiler.

Withdrawal of the Lochgorm Bogies started in March 1913 when 31 was sold for scrap. 74 also was withdrawn after bequeathing its boiler to 67 but was patched up with another in 1914 and returned to traffic until 1918, as earlier described. 71A was less fortunate, being withdrawn in 1915 and put up for sale in September, one of only two Highland engines to be taken out of service during the 1914-18 war. Some major defect must have been the cause. 75 fared better, being withdrawn in 1915 but reinstated with a repaired boiler.

Thus at the demise of the Highland at the end of 1922 five Dukes still existed, one Bruce, old 67, and four Lochgorm Bogies, 72A, 73A, 75A and 84A. All seem by then to have been out of use except 75A which was shunting at Inverness on 18th July 1923. Of the others 67 (now renumbered 70A) and 72A were stored at Culloden Moor in August 1923, the latter being sold to Arrol, Jackson for scrap in December of that year. 70A was broken up eventually at Kilmarnock in 1925. 84A was stored at Aviemore in August 1923 and was still there a year later, probably being sold soon afterwards. 73A and 75A also disappeared about the end of 1923. The question of

Fig 50   84A *Dochfour* laid aside at Aviemore in August 1924. Plain Drummond chimney.

(Photo: A.G. Ellis Collection)

the retention by the Highland of so many old and largely unserviceable engines at grouping is considered in greater detail when dealing with the Clyde Bogie Class.

Thus the last survivors of this notable class clung tenaciously to life, as befitted their strong and purposeful build. They were worked hard during the first fifteen years of their life, gradually easing off as the later classes, of which the Dukes were the direct ancestors, took over. Their design certainly put the

Highland in the forefront of locomotive development in 1874 and they clearly demonstrated the virtues of a straightforward, free steaming engine.

In the course of refurbishing Wick and Thurso stations in 1985 a large screen some 18 feet long was erected at the buffer end of each station, bearing an excellent line drawing of the appropriately named Duke 68 *Caithness*, forming a delightful link with past history (Fig 51).

Summary of Class

original	*H R No.* later	Name	Maker	Works No	Built	Withdrawn
60		*Bruce* (III) /*Sutherland* (IV) (6/1884)	Dübs & Co	714	6/1874	8/1908
61		*Sutherlandshire* /*Duke* (1/1877)	,,	715	,,	8/1907
62		*Perthshire* (I) /*Stemster* (1889) /*Huntingtower* (1899) /*Ault Wharrie* (1903)	,,	716	,,	8/1908
63		*Inverness-shire* /*Inverness* (II) (in 1890s)	,,	717	7/1874	11/1907
64		*Morayshire* /*Seafield* (III) (c.1889)	,,	718	,,	9/1909
65		*Nairnshire* /*Dalraddy*	,,	719	,,	9/1908
66		*Ross-shire* /*Ardvuela*	,,	720	,,	11/1907
67	70A (2/1923)	*The Duke* /*Cromartie* (1/1877)	,,	721	8/1874	8/1923
68		*Caithness-shire* /*Caithness* (II) /*Muirtown*	,,	722	,,	11/1907
69		*The Lord Provost* /*Sir James* /*Aldourie* (III) (c.1903)	,,	723	,,	1/1909
4	31 (1899)	*Ardross* (II) /*Auchtertyre* (1901)	Lochgorm	—	7/1876	1913
71	71A (7/1912)	*Clachnacuddin* (II)	,,	—	12/1883	1915
72	72A (7/1913)	*Bruce* (IV) /*Grange* (1886)	,,	—	7/1884	8/1923
73	73A (12/1916)	*Thurlow* /*Rosehaugh* (1898)	,,	—	1/1885	8/1923

original	H R No. later	Name	Maker	Works No	Built	Withdrawn
74	74A (12/1916)	*Beaufort*	,,	'—	9/1885	1918★
75	75A (3/1917)	*Breadalbane* (III)	,,	—	10/1886	8/1923‡
84	84A (4/1917)	*Dochfour*	,,	—	12/1888	8/1923

★ 74 was withdrawn in 1913 and reinstated in 1914.
‡ 75 was withdrawn in 1915 and reinstated in 1916.

Fig 51   Line drawing of **68** *Caithness* displayed at the buffer end in Thurso station. There is a similar display at Wick station. January 1968.

(Photo: Hamish Stevenson)

2.12 Raigmore II Class 2-4-0
Jones 6 ft 3 in Engines

These two engines were in the nature of a reversion to the previous decade's practice. They were built for working local passenger and branch trains with the Inverness-Tain services particularly in view for which duties the Board insisted that a 2-4-0 was adequate although Jones wanted a 4-4-0 design. It is not difficult to confuse the 1877 *Raigmore* with its venerable ancestor of 1855. Moreover both the Raigmore II engines later bore new numbers within the Glenbarry series, making confusion even easier.

Nominally the two engines were 'renewals' of two of the original Raigmore Class, Nos 1 and 3, the former having been converted from a 2-2-2 to a 2-4-0 in 1869 and laid aside in 1873 and the latter, still as a 2-2-2, ceasing work in 1869. Both however remained nominally in stock, as we have already seen, although very largely dismantled. The Raigmore II replacement engines were constructed of new materials apart from the wheels and axles of the old No 1 which went

to its successor, thicker tyres evidently being fitted increasing the diameter from 6 ft 0 in to 6 ft 3 in. The boilers were supplied from outside, possibly by Neilson, while cylinders, frames and probably other parts were similarly bought in. The tenders however were put together from spare parts and other bits and pieces on hand.

The Raigmore II Class again conformed to the Crewe pattern with deep outside framing, Allan gear, compensating levers between the laminated springs of the coupled axles and the Jones louvred chimney and cab. The domed boiler contained 223 tubes of 1¾ in diameter and had a flush firebox carrying a pair of Thomas Adams safety valves arranged transversely. The steam brake was of course fitted originally but the vacuum brake was provided around the mid-1880s. The two engines were built at Lochgorm in 1877 and were numbered 3 and 1 in order of construction (Figs 52-54).

Fig 52   1 *Raigmore* at Keith 1895-8, fitted with new firebox and with lock-up safety valves replacing the Adams
pattern. Probably Jones apple-green livery.   *(Photo: J.L. Stevenson Collection)*

Fig 53   29 (ex-1) *Raigmore* on branch train at Fort George about the time of its opening in 1899. Coal rails on tender.

(Photo: J.L. Stevenson Collection)

Dimensions

Cylinders (2 outside)	16″ × 22″
Boiler	
Maximum external diameter	4′ 1″
Length of barrel	9′ 5½″
Pitch	6′ 3½″
Heating surface	
Tubes	1,004 sq ft
Firebox	93 sq ft
Total	1,097 sq ft
Grate area	16.2 sq ft
Boiler pressure	140 lbs
Diameter of wheels	
Leading	3′ 9″
Coupled	6′ 3″
Tender	3′ 9″
Tractive effort (85%)	8,936 lbs
Length over buffers	47′ 3″
Wheelbase	
Engine	6′ 2″ + 8′ 4″
Tender	5′ 9″ + 5′ 6″
Total	34′ 3″
Weights	
Adhesion	23 tons
Engine	35 tons
Tender	27 tons
Total	62 tons
Water capacity	1,800 gallons
Coal capacity	3 tons

Renumbering

The two engines were renumbered in July 1898 to free the numbers for the Bens to be delivered that year. Nos 1 and 3 became 29 and 30 respectively. Later 29 was transferred to the duplicate list as 29A in August 1910.

Livery

On entering service the pair were finished in the usual mid-green of the period with triple lining and dark green border. Presumably they would later receive the 1885 apple green with lining and red-brown frames and steps. The Jones number plate was carried. Subsequently they were given the Drummond olive green with black and double white lining and claret framing, while at the end they were in unlined olive green, both retaining 'H . R' on the tender although this was very faint on 29 (ex-1). Each showed traces of lining on the splasher from earlier styles.

Names

Once more directors' residences were the source:

Ballindalloch The castle of this name on Speyside in Banffshire was the residence of Sir George Macpherson Grant, a director and from 1897 to 1900 Chairman of the Board. 141 *Ballindalloch Castle* appeared in 1900 but old 30 seems to have kept its name.

Raigmore   This name was repeated from the original No 1.

Detail Alterations

The engines were provided in the mid-1880s with the vacuum brake. Both were retubed and given a new firebox by Neilson in October 1895, and No 1 received lock-up safety valves probably at the same time and certainly by 1898. Neither engine underwent rebuilding.

Tenders

These were generally similar to those of the Glenbarry, Small Goods and Medium Goods Classes with unequal wheel spacing. The tool box was on the rear platform.

Allocation and Work

The pair mainly worked local passenger trains between Inverness and Tain also between Inverness and Keith, the type of work for which they had been designed. In 1901 29 (ex-1) was stationed at Aviemore and 30 (ex-3) was at Inverness but by 1904 the latter was back at Tain. In November 1905 it was at Aviemore as snowplough engine and reported to be in good working order. 29 had a spell on the Thurso branch in the early 1900s and was also for a time on the Fort George branch. Unfortunately working details are scanty.

Withdrawal

30 (3) was laid aside in July 1909 and sold for scrap in March 1910. The decision to sell 29A (1) was taken on 25th June 1912 and the sale took place in October.

In spite of their limited capacity the two engines were quite efficient in performing the secondary duties for which they had been designed.

Fig 54   30 (ex-3) *Ballindalloch* retaining Adams safety valves. Drummond 1903 livery but with traces of Drummond lining on splashers.
(*Photo: Real Photographs*)

Summary of Class

No	Name	Maker	Built	Withdrawn
3 /30 (7/1898)	*Ballindalloch*	Lochgorm	7/1877	Sold 3/1910
1 /29 (7/1898) /29A (8/1910)	*Raigmore* (II)	,,	11/1877	Sold 10/1912

2.13 Jones Tank Class 2-4-0T (later 4-4-0T)
Jones 4 ft 9½ in Engines

The need, which the Highland and its predecessors had earlier recognised, for shunting engines has already been mentioned when dealing with the Lochgorm Tanks. These three had gone some way towards filling the need but they were very small engines, having been designed with the use of old Raigmore boilers in mind and, while ideal for such activities as working the Inverness Harbour and Canal Basin branches, they were hardly suitable for heavy yard shunting.

Jones therefore constructed at Lochgorm in 1878-79 three 2-4-0 tanks which followed the design of the earlier 2-4-0 tender engines, in particular that of the Raigmore II Class of 1877. Indeed it is arguable that the original intention had been to build additional 2-4-0s of this class but that plans were altered in favour of providing shunting tanks, by which time perhaps the frames had been ordered. The 2-4-0 rigid wheelbase would not be ideal for yard shunting and the tank engines were slightly heavier than the 2-4-0 tender engines. It may therefore be conjectured that, if Jones had set out from the start to provide a shunting tank design, he would have gone either for a 6-coupled engine, an enlarged version of the Lochgorm Tanks possibly, or for a 2-4-0T with a radial leading axle. The only use at that time of tank engines for train working was the operation of the Aberfeldy and Burghead branches which had been opened in the 1860s and were worked respectively by 2-2-2T 13 and 0-4-2T 17, neither of them satisfactory performers. It does not seem to have been Jones' immediate intention to use his new tanks as replacements, but, as we shall see, they were shortly to do service on these lines.

Whatever their background, parentage and purpose were in reality, the tanks were neat little engines, sitting square and low on the track and showing the Jones outline with outside frames but with the running board horizontal over the slide bars. The cylinders were inclined and the smokebox curved out over the cylinders as on the 2-4-0s, while once again Allan's straight link motion was used. There were compensating levers between the laminated springs of the coupled wheels but, in contrast to the 2-4-0s, the leading axle had inside bearings only. The Jones louvred chimney was fitted and there were transversely arranged lock-up safety valves on the firebox. The cab had a low domed roof and rounded corners above the side joints, the spectacle windows being nearly square. The steam brake was fitted at first but the vacuum was provided in the mid 1880s following its adoption by the Highland (Fig 55).

The three engines were given numbers 58, 59 and 17, the first of these entering service in 1878 and the other two in 1879. 17 was apparently regarded as a replacement for the old 0-4-2T of that number which then went onto the duplicate list as 17A. Subsequently the three tanks were altered from 2-4-0T to 4-4-0T as described later.

58 and 59 had a boiler of 3 ft 7⅞ in diameter pitched at 5 ft 9 in above rail level. This had 181 tubes of 1¾ in diameter and, according to a drawing dated May 1878, a raised firebox although later replacements were flush with the boiler top. The boiler of 17 is believed to have been of similar outside dimensions but had 210 tubes and was pitched 6½ in higher at 6 ft 3½ in. It differed also in having the dome located slightly further forward. Almost certainly it did not have a raised firebox. All three boilers were built new at Lochgorm and remained with their engines until withdrawal. The working pressure of 58 and 59 was 140 lbs initially, but is shown in the 1901 and 1922 Diagram Books as reduced to 130 lbs, whereas that of 17, which was probably 140 lbs when new, appears as 160 lbs in 1901 and 150 lbs in 1922.

Dimensions

Cylinders	16″ × 24″
Boiler	
Maximum outside diameter	3′ 7⅞″
Length of barrel	9′ 7½″
Pitch	5′ 9″ (58 & 59) 6′ 3½″ (17)
Length of firebox casing	4′ 6″
Heating surface	
Tubes	829 sq ft (58 & 59) 820 sq ft (17)
Firebox	70 sq ft (58 & 59) 93 sq ft (17)
Total	899 sq ft (58 & 59) 913 sq ft (17)
Grate area	16.2 sq ft
Boiler pressure	(see note) 140 lbs
Diameter of wheels	
Leading	3′ 9½″
Driving	4′ 7½″
Tractive effort (85%)	(at 140 lbs) 12,715 lbs
Length over buffers	30′ 4″
Wheelbase	5′ 9″ + 8′ 4″

Fig 55   59 *Highlander* as built as a 2-4-0T, showing the leading rigid axle with inside frames. The engine is evidently in works grey.

(Photo: F. Moore (L.P.C.))

Weights (full)	
Adhesion	25 tons
Total	36 tons
Water capacity	700 gallons
Coal capacity	1¼ tons

Note: Boiler pressures were altered during the lives of the engines, that of 17 being generally higher. See previous paragraph.

HR Renumbering

17 was renumbered 50 in 11/1900, so enabling a Small Ben to occupy the number. In 12/1912 the three were transferred to the duplicate list as 58A, 59A and 50A, their numbers being later taken by the 1917 Castles. Surprisingly they became 58B, 59B and 50B in 8/1922. This suggests transfer to non-revenue earning stock, but in fact all were in active traffic operation until withdrawal between 1928 and 1932.

LMS Renumbering

All three of the class came into LMS stock in 1923 and received new numbers 15010 to 15012. The first two however were in the opposite order, 58 and 59 becoming 15011 and 15010 respectively.

Livery

On the strength of a very early photograph it has sometimes been thought that 59, at least, was finished in Stroudley yellow, although along with Jones's usual lining and border, and with the name on the tank in some rather darker shade. But it is almost certain that this is a works photograph with the engine in grey. The first livery was mid-green with white, black and red lining and a green border. The name was painted in gold on the tank, and the Jones pattern of number plate was on the bunker side. In or after 1885 mid-green gave way to apple green, while frames and steps were red-brown. In due course 17 (later 50) and 58, at least, were in Drummond's olive green with double white and black lining and a green border, along with claret underframes and steps. On the tank 58 had 'H . R' widely spaced and 50 had its name *Aberfeldy*. Eventually all appeared in unlined olive green, including the frames, 58 at first having no lettering on the tank but all having 'H . R' on the tank before grouping. 59 received a Cumming style number plate.

After 1923 all were given the LMS lined red livery with 14 in numerals on the tank side and the crest on the bunker. In this form they looked very fine. There were some minor differences. 15010 had the lining on the upper cab side, above and below, carried round the corner to the front of the cab, while the tank lining likewise was carried round to the tank front. 15012 showed the former characteristic only, the front of the tank being lined separately. 15011 was again different in that it had separate lining on the upper side cab side, tank side and tank front. 15011 had numerals positioned midway between the cab entrance and tank front, but those on 15010/2 were in the middle of the tanks, giving an off-centred appearance. Only 15010 was given a smokebox number plate which it retained after it received unlined black livery in 1930. The number was now in 10 in numerals forward of the cab doorway. The others were withdrawn still in red.

Names

Burghead denoted the branch where 58 worked for a time. The name *Highlander* had no particular connotation but was perhaps applied to distinguish the engine from those of the other companies while working at Perth. *Breadalbane* (17), previously carried by the old 2-2-2T, had associations with the Aberfeldy branch and the name *Aberfeldy* was even more explicit.

The name *Highlander* was probably carried by 59 when new, but the other engines of course received their names only when drafted onto the branches. After they returned to shunting duties all became nameless, 58 *Burghead* and 59 *Highlander* in 1900, but 17 (50) retaining the name *Aberfeldy* for some years more as it appears to have continued in use at times on that branch. It was nameless by 1915.

Detail Alterations

The leading rigid axle may have proved fairly satisfactory for yard shunting but it gave trouble when soon after entering service the engines were transferred to branch line operation. All three were therefore converted to 4-4-0 tanks between 1885 and 1887, the leading bogie requiring the extension of the frames at the fore-end. 58 was the first to be dealt with, entering Lochgorm Works in February 1885 and not emerging until October. This length of time suggests that the conversion was difficult and certainly there may well have been problems in obtaining clearance for the new bogie as the engines sat so low on the track. Evidently thicker tyres were fitted at that time, increasing the diameter of the driving wheels from 4 ft 7½ in to 4 ft 9½ in. It has been suggested that 5 ft 3 in wheels were substituted, a view which is supported by the 1901 Diagram Book, but measurement of the diagram in question and of photographs indicate that 4 ft 9½ in was the correct dimension. Any further raising of the body of the engine would have required the deepening of the rear buffer beam and no such alteration can be discerned. The figure in the Diagram Book may have arisen from confusion between the Jones Tanks and the Yankee Tanks, the latter having 5 ft 3 in driving wheels (Figs 56 and 57).

As 4-4-0Ts the amended dimensions were as follows:

Diameter of driving wheels	4′ 9½″
Diameter of bogie wheels	2′ 7½″
Length over buffers (approx)	31′ 8″
Wheelbase	5′ 6″ + 6′ 1½″ + 8′ 4″
Weight	37 tons 12 cwts

In the mid-1880s, probably at the time of rebuilding as 4-4-0Ts, vacuum brake was fitted and much later all received steam heating equipment for use in their carriage shunting, 58 in 1/1912 and the other two probably about the same time. Also in Highland days coal rails were fitted to the bunkers, the date for 58 being between 1885 and 1892 while it was at Burghead.

Fig 56   58 *Burghead*, rebuilt as a 4-4-0T and with coal rails on the bunker, at Burghead between 1885 and 1892. Jones apple green livery.
(Photo: B.D. Matthews Collection)

Fig 57   50 (ex-17) *Aberfeldy* at Perth c1900 in Drummond's first style of livery. Coal rails not yet fitted.

(Photo: Major S. Forbes)

There is no record of any reboiling and LMS boiler records confirm that, with firebox renewals, the boilers remained with the engines for their fifty-odd years of service.

17 (50) was fitted with larger tanks about 1900, these having 850 gallons capacity (instead of 700) and the weight of the engine was thereby increased to 39 tons 10 cwts. This change is not shown in the 1901 Diagram Book, but nevertheless the new tanks were most probably fitted before this date.

By 1919 all had received a Drummond flare on the louvred chimney. Exact dates are not known but the chimney of 50 was in its original condition in 1915. In the process 58's chimney was shortened but those of the other two retained their original height and 50, already with the higher pitched boiler, looked very tall from a front view (Figs 58 and 59).

59 must have had a tablet catcher at one time as the fixing bolts were still evident on the cab side until the end. It is not clear which of its duties would have required such a fitment.

58 acquired two tool boxes over the left hand tank, but these were later removed.

The LMS applied the classification N13 to the Jones Tank boilers. This was the same as that which was used for the boilers of the Yankee Tanks, although the respective dimensions were quite different.

Allocation and Work

Mention has already been made of the 'promotion' of the trio from shunting to passenger and goods working on branch lines. In 1880 17 went to Aberfeldy where it replaced the failing 2-2-2T 12, and the previous year 58 had taken over the Burghead branch from the equally ineffective 0-4-2T 17A. 59 at Perth served as spare for the Aberfeldy branch but in 1884 went north for the opening of the Keith-Portessie line which it was still working five years later when it was involved in an accident at Keith on 17th June 1889. The engine collided side-long with some empty carriages while leaving with the 3.40 pm to Portessie, the train being a mixed one consisting of one goods wagon, a composite carriage, a brake van and a third class carriage. The engine sustained some superficial damage but no one was injured. The Inspecting Officer concluded that the principal blame lay with the pointsman but that the signalling arrangements and lack of interlocking were very unsatisfactory. The absence of the continuous brake would have been a further factor. The branch train had Newall's mechanical brake connecting the brake van and two passenger carriages but in any event operation of a continuous brake would have been prevented by the presence of the goods wagon at the front.

58 was taken off the Burghead branch in 1892 and sent to inaugurate the first section of the Inverness-Aviemore Direct line. Four trains a day were run between Aviemore and Carr Bridge commencing on 6th July of that year, the engine being housed in a small wooden shed provided at the latter station. How

Fig 58   50 as LMS 15012 in red livery at Perth. Drummond pattern flare on the louvred chimney.
(Photo: W.H. Whitworth)

Fig 59   59 as LMS 15010 in the black livery of 1930 on its usual work of passenger station pilot at Inverness
in May 1930.   *(Photo: A.G. Ellis Collection)*

long the engine remained on what was termed the 'Carr-Bridge Branch' is not known, but in July 1897 the completion of the next section of the route enabled trains to operate between Aviemore and Daviot and, as there was a turntable at Daviot, a tender engine would probably have been used. The Direct line was fully opened on 1st November 1898.

These spells of work in the country had finished for 58 and 59 before 1900 and both reverted to shunting duties, becoming nameless. However 17 (50 from 1900) *Aberfeldy* was at Perth and still appeared from time to time on the Aberfeldy branch for which, as will be recalled, it had been given larger tanks. This work seems to have ceased about 1910. It is interesting to note that in the H.R. Appendix for 1901 50 was designated as a 'Tank Branch Engine', whereas the two others were mere 'Shunting Engines'. They were generally at Inverness although there seem to have been occasional change-overs to allow engines to visit the shops.

50A (15012) became very well known as one of the Perth General Station pilots — others were provided by the Caledonian and North British — while at Inverness 59A (15010) was a particular favourite of travellers as it went about its duties which were quite arduous at the busier times, especially in mid-afternoon. It usually had 58A (15011) as an assistant but this never seems to have been quite so much in evidence. There is no record of any of the three on the North line branches.

Withdrawals

The first to go was 15011 (58) from Inverness in February 1928, its work on carriage shunting being taken over generally by a tender engine looking for a quiet job, and at the end of the following year 15012 (17/50) was withdrawn from Perth. However 15010 (59) soldiered on at Inverness until November 1932, after which a Standard LMS 0-6-0T was usually to be found as passenger station pilot, for some time regularly 16623 (later 7540). 15012 was broken up at Kilmarnock, the other two probably at their birth place Lochgorm.

The three tanks gave excellent service, spanning just over half a century without requiring a change of boiler. 15010 when it departed was the last of the early Jones design with the Crewe front end. Indeed its demise marked the end of over 75 years of this feature which will always be associated with the earlier days of the Highland and its antecedents.

Summary of Class

HR No. original	1922	LMS No	Name	Maker	Built	Converted to 4-4-0T	Withdrawn
58	58B	15011	*Burghead* /- (c.1900)	Lochgorm	12/1878	10/1885	2/1928
59	59B	15010	*Highlander* (II) /- (c.1900)	,,	6/1879	6/1887	11/1932
17	50B	15012	*Breadalbane* (II) /*Aberfeldy* (1886) /- (by 1915)	,,	12/1879	7/1887	11/1929

2.14 Skye Bogie Class 4-4-0
Jones 5 ft 3½ in Engines

The opening in 1870 of the Dingwall and Skye Railway over the first 53 miles to Strome Ferry created new problems for the Locomotive Department. Soon after leaving Dingwall the line climbs for four miles at 1 in 50 to Raven's Rock and a further stiff climb ensues from Garve to Corriemullie Summit, while eastbound there are some six miles of a pull up from Achnashellach to Luib Summit, again including some stretches at 1 in 50. Curvature is severe at many points and the line was fairly lightly laid from the start which for a long time precluded any thoughts of heavy engines.

Trouble was soon experienced with the 2-4-0s because of their rigid wheelbase, and, as we have seen, Jones converted two of the Seafields, Nos 7 and 10, to 4-4-0s in 1875 and 1873 respectively to meet this problem and at the same time to gain experience with bogie engines. The conversions were successful and set the pattern for a new class of 4-4-0s specifically designed for the Skye line.

The first Skye Bogie proper, as distinct from the Seafield conversions, figures in the Locomotive Committee minutes of 30th December 1881 when Jones informed the meeting that he had built "a new big engine". The Committee, presumably being already aware of what was afoot, agreed to charge it to capital — hence its occupation of a hitherto unused number 70 — and authorised Jones to construct at Lochgorm three additional engines of the same class, the expenditure to be spread over several years. He certainly heeded this instruction because ten years passed before the next three appeared, 85, 86 and 87 in 1892-93. 88 arrived in 1895, followed by a further three in 1897-98 at the time of the extension of the line forward from Strome Ferry to Kyle of Lochalsh, while the ninth and final engine came out in 1901. These last four, Nos 5, 6, 7 and 48, which appeared under Drummond's superintendency, were evidently regarded as 'renewals' and would no doubt be charged to revenue as they took over numbers of old 2-4-0s. The Skye Bogies were not named — officially at any rate — as they were always considered by the Highland as goods engines.

The class was in the nature of a small-wheeled version of the Dukes. They certainly looked smaller because their 5 ft 3½ in driving wheels enabled the

Fig 60   88 at Dingwall about 1900 resplendent in Drummond lined livery.   (Photo: F. Moore (L.P.C.))

Fig 61   86 on the turntable at Kyle of Lochalsh with metal cab doors fitted. Unlined olive green with small numbers on the back of the tender.   (Photo: Real Photographs)

boiler to be pitched 3 in lower than that of the Dukes and a correspondingly higher chimney was a prominent feature. This had the advantage of keeping the smoke clear of the cab and may also have cooled down a little the sparks which they emitted very freely when they were driven hard as they had to be on the gradients. The boiler barrel was of the same diameter as that of the Dukes but 5½ in shorter (Figs 60 and 61).

In general the design conformed to the typical Jones pattern with outside framing but in this case with horizontal rather than inclined cylinders because of the smaller driving wheels. The first five received louvred chimneys but the last four came out under the superintendency of Peter Drummond who fitted them with his own pattern of flared chimney (Figs 62 and 63). On these engines he discarded Jones compensating levers between the laminated springs of the coupled axles and fitted instead laminated springs on the driving axle and helical springs on the trailing coupled axle. Otherwise all nine were identical in their main features, having Allan link motion, a round-cornered cab, smokebox combined with the cylinders and lock-up safety valves placed transversely. Automatic vacuum brake was fitted at building to all the class except the 1882 engine, 70, which had the steam brake only when built but received the vacuum some three years later. All the

Jones Skye Bogies had plug type regulators, but the Drummond engines had the vertical face type which subsequently was fitted to the earlier engines when heavy boiler repairs were effected.

Dimensions

Cylinders	18″ × 24″
Boiler	
Maximum outside diameter	4′ 2″
Length of barrel	10′ 3″
Pitch	6′ 3″
Length of firebox casing	5′ 5½″
Heating surface	
Tubes (223 of 1¾″)	1,123 sq ft
Firebox	93 sq ft
Total	1,216 sq ft
Grate area	16.2 sq ft
Boiler pressure	150 lbs
Diameter of wheels	
Bogie	3′ 2½″
Coupled	5′ 3½″
Tender	3′ 9½″
Tractive effort (85%)	15,552 lbs
Length over buffers	52′ 7″*
Wheelbase	
Engine	6′ 0″ + 6′ 9″ + 8′ 9″
Tender	6′ 0″ + 6′ 0″
Total	42 ft 9 in

Fig 62   32 (ex-5) at Inverness. Built by Drummond in 1897 and fitted with his design of unlouvred chimney.
(Photo: F. Moore (L.P.C.))

Fig 63   48, the last of the class to be built, in 1901, spent some of its early years on the Invergarry and Fort Augustus Railway. It is shown here on a train in the spacious station at Fort Augustus.
(Photo: J.L. Stevenson Collection)

Weights (full)	
Adhesion	28 tons
Engine	43 tons
Tender	30 tons
Total	73 tons
Water capacity	2,100 gallons*
Coal capacity	4 tons

*Some of these tender dimensions do not apply to 70 which had a shorter tender, like that of the Dukes. It had a wheelbase of 5 ft 6 in + 5 ft 6 in and a water capacity of only 1,800 gallons. The length over buffers of this engine and tender was some 4 ft less than that of the others.

HR Renumbering

Some renumbering took place under the Highland, mainly between the capital and duplicate lists. 70 became 70A in 1915 but was returned to capital stock in 2/1923 following reboilering. Its original number was now occupied by a Loch and it therefore took the number of the Duke, 67 *Cromartie*, which had provided the boiler. 85 hovered between capital and duplicate lists, becoming 85A (4/1918), 85 (9/1919) and again 85A (11/1919), thereafter remaining on the duplicate list and not being considered worth taking into LMS stock. 86 became 86A in April 1918 but reverted to 86 in September 1919. Finally Nos 5, 6 and 7 were renumbered 32, 33 and 34 respectively in 1899 so that the Small Bens, which were then beginning to appear, could be numbered in sequence.

LMS Renumbering

All the Skye Bogies were in existence at 1st January 1923 but, as already stated, 85A was not taken on by the new regime. The rest were allocated LMS numbers 14277 and 14279-85 in order of construction. The renumbering of 70A to 67 seems to have caused some confusion whereby the class did not receive their numbers in sequence, the intervening 14278 being a Clyde Bogie, 82A of 1886. No 87 and 88 were withdrawn at the end of 1926 without carrying the allocated LMS numbers 14280 and 14281.

Tenders

The original tenders had the springs behind the outside framing, other than that of 70 which, as mentioned, had a shorter Duke type of tender with outside springs. Later there were some exchanges with the Duke class (Bruce series and perhaps No 4 of the Lochgorm Bogie series) with the result that tenders with outside frames appeared also behind all the rest except 48. However 86 and 87 got back the original type of tender about 1923. 70, which had a Duke tender, in 1923 received one which had the tank

extended over the rear space previously occupied by the tool-box.

Towards the end of 1927 the LMS introduced tender numbers in advance of the transfer of the engine numbers from tender to cabside. The Skye Bogie tenders were numbered as follows:

Engine No	Tender No
14277	379
14279	380
14282	381
14283	382
14284	383
14285	384

In August 1925 14277 ran for a time with the tender of 14282 bearing the latter's number, while its own tender had a leak repaired.

Livery

The first engine, 70 was painted in brunswick green with white, black and red lining and an olive green border, the outside framing, steps etc being in red-brown. 85-88 were finished in the apple-green introduced in 1885 with the other details as on 70. Nos 5-7 and 48 were at first in Drummond's first style, olive green with black and double white lining, the framing being in claret.

Drummond's lined style was also applied later to 70 and 88 at least, but from 1903 the class began to appear in overall olive green unlined. Later 70, 86, 87, 32, 33, 34 and 48 were in lighter green, again unlined. With the unlined styles 'H . R' on the tender was omitted, at least for a time, from 85, 86 and 32, but later it was restored on 86.

The number plate was of the Jones pattern, even on the last four which were completed under Drummond. About 1915 34 lost its plates and had the number painted high on the cab side in the Smith style. 88 received a Cumming style number plate about 1920.

The six engines which ran with their LMS numbers were given the red passenger livery with the usual yellow lining, crest on the cab side, number in 18 in numerals on the tender and a smokebox number plate. The red livery was even applied, with lining, to the outside framing of the engine and to that of the tenders where found, i.e. on 14277/82/3/4.

There is no evidence of the 1928 livery, but there is just the possibility of a transitional one. A late photograph of 14282, dated 1928, shows the engine painted very dark but with the lining, tender number and crest very bright, suggesting that the engine might have been recently repainted black. Three Small Bens certainly became black while retaining the large tender number but with this Skye Bogie it cannot be proved.

Fig 64   33 as LMS 14283 at Kyle of Lochalsh. Jones chimney from 70A replacing the Drummond pattern.

(Photo: W.H. Whitworth)

Detail Alterations

The Skye Bogies underwent few changes and retained their quaint appearance to the end of a life spanning nearly 50 years.

No 70, first of the class, was built with an exhaust steam feed water heater under the footplate. It is not known how long this was retained. Initially provided with steam brake only on the engine, it received the vacuum after some three years. The rest of the class, as we have seen, were so equipped from the start.

Two at least were given steel fireboxes, 85 in 9/1917 and 33 early in 1916, the latter receiving a copper replacement in 6/1919. No 88 is believed to have had heavy repairs about 1920.

A Highland allocation of 1919 makes no mention of 70A which suggests either that the compiler of the list forgot about it or that it was laid aside at the time. It may well have been in limbo because its louvred chimney and possibly other components were used to rehabilitate 33 in 1922, which gave rise to a rare instance of the replacement of a Drummond chimney by a Jones one (Fig 64). But early in 1923 70A was resurrected when it received the boiler, smokebox and chimney of a Duke, 67, the boiler in question dating from 1898. The dimensions of this boiler would have been slightly different from those of the Skye Bogie's original boiler, but 70A was duly rejuvenated and reinstated to capital stock, becoming 67 by exchanging numbers with the donor of the boiler.

Chimney alterations occurred in some cases. A flared top was fitted to the louvred chimneys of 87 and 88 by 1922 and to that of 14279 (86) after grouping (Fig 65). Three of the last four, which were built with Drummond chimneys, had these shortened, no doubt because the top had been burnt away. These were 33 prior to its reboilering in 1922, 34 by 1923 and 32 probably well before 1927 (Fig 66). Only 48 retained the Drummond pattern throughout at the original height. In no case were the lock-up safety valves replaced as on other Jones classes.

The LMS allocated Class N22 to the Skye Bogie boilers, the same classification being used for the boiler on 14277.

A Lochgorm builder's plate of one of the two 1897 engines is preserved in the Glasgow Museum of Transport (Fig 67). On 14285 an LMS plate "L.M.S. built 1901 Inverness" replaced the Lochgorm plate.

Allocation and Work

The Highland may have had ideas of using the class widely over their system because the 1897 Appendix shows the loads which they could take over all the main lines, for example 23 loaded wagons from Blair Atholl to Dalnaspidal (as against 28 for the Big Goods). But they were primarily intended for the Skye line and the great bulk of their work was done here. They proved to be very capable performers and excellent climbers. Indeed they seemed able to tackle

Fig 65   86 as LMS 14279 on a Kyle goods at Achterneed. Drummond flare on the louvred chimney.

(Photo: A.G. Ellis Collection)

Fig 66   34 as LMS 14284, with the Drummond chimney shortened, setting out from Dingwall for Kyle on a goods near Fodderty Junction.   *(Photo: J.L. Stevenson Collection)*

Fig 67

Works plate off 32 or 33 preserved in Glasgow Museum of Transport.

(Photo: J.L. Stevenson)

loads out of proportion to their small size. Their protracted delivery was due partly to financial considerations but was related also to the very limited service which was operated in early days over the 53 miles between Dingwall and Strome Ferry. The February 1878 timetable, for example, shows only one train (mixed) in each direction which in theory could have been covered by the two converted Seafields Nos 7 and 10. The service had improved by February 1881 with two trains each way, while in the following summer there were three, one passenger, one mixed and one goods, requiring at least three engines. Thus the arrival of 70 in 1882 was welcome.

Reference has already been made under the Duke class to the running battle conducted in correspondence between the Company and the Board of Trade on the subject of mixed trains. Despite the near disaster at Achnashellach in 1892 things were going on five years later much as before with the passenger portion marshalled behind the loose-coupled wagons. Matters at last came to a head when a serious accident was only narrowly averted, the train involved being the 6.15 pm from Dingwall to Strome Ferry on 25th September 1897. The engine was Skye Bogie 88 and on a wet and stormy night a coupling broke a quarter of a mile short of the summit of the 1 in 50 climb to Raven's Rock. The engine was left with the first five wagons and the rest of the train, including the passenger coaches, started to run back. The vehicles clattered through Achterneed station and, traversing the sharp curves, passed Fodderty Junction signal box at speed. Here fortunately the line levels out and, although demolishing one set of level crossing gates outside Dingwall, the runaway finally came to rest a few hundred yards short of the station. Happily no one was physically injured.

At last the Company realised that they could delay no longer in meeting the Board of Trade's demands on the marshalling of mixed trains, which incidentally were based on the Regulation of Railways Act of 1889. Not only did they take immediate steps to comply but the number of mixed trains was forthwith reduced throughout the system. In the early 1890s 113 mixed trains were being run daily — almost half the service in fact — but from 1st November 1897 no fewer than 50 additional trains were introduced, passenger and goods, which eliminated a good proportion of the mixed operation.

The extension of the line from Strome Ferry to Kyle of Lochalsh, opened in November 1897, saw four daily trains on the line, two passenger, one mixed and one goods, now with through services in most cases to and from Inverness. The timings of these were such that at least seven engines were required daily but by now eight of the Skye Bogies were in service, although the two old Seafields had at last given up the struggle. The summer timetable soon showed no fewer than five trains each way and until the outbreak of war in 1914 the Skye Bogies pretty well monopolised the line, becoming very much part of the Ross-shire landscape. However the larger-wheeled 4-4-0s did appear on occasions during this period with the exceptions of the Lochs which were not seen at Kyle until the 1920s and the Big Bens which seem to have been excluded.

In the last months of the 1914-18 war the Skye line was largely used to carry U.S.A. naval supplies from Kyle of Lochalsh to Belleport Sidings at Alness, adjacent to Invergordon. In February 1918 no fewer than four Express Goods trains were booked daily from Kyle with the return workings on empty wagons, ordinary services being reduced to a single daily passenger train each way between Kyle and Inverness and one goods train between Kyle and Dingwall. Although the Skye Bogies no doubt played their part in working these naval trains, other types, both Highland and 'foreign' engines on loan, were used and reference is made elsewhere to an incident which occurred to a Strath when so engaged, requiring its rescue by a Caledonian 4-6-0.

When the war ended, the Skye Bogies resumed the near monopoly of their line and were to be found on most services, goods and passenger, until the mid-1920s, when the Small Bens were becoming quite common. A great deal was done by the LMS to relay and strengthen the permanent way and thoughts were turning towards using six-coupled engines. Thus the first Superheated Goods, 17950, was recorded at Kyle on 26th July 1928. Small Ben 14415 was there too but the Old Guard was still represented by Skye Bogie 14282. The following month a Big Goods also was seen there, but this must have been in the nature of a trial as they did not run regularly to Kyle until 1934. With the arrival of the Superheated Goods, supplemented by Small Bens and now by the occasional Loch, the little Skye Bogies were soon to be seen no more at Kyle.

Despite their obvious suitability for the Skye line, the class did occasionally appear elsewhere. The most interesting working was that of 48 which was one of the engines sent by the Highland to operate the Invergarry to Fort Augustus Railway, taking over from Yankee Tank 52 soon after the Highland became responsible for the working of the line in July 1903. 48 stayed here until April 1907 when the Highland thankfully handed over the working of the 24-mile line to the North British, as not surprisingly it had become clear that the traffic prospects were extremely poor. But at least the Highland by working the line had checked for good any attempt by the North British to reach Inverness through the Great Glen. The winter service had consisted of two trains each way only, one of them mixed, but this was doubled during the summer with the added interest that one and at times two of these trains ran also over the short-lived Fort Augustus Pier branch with its massive engineering works. During this spell 48 had its moments of glory when it hauled a shortened version of the Royal Train conveying King Edward VII to Invergarry in 1905. By now the Balquhidder to Perth line was open throughout and the timings have survived of the return journey which was made to Ballater using this route. The train left Invergarry at 11.15 am and reached its destination at 6.40 pm, the Highland engine handing over to the North British at Spean Bridge. 48 was decorated for the occasion.

In the early 1920s 48 and 86, also possibly others,

were working the Inverness-Tain locals, both passenger and goods. In 1928 14277 had a spell on the Fortrose branch and about the same time 14283 was at Fort George.

The Skye Bogies were very popular with the enginemen. One of their firemen, Murdoch Finlayson, described his charge, 48, as "splendid, travelling like a motor car and one of the finest engines I have ever fired on". He is the authority for revealing the delightful nicknames which some of the engines bore. These were variations on the theme of Mary and were as follows:

70	*Queen Mary*
85	*Lady Mary*
87	*Princess Mary*
33	*Fiery Mary*
48	*Enchanting Mary*

Withdrawal

85 was the first to go, being laid aside in April 1922 with its boiler condemned and with broken frames. It was however still regarded as being in Highland stock at grouping but was withdrawn in August 1923 without being taken into LMS stock and sold for scrap in 12/1923 to Arrol, Jackson & Co. At that time it was to be found in the locomotive cemetery at Culloden Moor to which further reference is made under the Clyde Bogies. Withdrawal of the rest started at the end of 1926 and the last survivor was 14284 which was awaiting cutting up at Kilmarnock in June 1930, keeping fascinating company with the last Clyde Bogie, 14278, and two Straths, 14272 and 14276.

Epilogue

Not many engines have had songs written about them, but one of the Skye Bogies had this distinction. The following, to the tune of 'Ho-ro Mo Nighean Dhonn Bhoidheach' (Ho-ro My Nut Brown Maiden) appeared in the *L.M.S. Magazine*:

> Ho-ro, my old Skye Bogie,
> Hi-ri, my old Skye Bogie,
> My Davie Jones's Bogie,
> My One-four-two-eight-three.
> In Dawsholm and Polmadie
> Are engines fair to see,
> But ne'er a Midland Compound
> Can lure my heart from thee.

In fact 14283 was a Drummond engine, but with its louvred chimney it had almost all the Jones features!

Summary of Class

HR No	LMS No	Maker	Built	Withdrawn
70/70A (1915) /67 (2/1923)	14277	Lochgorm	5/1882	12/1929
85/85A (11/1919)	—	,,	8/1892	8/1923
86	14279	,,	2/1893	10/1927
87	(14280)	,,	12/1893	12/1926
88	(14281)	,,	4/1895	12/1926
5/32 (1899)	14282	,,	8/1897	9/1929
6/33 (1899)	14283	,,	11/1897	8/1929
7/34 (1899)	14284	,,	7/1898	4/1930
48	14285	,,	12/1901	10/1928

2.15 Clyde Bogie Class 4-4-0
Jones 6 ft 3½ in Engines

This class has sometimes but incorrectly been regarded as a third series of the Duke Class. Certainly it bore a considerable resemblance to the Duke design but there were several differences. It is fair to say that the Clyde Bogies stood in development midway between the Dukes and the Straths and so deserve recognition as forming a class on their own.

The louvred chimney, deep external framing, Allan motion, compensating levers, cab and locomotive wheelbase were the same as on the Dukes as were the cylinders, also inclined at 1 in 12. Boiler diameter was unchanged and there were, as in the Duke Class (Bruce Series), 223 tubes of 1¾ in diameter. But changes in design were made with a view to improvement in the light of experience, principally the shortening of the boiler barrel by 11 in and the enlargement of the firebox. The pitch of the boiler was the same as on the Dukes at 6 ft 6 in above rail level and the lock-up safety valves were arranged in the usual transverse position. The tender was longer than that of the Dukes and had a valuable increase in water capacity. The vacuum brake was fitted at building as was once again the counter-pressure brake, to which reference has already been made when dealing with the Dukes. Overall the Clyde Bogies had a solid symmetrical appearance very similar to the Dukes, but the two classes could be readily distinguished at some distance because the Clyde Bogies' dome was located further back than the Dukes' and was nearer to the safety valves than to the chimney. This was because the Clyde Bogie boiler, being shorter than the Dukes', was made up of two rather than three rings (Figs 68 and 69).

The Board at their meeting on 1st September 1885 considered a request from Jones for additional engines and resolved to order six "new bogie engines". At their following meeting on 29th September they appeared to have been pleasantly surprised at the level of the tenders received because they decided to order eight from the Clyde Locomotive Co Ltd at a price of £2,395 each. The engines thus acquired their class name. Delivery started in April 1886 and the new arrivals took numbers 76 to 83.

It may be appropriate to give here a note on this short-lived company whose first production these engines were. In 1876 a disagreement between Neilson and Reid, partners in the firm of Neilson & Co., Hydepark, Glasgow, led to the former finding himself out of his own business. Eight years later he founded the Clyde Locomotive Works, situated close to his old firm but separated from it by the line of the North British Railway. However very soon afterwards, in 1888, the firm of Sharp, Stewart & Co transferred their business from Manchester to Glasgow and purchased the Clyde Locomotive Works, changing the title to the Atlas Works, by which title their old premises in Manchester had been known.

Dimensions

Cylinders (2 outside)	18″ × 24″
Boiler	
Maximum outside diameter	4′ 2″
Length of barrel	9′ 9½″
Pitch	6′ 6″
Length of firebox casing	6′ 2½″
Heating surface	
Tubes	1,038 sq ft
Firebox	102 sq ft
Total	1,140 sq ft
Grate area	18.83 sq ft
Boiler pressure	160 lbs
Diameter of wheels	
Bogie	3′ 9½″
Coupled	6′ 3½″
Tender	3′ 9½″
Tractive effort (85%)	14,100 lbs
Length over buffers	53 9″
Wheelbase	
Engine	6′ 0″ + 6′ 9″ + 8′ 9″
Tender	6′ 6″ + 6′ 6″
Total	44′ 0″
Weights (full)	
Adhesion	28 tons
Engine	43 tons
Tender	31 tons 10 cwts
Total	74 tons 10 cwts
Water capacity	2,250 gallons
Coal capacity	4 tons

Renumbering

All eight engines were transferred to the duplicate list and were given 'A' suffixes to their numbers. 81 in 12/1916, 76-80 and 82 in 3/1917 and 83 in 4/1917. All of the class were in HR stock at the end of 1922 but only one was allocated an LMS number, 82A which became LMS 14278.

Fig 68   82 *Fife* in original condition c1900. First Drummond livery.   *(Photo: Real Photographs)*

Fig 69   76 *Bruce* at Perth in the 1903 unlined olive green.   *(Photo: J.F. McEwan Collection)*

Names

Once again the directors and their residences were commemorated by the names, all but four of which had been used on earlier classes and have already been explained. The new names had their origins as under:

Lochalsh   This apparently referred to Sir Alexander Matheson of Lochalsh who was Chairman of the Inverness & Aberdeen Junction Railway throughout its existence and thereafter of the Highland from its formation in 1865 until he was succeeded by The Hon. T.C. Bruce (after whom 76 was named) in 1885. Matheson remained a director until his death in July 1886.

Colville   Lord Colville of Culross, appointed a director in 1885.

Durn   The residence near Perth of A.E. Pullar, director and for a time Deputy Chairman.

Monkland   The residence at Nairn of William Whitelaw who was Chairman of the Highland from 1902 to 1912 and previously a director.

82 *Durn* lost its name to the new 4-4-0 74 in 1916 and thereafter ran nameless which was unfortunate as the engine outlived the others by some seven years until 1930.

Exhibition of 76

When new 76 was sent to the 1886 Edinburgh Exhibition where it earned a gold medal. Using track laid temporarily, the engine was towed from Lothian Road Goods Yard via Tollcross to the Meadows. The tender however was run over the horse tram tracks. As prepared for exhibition the livery showed a few differences from the standard finish while the chimney, as far as can be judged from a photograph (which has perhaps been retouched), lacked the top rim which made the tiny flare of the Jones chimney much more noticeable. Also there was an extra cylinder lubricator over the piston head. The special livery, which was applied for the Exhibition only, consisted of dark gamboge. This lining looked not very different from that which Drummond later used, but was thinner and finer even being continued along the narrow coupling rod cover between the splasher and cab. The frames were apparently standard red-brown and the cylinders were separately lined out with a panel. The number plate was of standard pattern.

After the Exhibition the builders complained that they had incurred some £1,000 in expenses and they sought a contribution from the Highland Board who however promptly declined!

Tenders

With a wheelbase of 13 ft the tenders had the merit of some increase in water capacity over the Dukes and Skye Bogies, the standard design of which tenders had wheelbase of 11 ft and 12 ft respectively. The axles had both inside and outside bearings and were interchangeable with the leading axles of the 2-4-0s.

As time went on however there were some exchanges among the three types of tender. At the turn of the century the tender of 76, emblazoned 'THE HIGHLAND RAILWAY', had apparently come off a Skye Bogie and similar tenders were behind 77 and 83 in their later days. 79 had a shorter tender latterly, perhaps from a Lochgorm Bogie, while 78 and 82 had in later Highland days outside framed tenders from the Bruce series. 76 (76A) recovered a Clyde Bogie tender by 1923, and 82A received a Skye Bogie one, probably at repainting in LMS livery.

As with all Jones tenders, the tool box on the rear platform was usually removed quite soon but there is no evidence in this class of the extension of the tank. However the Skye Bogie tender which ran behind 76 appears to have been so lengthened. It also had acquired by 1915 a weather board with two circular spectacle windows and the top rounded to the shape of the cab roof. This was for the protection of the crew on the descent from Dalnaspidal to Blair Atholl. 82A had a similar fitting for a time about 1914 on a tender which was still complete with its tool-box. After the arrival of the 0-6-4 tanks in 1909-11 the use of tender engines for banking at Blair Atholl was infrequent until 1940.

The only Clyde Bogie tender in LMS livery, that of 14278 (82A), was given the number 690 in 1927.

Livery

The Clyde Bogies arrived on the scene just in time to receive the new style introduced by Jones, namely apple green with white, black and red lining and a darker green border, along with red-brown frames and steps. The number plates were of the Jones pattern.

In due course five at least of the class received the Drummond lined style of olive green with double white lining. Tender lettering varied, 76, 79, 81 and 83 having 'THE HIGHLAND RAILWAY' on the tender, while 82 had 'H . R'. Outside frames in claret accompanied this style. Later the whole class were in unlined olive green, but tender lettering was not always applied. 76, 78, 79, 81 and 83 at least had 'H . R' on the tender but for a time 77, 80 and 82 had unlettered tenders. 78 lost its number plate about 1915 and had the number painted high on the cab side in the Smith style, the numeral '8' being unusual in having a flat top as if the painter had started to form a '3'. For some reason 81A received a new number plate of the Cumming type in 1919. This showed

'81A' in contrast to the usual practice with duplicate engines which kept their plates and had 'A' (or 'B') painted above the number.

The only Clyde Bogie which entered LMS stock, 82A which was by then nameless, appeared by August 1926 as LMS 14278 in standard red livery with a smokebox number plate, and so remained until withdrawn in April 1930.

Detail Alterations

Information is available on the boiler and firebox repairs which the Clyde Bogies received in their early years and it may be of interest to quote these, although they were largely in the nature of routine maintenance.

76 Retubed, new half tubeplate in firebox and new half backplate in firebox May 1895.

77 Retubed (brass) August 1890. Firebox renewed April 1896.

78 Retubed February 1895, also new half tubeplate and doorplate in firebox.

79 Retubed (red metal) November 1889. New firebox April 1896.

80 Retubed December 1889. New firebox October 1899.

81 Retubed July 1893. New firebox tubeplate November 1894.

82 Retubed May 1890. New firebox 1896.

83 Retubed June 1890. Partial retubing September 1894. Half tubeplate in firebox September 1894.

During and just after the First World War three of the class were repaired by outside firms, namely:

77A	(not known)	1915
	Yorkshire Engine Co.	1920
81A	R. Stephenson, Darlington	c.1916
	Hawthorn, Leslie	1920/1
82A	Yorkshire Engine Co.	1920

However neither then nor at any time were any radical changes made to the class, although there were some alterations to the boiler mountings. In 1919 81A had the chimney shortened and received a broad flattened dome also Ross pop safety valves in line, the work presumably being done by Hawthorn, Leslie. It has been stated that the boiler pressure of this engine was raised to 170 lbs in 1916, perhaps after its visits to Darlington, but this seems unlikely as the boiler would then be 30 years old. In any event an official circular dated 21st June 1922 states that the pressure of 76A to 83A was 160 lbs. Five acquired a Drummond pattern flare on the louvred chimney, namely 76 (by 1915), 77A subsequent to its visit to the Yorkshire Engine Co), 78A (while in the Smith livery), 82A (by 1926) and 83A (by 1922). The last named had its chimney shortened at the same time (Fig 70). Finally 14278 (82A) after receiving the LMS livery but by May 1928 had been given a Drummond

pattern flared chimney, i.e. without louvres.

The boiler of 14278 was put into Class N18 by the LMS.

Allocation and Work

The allocation cycle of the Clyde Bogies was like that of most of the Highland passenger classes. When new they were on the main Inverness-Perth trains but were displaced by larger types, the Straths, Lochs and Castles, and moved partly to the North line and also to local services elsewhere. In their declining years they could sometimes be found on branches. The allocation of the class in 1900-01 was as follows:

Inverness	76, 79, 80, 83
Blair Atholl	77
Wick	78
Kingussie	81
Helmsdale	82

In 1919 the distribution had not materially altered, namely:

Inverness	76A, 77A, 78A, 80A, 82A
Wick	83A
Thurso	79A
Kingussie	81A

An accident occurred at Dalwhinnie on 2nd December 1890, involving 76 and 77, and is of particular interest as giving an insight into a very strange operating practice. 76 was train engine of the 10.10 am Up Mail from Inverness to Perth, consisting of three fish wagons, five coaches and four assorted passenger vans. At Kingussie 77 was attached ahead to assist to Dalwhinnie, such assistance being evidently provided either in front or in the rear depending on the ideas of the drivers. In accordance with what appears to have been common practice, the pilot was detached whilst the train was in motion some ¾-mile short of Dalwhinnie by the fireman of the train engine. It then ran ahead, whistling to the signalman who altered his points to admit the engine to the Down loop, passing the home signal at danger, whereupon the points were re-set to normal and the home signal cleared. Unfortunately, due to a defect in the mechanism the points did not fully close, derailing 76 and all except the rear three vehicles. Fortunately there were no casualties.

The Inspecting Officer, Major Marandin, dealt surprisingly lightly with the Company over the affair, but reported that this method of detaching a pilot engine appeared to be "a practice unusual and open to objection''. He pointed out that there was a distinct breach of absolute block working, that it was wrong for the pilot to pass the home signal at danger and that the uncoupling of the pilot when running at some 25 mph was "one not unattended by risk to the fireman who performs it''. He also drew attention to the need for the train engine to pass at danger the

Fig 70   83A *Monkland* shunting at Inverness in July 1922. Chimney slightly shortened and fitted with a
Drummond flare.   *(Photo: LCGB Ken Nunn Collection)*

distant signal which on the Highland at that time was
to be treated as an absolute stop signal when at
danger. His final comment was that the manoeuvre
seemed unnecessary anyway as the train was booked
to stop at Dalwhinnie and the pilot could have been
detached in the normal way with little if any loss of
time. The Major concluded "I should hope that it
may be found possible to follow upon this line the
usual practice when pilot engines are detached upon
other lines".

How long it took the Company to comply with this
admonition is not known, but one strange practice
which remained was that of detaching the pilot from
Up trains at Dalwhinnie when the hardest part of the
climb lies ahead, from Dalwhinnie to Dalnaspidal, in
particular the restart at 1 in 80. However it seems to
have been quite common to give rear end assistance
for half a mile or so and the Inspecting Officer may
have thought it better not to enquire on this point!

76 was in trouble again on 7th July 1891 when,
piloting Duke 67, it was derailed on a passenger train
at Ballinluig. Later for some years it was pilot at
Helmsdale but then moved south again to Blair Atholl
for local and banking duties, for which work it
received the tender weather board, already
mentioned. Soon after 1918 it was shunting at
Inverness, still with the weather board, and was last
seen in traffic at Forres on 18th July 1923 and at
Inverness on 27th August (Fig 71).

77 is credited with a particularly fast run from
Inverness to Perth some time during the First World
War, the train being a one-coach special to convey
General Coombe of Strathconon who had been
urgently recalled from leave. The Traffic Superintendent told the driver that the line would be
cleared for him and that he could go as fast as he liked
(or perhaps as fast as he dared!). Perth (118 miles) was
reached in 2½ hours. In the early 1920s 77A, as it had
become, was on less energetic work on the Inverness-
Tain locals.

79A was on the Thurso branch in 1919 and 80A was
recorded about the same time at Kyle of Lochalsh,
one of the comparatively few appearances of the class
on the Skye line. Although it worked for some years
between Inverness and Wick, 81A also spent a lot of
its time at the small shed at Kingussie which provided
pilot assistance to Dalwhinnie and also had a daily
turn to Inverness. Its last recorded active appearance
was on the Fortrose branch on 30th August 1923, but
— see Withdrawals — it was evidently retained for
some purpose during the ensuing winter, as was 76A
(Fig 72).

Finally 82 was at Aberfeldy in 1913-14 and again
around 1920, during which periods it could also be
seen at Blair Atholl. Surviving the rest of the class by
some seven years, on the strength of a major boiler
overhaul in 1913, it spent this borrowed time at
Forres on shunting and local work as well as having

Fig 71   76A *Bruce* still in use at Inverness on 27th August 1923. Drummond flare to chimney and spectacle
plate on tender fitted for banking duties at Blair Atholl.   *(Photo: A.W. Croughton)*

spells as the Fochabers Town branch engine, a red
but nameless 14278 (Fig 73).

Withdrawals

77 was withdrawn in 1915 but was reinstated in the
following year, having been overhauled by an
unknown firm or railway works. The Highland could
not afford to lose anything capable of movement at
that difficult time when they had just been denied the
use of the Rivers. No further withdrawals of the Clyde
Bogies took place under the Highland so that all eight
were in stock at grouping in 1923, although about half
were unserviceable.

The reason for the retention by the Company of so
many old engines after the end of the war in 1918 has
never been clear. With the arrival of 24 new engines
between 1916 and 1921 one would have expected at
least a corresponding drop in the numbers of the more
decrepit classes as traffic fell to normal levels after
1918, but in fact no withdrawals were recorded by the
Highland after Duke 74 was broken up in 1918.
Nevertheless many engines came to be stored
unserviceable and were clearly not worth repairing.
Probably the directors thought that they could strike
a better deal with the LMS by having this large
number of engines on the books but it has also been
suggested that the retentions were connected with the
settlement of debts due to the Company by the
Government under the Delayed Repair and Maintenance Scheme.

Whatever the reason, there were 173 engines in
Highland Railway stock at the end of 1922 but only
150 of these were taken into LMS stock and allocated
new numbers, the 23 engines which thus found themselves in limbo including seven of the eight Clyde
Bogies. A few of the 23 were allowed to perform light
duties until the final take-over by the LMS on
1st September 1923, among them two Clyde Bogies,
76A and 81A, as we have seen. By that time all the
other 'unwanted' engines had been laid up at three or
four locations and were regarded as withdrawn, but
Bruce and *Colville* had a short reprieve and were not
recorded as being taken out of stock until 1924 when
they were scrapped at Inverness. One can only
suggest that they were regarded as non-revenue-
earning stock and retained solely for snow plough or
ballast working or for steam heating during the winter
of 1923-24.

Of the other Clyde Bogies 77A seems to have been
in the poorest condition and had been laid off in 1919
awaiting a heavy repair. This was not carried out but
it was evidently patched up sufficiently to be seen on
a ballast train at Clachnaharry in August 1921.
Thereafter it was briefly on the Inverness-Tain locals
but soon threw in the towel and was to be found for
a time at the back of Inverness coaling stage at the
head of a sad silent line of Jones engines. The tops of
their chimneys could just be seen over the head of the
high wall which frustrated generations of railway
enthusiasts anxious to see the goings-on in the
roundhouse area from Eastgate.

106

Fig 72   81A *Colville* as branch engine at Fortrose on 30th August 1923, one of its last days in revenue-earning service. Shortened chimney, flattened dome and pop valves in line.   *(Photo: A.W. Croughton)*

Fig 73   82A as LMS 14278 awaiting scrapping at Kilmarnock in 1930. Full length chimney without louvres fitted by May 1928, similar to that of a Skye Bogie.   *(Photo: J.L. Stevenson Collection)*

The storage points for the withdrawn engines, as far as they are known, were as follows:

Culloden Moor
Small Goods 2-4-0: 27A
Dukes: 70A and 72A
Clyde Bogies: 77A, 78A and 80A
Straths: 96A and 97A
Skye Bogie: 85A
2-4-0T: 118A

Aviemore
Duke: 84A
Clyde Bogies: 79A and 83A
Straths: 90A, 91A, 93A and 99A
also probably Glenbarry Class 2-4-0 35A which was noted here, apparently serviceable on 27th August 1923.

Inverness
Three probably finished up here, namely
Medium Goods 2-4-0: 37A
Dukes: 73A and 75A

Kingussie
It is stated that two engines were stored here, possibly 76A and 81A

Reverting to the Clyde Bogies themselves, there was some haste to dispose of all the stored engines and 78A and 80A were bought for scrap by Arrol, Jackson & Co in November 1923 while 83A went the same way in January 1924. 77A and 79A are understood to have been scrapped at Kilmarnock in 1925. The boiler of 81A, which was scrapped at Inverness with 76A in 1924 (or possibly 1925), was retained as a stationary installation. The survivor of the slaughter, 14278, was broken up at Kilmarnock in mid-1930, still with an original boiler, 88 of 1886.

So passed a very reliable class of main line passenger engine, slightly better than the Dukes but more quickly superseded, in this case by the Straths of 1892 and the Lochs of 1896.

Summary of Class

Nos	Name	Maker	Works No	Built	Withdrawn
76 /76A (3/1917)	*Bruce* (V)	Clyde Locomotive Co.	1	4/1886*	1924
77 /77A (3/1917)	*Lovat* (III)	,,	2	5/1886	8/1923†
78 /78A (3/1917)	*Lochalsh*	,,	3	6/1886	8/1923
79 /79A (3/1917)	*Atholl* (II)	,,	4	,,	1923
80 /80A (3/1917)	*Stafford* (III)	,,	5	7/1886	8/1923
81 /81A (12/1916)	*Colville*	,,	6	,,	1924
82 /82A (3/1917) /LMS 14278	*Fife* (II) /*Durn* (I) (1900) /- (1916)	,,	7	9/1886	4/1930
83 /83A (4/1917)	*Cadboll* (II) /*Monkland* (1900)	,,	8	10/1886	8/1923

* Not taken into stock until 12/1886, i.e. after being shown at the Edinburgh Exhibiton.
† Withdrawn in 1915 and reinstated in 1916.

2.16 Strathpeffer Tank Class 0-4-4T
Jones 4 ft 3 in Engine

This solitary tank was built at Lochgorm in 1890 to replace the 2-2-2T (rebuilt from the Belladrum class 2-2-2), 12 on the Strathpeffer branch. It has been stated that the boiler came from old 2-2-2 13, but the LMS boiler list records this as (172) built in 1890. Pitched at 5 ft 9 in above rail level, it contained 158 tubes of 1¾ in diameter. Frames were inside and the valve gear was presumably Allan as in all other Jones engines. The saddle tank with straight sides and an arched top, was placed over the boiler barrel while the dome, which was surmounted by a spring balance safety valve, was set on the raised firebox. The chimney had no louvres but was otherwise of Jones pattern, and the cab rather resembled that of Stroudley's Lochgorm tanks but had rounded corners. Vacuum brake was fitted early in the 1890s.

Even when it was new, the engine looked old fashioned, like a product of the 1860s rather than of 1890. It is notable as being the only inside cylinder engine which Jones designed for the Highland, although he had built two of the Lochgorm Tanks to Stroudley's design. The latter's cylinders and those of this 0-4-4T were identical. Its cab windows were square and remained thus after the rebuilding (Figs 74 and 75).

The new engine, which cost £1,214, took the number 13, old 13 being withdrawn at the same time.

Dimensions

Cylinders (2 inside)	14″ × 20″
Boiler	
Maximum outside diameter	3′ 6½″
Length of barrel	?
Pitch	5′ 9″
Heating surface	
Tubes	578 sq ft
Firebox	62 sq ft
Total	640 sq ft
Grate area	12.5 sq ft
Boiler pressure	100 lbs
Diameter of wheels	
Coupled	4′ 3″
Rear Bogie	2′ 7½″
Tractive effort (85%)	6,533 lbs
Length over buffers	29′ 6″
Wheelbase	6′ 0″ + 6′ 6″ + 5′ 6″*
Weights (full)	
Adhesion	20 tons
Total	32 tons
Water capacity	820 gallons
Coal capacity	1½ tons

* The bogie pin was placed 6 in off-centre, nearer to the rear bogie axle.

Renumbering

The engine was renumbered 53 in December 1899 as its original number 13 was required for a Small Ben. It was put onto the duplicate list as 53A in March 1917, making its capital number available for a Clan. When taken into LMS stock it became 15050.

Names

These were of the two branches which the engine worked. The name *Lybster* was not retained when LMS red livery was applied.

Livery

This was originally apple green with white, black and red lining and an olive green border with the frames and steps in red-brown. The name in gold letters ran along the saddle tank and the Jones number plate was on the bunker side. Prior to renumbering as 53 the engine was already in the first Drummond livery of olive green with double white and black lining and a claret frame edge and this style was continued after the 1899 renumbering and the 1901 rebuilding. However in 1903 unlined olive green replaced the previous colours when also the name *Lybster* took the place of *Strathpeffer* on the side tanks. Nevertheless some photographs show faint traces of lining showing through. By 1927 the LMS red livery had been applied with 14 in tank numerals, emblem on the bunker and number plate on the smokebox door. The lining on the cab side was now carried round the corners in the Jones manner. The engine was never in black.

Rebuilding

Drummond rebuilt 53 as a side tank in October 1901 at Lochgorm, rebuilding plates appearing on the splashers. Apart from new side tanks, the boiler was given lock-up safety valves on the dome which was now in mid-boiler position. Otherwise the engine was unchanged but its appearance was much improved and indeed it looked, if anything, better proportioned than the Drummond passenger tanks of 1905-6 the design of which was based on 53. The boiler was

Fig 74   13 *Strathpeffer* in original condition as a saddle tank. At Strathpeffer soon after entering traffic in 1890.
(Photo: *L.G.R. Photographs*)

Fig 75   13 *Strathpeffer* on a mixed train at the branch terminus, with the staff suitably posed, in he 1890s.
The vacuum brake has now been fitted.   (Photo: *B.D. Matthews Collection*)

pitched 3 in higher at 6 ft and the heating surface appears to have been altered, while a new firebox was provided, more or less identical to that of the 1905 design (Figs 75-76). Dimensions which differed from the original were as follows:

Heating surface

Tubes	623 sq ft
Firebox	67.5 sq ft
Total	690.5 sq ft
Grate area	13 sq ft
Boiler pressure	140 lbs
Tractive effort (85%)	9,146 lbs
Weights	
Adhesion	19 tons 10 cwts
Total	34 tons
Water capacity	900 gallons

Steam heating apparatus was fitted in December 1917.

Allocation and Work

As indicated by the name, the engine was stationed at Dingwall for the first thirteen years and employed on the Strathpeffer branch, five miles in length, rising fairly easily at around 1 in 200 from Dingwall and after the first half-mile or so almost dead straight. Six or seven round trips a day were scheduled so the work was not unduly strenuous. In July 1903 the Wick and Lybster Light Railway was opened and 53, as it now had become, was there from the start, being photographed suitably decorated arriving at the branch terminus with the first train from Wick (Fig 77). It worked there off and on until the end of its life, with a Drummond 0-4-4T or a Yankee 4-4-0T at times taking its place. Occasionally it was sent to work the Dornoch branch where it was to be seen as LMS 15050, in August 1927. Shortly before its withdrawal it was back on its old ground at Dingwall.

Withdrawal

This took place in December 1929 and scrapping was carried out at Lochgorm. To see its fortieth year was a good feat of survival for a solitary engine.

Fig 76   53 (ex-13) at LMS 15050 in red livery. Rebuilt as a side tank. The plate on the splasher reads "Rebuilt 1901"
(Photo: W.H. Whitworth)

Fig 77   53 *Lybster* entering Lybster on the first train from Wick on 1st July 1903. Drummond unlined livery.
(Photo: J.L. Stevenson Collection)

Summary of Class

HR No.	LMS No	Name	Maker	Built	Rebuilt	Withdrawn
13	15050	*Strathpeffer* (**II**)	Lochgorm	5/1890	10/1901	12/1929
/53 (12/1899)		/*Lybster* (5/1903)				
/53A (3/1917)		/ — (by 1927)				

2.17 Strath Class 4-4-0
Jones 6 ft 3½ in Engines

Also known as the Glen class, this was a development of the Clyde Bogie. The Crewe framing was continued with the cylinders contained within the outward and downward curve of the smokebox, while the Jones fittings were again evident in the louvred chimney, the tall brass safety valves transversely arranged with the whistle beside them and just ahead, and the round-cornered cab. The boiler, pitched at 7 ft 4 in, was of increased diameter — 4 ft 6 in as against 4 ft 2 in on the Clyde Bogies — and contained 242 tubes of 1¾ in diameter made of Everitt's red metal. Steam distribution was by Allan link motion and there were compensating levers between the laminated springs of the coupled axles. The tender was practically identical with that of the Clyde Bogies, though with slightly increased coal capacity. Fore-end lubrication was by a Vacuum Oil Coy's sight feed lubricator for steam chests and by Jones patent lubricators for the cylinders. A notable feature was that they were the first Scottish engines to have combination injectors (Gresham & Cravens No 8),

these later becoming universal on all the Scottish railways except the Glasgow & South Western.

While the Straths were tidily designed and typical of Jones's work, they lacked the regular lines of his earlier express engines or, for that matter of his later Lochs. In the Straths the larger diameter boiler on the Clyde Bogie length of framing somewhat spoiled the proportions, as did the handrail which ran lower than the central flange across the cab. The original intention was to build eight of the class, for which Neilson quoted a price of £2,525 each, but when the Board discussed the matter on 7th October 1891 they noted that Neilson, who clearly knew their customer, had indicated that if the order were increased to twelve they would give a reduction of £50 per engine. The offer was accepted and the twelve engines were delivered the following year under Neilson Order E693 at a cost of £2,475 each. The Board minute refers also to "alterations in four of the boilers at an extra cost of £80". They took numbers 89 to 100 and all bore names (Figs 78 and 79).

Fig 78   93 *Strathnairn* at Inverness as built. Drummond lined livery.   *(Photo: Real Photographs)*

113

Dimensions

Cylinders (2 outside)	18″×24″
Boiler	
Maximum outside diameter	4′ 6″
Length of barrel	9′ 9½″
Pitch	7′ 4″
Length of firebox casing	6′ 2½″
Heating surface	
Tubes	1,127 sq ft
Firebox	115 sq ft
Total	1,242 sq ft
Grate area	18.83 sq ft
Boiler pressure	160 lbs
Diameter of wheels	
Bogie	3′ 9½″
Coupled	6′ 3½″
Tender	3′ 9½″
Tractive effort (85%)	14,100 lbs
Wheelbase	
Engine	6′ 0″ + 6′ 9″ + 8′ 9″
Tender	6′ 6″ + 6′ 6″
Total	44′ 0″
Length over buffers	54′ 1½″
Weights	
Adhesion	29 tons 10 cwts
Engine	45 tons
Tender	31 tons 10 cwts
Total	76 tons 10 cwts
Water capacity	2,250 gallons
Coal capacity	4½ tons

HR Renumbering

None of the class had its number changed by the Highland but all were placed on the Duplicate list in 1919 with the addition of 'A' to the existing number. Within a few months all were returned to capital stock but most were later to go onto the Duplicate list again. Details are as follows:

Original Number	Later Numbers
89	89A (5/1918); 89 (9/1919); 89A(11/1919); 89 (8/1922)
90	90A (5/1918); 90 (9/1919); 90A (11/1919)
91	91A (6/1918); 91 (9/1919); 91A (11/1919)
92	92A (6/1918); 92 (8/1918); 92A(4/1919); 92 (9/1919); 92A (7/1921)
93	93A (4/1919); 93 (9/1919); 93A (8/1921)
94	94A (4/1919); 94 (9/1919)
95	95A (4/1919); 95 (9/1919)
96	96A (4/1919); 96 (9/1919); 96A (5/1922)
97	97A (4/1919); 97 (9/1919); 97A (5/1922)
98	98A (7/1919); 98 (9/1919)
99	99A (7/1919); 99 (9/1919); 99A (8/1922)
100	100A (7/1919); 100 (9/1919)

LMS Renumbering

The whole class was in existence at grouping but six were not taken into LMS stock and therefore were not allocated LMS numbers, viz. 90A, 91A, 93A, 96A, 97A and 99A. The remaining six were given numbers

Fig 79   97 *Glenmore* on an Up train near Dingwall about 1910.   *(Photo: D.C. McBean)*

14271-76 in the order of their former numbers but, although surviving until 1925, 94 did not carry its allocated number 14273.

Names

Apart from *Snaigow* and *Durn* of 1916, the Straths were the last class to be given the names of directors and their residences, the origins of the names of the first two being as follows:

Sir George   Sir George Macpherson Grant, a director and later to be Chairman from 1897 to 1900.

Tweeddale   Marquis of Tweeddale, a director.

Grandtully   Residence near Aberfeldy of W. Steuart Fothringham, a director.

With these exceptions the class was named after Highland glens and straths, a strath being usually a broad-bottomed valley, often carrying a highway and on a larger scale than a glen. The movement had started towards a uniform set of names for each class, first realised in the Lochs.

Before delivery there was confusion over name allocation. 94 was at first expected to be named *Strathglass*, 97 to be *Glenbruar* and 100 to be *Glenmore* but in the event the three were named as shown in the summary.

The often quoted statement that 92 was for a time named *Glendean*, *Glendeane* or even *Glendearne* is without foundation.

The locations of the geographical names will mostly be familiar, in particular Strathspey, Strathnairn and Strathtay. Less obviously, Strathdearn carries the River Findhorn on its course northward, while the Kyle line runs down Strathcarron from its summit west of Achnasheen to Strathcarron station. Glentilt runs south to Blair Atholl, Glenmore is of course the Great Glen, Glentruim is occupied by the railway from south of Dalwhinnie to Newtonmore, Glentromie runs north to join the Spey valley near Kingussie and the foot of Glenbruar lies three miles north-west of Blair Atholl.

Livery

The original livery was the apple-green style introduced by Jones in 1885 with white, black and red lining and darker green border, while the outside framing and cab steps were in red-brown. The number plate was of the standard Jones pattern. By 1902 several had received the earlier Drummond colours of olive green with black and double white lining and claret framing etc. These included at least 90, 93, 94, 96 and 99. The tender lettering of 90 and 94 was 'THE HIGHLAND RAILWAY' and of 93 and 99 'H . R'. That of 96 is not known.

From 1903 onwards the class was repainted in the unlined olive green, generally with 'H . R' on the tender, although for a time 91, 93, 94 and 96 had no tender lettering, 93 later recovering it. 96 had the number plate removed about 1915 and until 1918 had the Smith livery with the number painted high on the cab side. The Cumming style of number plate was fitted after repair to 93 and 96 (in 1918), to 98 (in 1920) and to 100 (in 1921).

14271 (89), 14272 (92), 14275 (98) and 14276 (100) received LMS lined red livery with the number in 18 in figures on the tender, crest on the cab side and smokebox number plate. By 1929 14275 had been given lined black livery, retaining the smokebox number plate. 95 missed red paint but in 1928 appeared as 14274 in lined black without a smokebox number plate. In black 14274 and 14275 had the number in 10 in unshaded figures on the cab side and LMS on the tender.

Detail Alterations

The first noticeable external change was the fitting of a Drummond flare to the louvred chimney of seven engines, namely 89 about 1913, 90 possibly about 1917, 91 by 1912, 93 by 1913, 94 at an unknown date, 95 by 1912 and 97 probably from 1916. The effect upon the eye has been described as "rather shark-like" but to some was not unpleasing (Fig 80).

From 1915 onwards all the Straths were overhauled by outside firms and other companies' works as follows:

89	Yorkshire Engine Co*	1916
	Yorkshire Engine Co‡	1921
90	Yorkshire Engine Co*	1917
91	North British Loco Co*	1916
92	Hawthorn, Leslie*	1916
93	Hawthorn, Leslie*	5/1918
94	NER Gateshead Works*	1916
	Beardmore, Dalmuir‡	1920
95	Hawthorn, Leslie*	1916
	Beardmore, Glasgow‡	1921
96	GNSR Inverurie Works	1915
	Hawthorn, Leslie*	5/1918
97	Yorkshire Engine Co	1916
	? *	2/1918
98	Hawthorn, Leslie‡	7/1920
99	Yorkshire Engine Co	1916
	? *	2/1918
100	Hawthorn, Leslie‡	7/1921

* Steel firebox fitted
‡ Copper firebox fitted

In addition to the fitting of new fireboxes as indicated above, 92 received a copper firebox around 1920, while 98 and 100 were given reconditioned boilers, presumably with copper fireboxes, in 7/1920 and 7/1921 respectively by Hawthorn, Leslie. At the same time they had the original chimneys shortened, that of 98 at the base and 100's at the top and base

Fig 80   93 *Strathnairn* at Inverness in 1913. Drummond flare on the chimney and fitted with cab doors. Unlined olive green.   *(Photo: L.G.R. Photographs)*

Fig 81   98 *Glentruim* at Forres in LMS days with shortened chimney, flattened dome and pop valves in line, fitted by Hawthorn, Leslie in 1920. No coal rails on tender. Cumming number plate. *(Photo: W.H. Whitworth)*

(Fig 81). Only the engines with copper fireboxes continued in service after 1923.

Other changes to boiler mountings were made when 95 received a wider dome and 93, 96, 98 and 100 were given domes which were both flatter and wider. Safety valves also were altered. Ross pop valves arranged in line were fitted to 93, 96, 98 and 100, but 95 had the original tall lock-up valves re-arranged in line instead of, as built, transversely (Fig 82). 95 later — some time after 10/1926 — received pop valves in line. Finally extra wash-out plugs in the firebox were fitted to 93, 95, 96, 98 and 100.

The Strath boiler was classified N33 by the LMS.

Tenders

The tool box fitted to the back of the tender was in all cases removed and in a number of them the tank was lengthened over the space so left. 91, 93, 95, 96 (from c1918), 97 and 99 were recorded with tenders thus modified, slightly increasing the water capacity. There may have been exchanges within the class or with the Clyde Bogies and this makes it difficult to be precise on the number of extended tenders.

The LMS in 1927 allocated the undernoted tender numbers:

Engine No	Tender No
14271	685
14272	686
14274	687
14275	688
14276	689

Allocation and Work

The Straths were intended for the main Inverness-Perth line and were put to work on the principal trains, only to be partially ousted by the appearance in 1896 of the Lochs with increased power and other improvements. However the weight of the trains continued to increase, helped by the opening of the Aviemore Direct line in 1898, and this led to an increase in double-heading which kept Straths in evidence on the main south trains for some more years. Soon however some moved to the Inverness-Wick trains, particularly 96 and 98 which worked here for several years, while 100 surprisingly had a spell on the Skye line.

The allocation of the class in 1900 was:

Inverness:	89, 91, 94, 96
Keith:	90
Forres:	92, 93, 97
Wick:	95
Aviemore:	98
Blair Atholl:	99
Kyle of Lochalsh:	100

In the *Railway Magazine* of August 1904 T.R. Perkins, writing of a journey on the 9.50 am train north from Inverness, describes it as consisting of 19 vehicles, "most of them bogie carriages", the engine being 98.

As they became older the Straths were employed more on local passenger work and on piloting and banking to Druimuachdar and Dava. They also became more common on the Skye line, particularly

Fig 82   95 *Strathcarron* at Elgin (GNS) shed in October 1926. Drummond flare on chimney and lock-up safety valves arranged *in line*.

(Photo: A.W. Croughton)

Fig 83   95 *Strathcarron* as LMS 14274 in 1928 black livery and now fitted with pop valves, assisting a Standard LMS Mogul north from Aviemore on a train of empty stock.   *(Photo: J.L. Stevenson Collection)*

Fig 84   96A *Glentilt* heading a line of engines awaiting scrapping, at Culloden Moor in August 1923. Drummond flare on chimney, wider dome and pop valves. Those behind are 72A, 77A, 70A and 97A.
(Photo: LCGB Ken Nunn Collection)

94 and 100. About 1914 89 was on the Thurso branch and Blair Atholl was another shed which had the class, mainly for local work to Perth, although they seem to have moved by 1922. The Straths' allocation in the summer of 1919 was:

Blair Atholl: 96-100
Forres: 90, 92, 93, 94
Helmsdale: 95
Wick: 89, 91

In the early 1920s 98 and 99 were on the Inverness-Tain locals, while 95 was at Thurso in 1923. But the last survivors were then generally to be found around Forres, which depot could always be relied upon to produce a few light turns for engines in their old age. 14272 (92), 14275 (98) and 14276 (100) were here at the end while 14274 (95) was on the Fochabers Town branch in May 1930. The last-named however made a surprising appearance at Aviemore piloting a Mogul northbound on a heavy train of what appeared to be empty stock, probably in the summer of 1929 (Fig 83). 14271 (89) was a familiar sight shunting in the Civil Engineer's sidings at Inverness for the last three years or so of its life.

The Straths had their share of mishaps and adventures. There is a photograph of 97 with a broken axle at Struan, probably prior to 1914, while in *The Skye Railway* John Thomas relates an incident which befell 94. In the winter of 1917-18 the engine failed on the 1 in 50 climb from Garve to Raven's Rock while working a train of American naval stores from Kyle to Invergordon. Help was provided by Caledonian 5 ft 0 in 4-6-0 53, then on loan to the Highland, an unusual if not unprecedented use of a six-coupled engine on the Skye line. It was sent from Dingwall

with a fitter on board and was duly joined at Achterneed by the failed engine's fireman who had walked through the section with the tablet. When 94 was reached the fitter removed some broken piston rings so allowing it and its train to be hauled forward to Dingwall.

Withdrawals

The six Straths which were not allocated LMS numbers did little if any work after 1st January 1923 and indeed most, if not all of these were out of use before that date. (Reference is made under the Clyde Bogies to the matter of the Highland engines in existence in 1923 but not taken into LMS stock.) Four were stored at Aviemore where 90A and 91A were in the carriage shed in company with Duke 84A in August 1923 while 93A and 99A were in a siding beside the locomotive shed. The other two unwanted, 96A and 97A, had joined the array of old iron at Culloden Moor (Fig 84). Five of these were sold later in the year to Arrol, Jackson & Co for scrap, 97A in November and 90A, 93A, 96A and 99A in December while 91A was taken to Kilmarnock in 1924 for breaking up. 94 had similar treatment in St Rollox Stores yard in 1925. But the rest lasted until 1930. 14271/2/6 were lying in Kilmarnock Works yard in September 1930 awaiting breaking up.

So ended a strong, well-built class, very much in the Highland tradition, put rather in the shade from early days by the Lochs and Castles but still doing valuable work. They were well liked by their crews, steamed freely and with their 6 ft 3½ in driving wheels could show a good turn of speed.

Summary of Class

H R No. 1892	1922	LMS No	Name	Maker	Works No	Built	Withdrawn
89	89	14271	*Sir George*	Neilson & Co	4428	5/1892	9/1930
90	90A	—	*Tweeddale /Grandtully* (1897)	,,	4429	,,	8/1923
91	91A	—	*Strathspey*	,,	4430	,,	8/1923
92	92A	14272	*Strathdearn*	,,	4431	6/1892	2/1930
93	93A	—	*Strathnairn*	,,	4432	,,	8/1923
94	94A	(14273)	*Strathtay*	,,	4433	,,	3/1925
95	95	14274	*Strathcarron*	,,	4434	,,	1/1931
96	96A	—	*Glentilt*	,,	4435	,,	8/1923
97	97A	—	*Glenmore*	,,	4436	,,	8/1923
98	98	14275	*Glentruim*	,,	4437	,,	1/1931
99	99A	—	*Glentromie*	,,	4438	,,	8/1923
100	100	14276	*Glenbruar*	,,	4439	,,	2/1930

2.18 Yankee Tank Class 4-4-0T
Dübs 5 ft 3 in Engines

In 1892 the Highland, possessing only nine tank engines two of which, 12 and *Needlefield*, were barely serviceable, found itself short of power for the various branches then being opened or planned. Word got around of five small tanks which had been ordered from Dübs by the Uruguay Eastern Railway in 1891. However the Uruguayans had apparently been unable to pay for the engines and the position had been complicated by a change of government. Dübs therefore wrote to all railways likely to be interested indicating that two of the tanks were on their hands completed with a further three under construction. This led to an offer to the Highland of a trial with a view to purchase, which was readily accepted. On 7th September 1892 the Board considered a letter from Jones stating that he had examined the two tank engines which Dübs had for sale and he recommended their purchase at a price of £1,500 each. The Board, recognising that this was a bargain, assented and the two completed engines arrived later that month for a year's trial in the first place, purchase

being confirmed the following year. They were allocated numbers 101 and 102. The other three also were purchased in 1893 and took the numbers 11, 14 and 15. As they were in a less forward state of construction, one or two modifications (see below) were incorporated to meet the requirements of the new owners before delivery towards the end of 1893. The designer is unknown but was probably the makers.

The engines' neat and tidy design made them look perfectly at home on the Highland and in no way suggested that they had been intended to spend their lives some 7,000 miles distant. The 3 ft 11¾ in diameter boiler, pitched at 6 ft 8 in carried Ramsbottom safety valves, a shapely dome and, in the case of 101 and 102, a tall elegant chimney with a copper flare which would not have looked out of place on the Isle of Man. The appearance of the other three however was altered by their having a Jones chimney without louvres and tank capacity increased from 700 to 900 gallons, this being effected by making the tanks 3 inches wider on the boiler side. The cylinders were

Fig 85   Works photograph of the first of the 4-4-0 tanks built by Dübs for the Uruguay Eastern Railway, and purchased by the Highland.   *(Photo: J.F. McEwan Collection)*

outside, inclined at 1 in 25, with slide valves above actuated by Stephenson link motion and rocking levers. There were compensating levers between the laminated springs of the coupled wheels (Fig 85). The engines differed in one respect from all Highland classes in being arranged for right hand drive and in consequence the vacuum ejector exhaust pipe, which was carried outside the boiler above the handrail, was on the right side. When reboilered in 1906 102 was altered to left hand drive.

101 and 102 were built with a cowcatcher and an American style of headlamp in front of the chimney but these were removed before delivery to the Highland. However they did retain covers over the piston rods and crossheads which had been meant for South American conditions but which Jones thought might be valuable on the Burghead branch. This was for a long time troubled with sand driven by high winds, a problem eventually solved by planting strong growing grass. The covers however made access to the motion difficult and were soon removed. These two engines are said to have had the letters 'F.C.U.del E.' on parts of their motion. The later three, which were completed for the Highland, never received the foreign fittings nor initials (Fig 86).

The class was nicknamed 'The American Tanks' but this was soon altered to 'The Yankee Tanks', which was something of a misnomer. It is doubtful if South America would have been amused!

Dimensions

Cylinders (2 outside)	16″ × 22″
Boiler	
Maximum outside diameter	3′ 11¾″
Length of barrel	10′ 6″
Pitch	6′ 8″
Length of firebox casing	4′ 10″
Heating surface	
Tubes (150 of 1⅞″)	795 sq ft
Firebox	88 sq ft
Total	883 sq ft
Grate area	14 sq ft
Boiler pressure	(101 & 102) 140 lbs; (11, 14 & 15) 160 lbs
Diameter of wheels	
Bogie	3′ 0″
Coupled	5′ 3″
Tractive effort (85%)	(101 & 102) 10,638 lbs (11, 14 & 15) 12,158 lbs
Length over buffers	31′ 1″
Wheelbase	5′ 9″ + 7′ 4″ + 7′ 2″
Weights (full)	
Adhesion	(101 & 102) 29 tons (11, 14 & 15) 30 tons 5 cwts
Total	(101 & 102) 41 tons 12 cwts; (11, 14 & 15) 42 tons 10 cwts
Water capacity	(101 & 102) 700 gallons; (11, 14 & 15) 900 gallons
Coal capacity	1½ tons

Fig 86   101 on the branch train at Hopeman soon after the opening of the extension from Burghead in 1892. Apple green livery with triple lining. Number plate on tank.   *(Photo: B.D. Matthews Collection)*

Fig 87   101 as LMS 15013 in red livery at Wick. Fitted with new boiler in 1919 but virtually unchanged from its original appearance when stripped of foreign fittings.   *(Photo: W.H. Whitworth)*

HR Renumbering

All were renumbered by the Highland as follows:

101	101A (7/1919)	101 (8/1922)
102	102A (7/1919)	102 (8/1922)
11	51 (1899) 51A (12/1916)	51B (8/1922)
14	54 (10/1900) 54A (4/1918)	54B (1921)
15	52 (12/1900) 52A (3/1917)	52B (8/1922)

LMS Renumbering

The LMS allocated to the class numbers 15013 to 15017. The last two engines however were now placed in the opposite order, 52B (15) becoming 15016 and 54B (14) becoming 15017. 51B was withdrawn before receiving its new number 15015.

Livery

The first two engines were originally painted in the livery of the railway for which they were intended. A works photograph shows the first engine attractively finished in what is believed to be bright blue which perhaps covered also the smokebox and chimney. The tank and bunker sides were lined in black, which was double edged with white and had double corners. The cab side also was edged in black and white. The number '1', in white was fixed on the sides of the chimney, and the name *OLMOS* was on a panel on the tank side. On the bunker side was a round plate or panel, having the works number in the centre surrounded by the maker's name and 'F.C.U.del E. 1891' in larger print further encircling the panel, all the wording being light against a dark background. The second engine, as numbered 2, was painted likewise. However when these two came to the Highland for trial the foreign names and number plates were removed, although it seems likely that the original livery was retained.

When taken into Highland stock the whole class was in apple green, lined in white, black and red, and with an olive green border, also a red-brown running board. The Jones number plate was placed not on the bunker but in the centre of the tank side, while the diamond-shaped maker's plate was generally on the upper cab side, although 101 had it on the bunker.

11 and 15, at least, received the Drummond olive green with black and double white lining, the usual border, claret running board etc. 51 (11) had 'THE HIGHLAND RAILWAY' on the tank, whereas 52 (15) and 54 (14) showed their names there. In these cases the number plates were removed from the tank to the bunker.

In due course the class were all in unlined olive green with number plate on the bunker and, if not named, with 'H . R' on the tank, the only exception being 52 (15) which after losing its name in 1903 was unlined with 'THE HIGHLAND RAILWAY' on the tank for a few years some of which were spent on the Invergarry & Fort Augustus Railway. No doubt the Highland would wish to proclaim its presence there! By 1920 101 had the letters 'H . R' painted more closely together and also showed a Cumming number plate high on the cab side. This was a particularly clean and well kept engine, especially when the copper cap to the chimney was polished.

All except 51B were repainted in LMS lined red after 1923, the number being in 14 in numerals on the tank side and the LMS emblem in front of the cab doorway (Fig 87). Smokebox number plates were fitted. 15014 was given lined black livery by 1930, the number in 10 in numerals taking the place of the crest in front of the cab door. The smokebox number plate was retained on 15014 but was missing from 15013 in its last year.

Names

As we have seen, the first engine carried the name *Olmos* after a town in Uruguay. The name of the second is unknown. All were nameless on delivery to the Highland but subsequently three were named after places on the branches which they worked. 54 (14) became *Portessie* and 52 (15) *Fortrose* both in 1901, and 102 was named *Munlochy* in 1910. However all names were removed during Highland ownership, *Fortrose* and *Portessie* as early as 1903 and *Munlochy* by 1919.

Detail Alterations

Reference has already been made to the early removal of the covers over the piston rods on 101 and 102. The former ran for a time with a painted and lined screen over the cab cut-out shortly after its arrival.

The only substantial change occurred in 1906 when 102 was reboilered at Lochgorm and a brass plate fixed to the frame recorded this. The new boiler was slightly larger and higher pitched but no dimensions have survived. The large dome was surmounted by lock-up safety valves and a Drummond chimney was fitted (Fig 88). Working pressure remained at 140 lbs. The engine was altered to left hand drive and the vacuum ejector exhaust pipe moved to the left hand side of the boiler, remaining outside (Fig 89). The tank capacity was increased to 900 gallons and later, probably in 1910 and certainly by 1913, the frames were slightly extended at the rear to allow a larger bunker to be fitted. Steam heating was provided. These changes raised the engine weight to about 44 tons. Apart from the provision of a new firebox in 1922 no further alterations were made.

Little change overtook the others. 52 appears to have received the old boiler off 102 in 1906 while 101 was given a new boiler more or less identical to the original in 1919. All Highland 4-4-0T boilers were classified N.13 by the LMS. 54 (15) had a tool box fitted over the tank on the left hand side against the cab by the time it was on the Fort Augustus line. All received coal rails round the bunker and 52 (15) had an extra handrail on the left hand side of the bunker where the number plate was missing from 1924 while the engine was still in Highland livery.

Allocation and Work

Their work lay on branch lines and at different times the class must have worked on every branch, except Dornoch where they were never recorded

and for which they were probably too heavy.

101 and 102 were sent to the Burghead branch just in time for its extension to Hopeman in October 1892. The branch was then very busy timber landed from Norway, fertilisers and building stone being the principal traffics. Indeed about this time there was a proposal to provide double track. Two engines were rostered to work it, and in 1897 the passenger engine was booked to run some 100 miles daily, these trips including a couple of goods trains, while the shunting engine also made trips to Hopeman and to Alves on goods and mixed trains. Thereafter services were gradually reduced until in the latter part of the 1914-18 war only three trains each way were shown to run (all mixed) and in fact the Burghead to Hopeman section was temporarily closed from January 1917 to June 1919. Nevertheless two engines seem to have remained at Burghead shed, 101 being there for some 25 years in all. By 1919 51A and 54A were at Burghead and 101 had moved to the Black Isle branch (Fortrose). In the 1920s it was to be found at Lybster, still in HR livery, and was there again in 1928 as LMS 15013. In its last year it was on the Strathpeffer branch where it took over from 15014 (102).

102 was reallocated more often and to places further afield. Starting its life by sharing the work on the Burghead branch with 101, in 1906 it was moved south to Aberfeldy, its re-equipment with larger tanks having been done with this branch specially in view. In 1910 it was transferred to the Black Isle branch, being named *Munlochy* accordingly, but by 1919, minus the name, it was back at Aberfeldy for a short time. In the 1920s it was shunter or spare engine at Inverness but in the early 1930s was on the Strathpeffer branch.

51 (11) was on the Strathpeffer branch about 1903-4 and at Burghead in 1919 but not much is known about its work otherwise. Indeed it almost succeeded in eluding photography.

14 was in its early days on the Burghead branch, and about 1901, in which year it became 54, it was on the short-lived Keith-Portessie line. At that time the branch engine was out-stationed in the two-road shed at Portessie but this was closed in November 1907 and services were thereafter operated from the Keith end. It was a line which presented a stiff haulage task as it climbed nearly 700 feet in some nine miles from sea level at Portessie. However 54 moved away in July 1903 when, in company with sister engine 52 (ex-15), it went far afield to work the Invergarry and Fort Augustus Railway which the Highland, after two years of legal wrangling, had won the right to work in preference to the North British. The Bill confirming this had been passed on 30th June 1903 and the Highland Board was immediately requested to send round an engine and coach for Board of Trade

re-inspection of the line which had been completed two years before but had since lain idle. Probably 52 and 54 were sent together, travelling via Dunblane and Crianlarich hauling three or four coaches to start public services which they managed to achieve as early as 27th July. Early photographs show 52 as the working engine but it was soon relieved by Skye Bogie 48, as mentioned under that class. The tender engine was no doubt more suitable but before its arrival the Highland had to instal a turntable at Spean Bridge. 54

Fig 88   102 *Munlochy* at Fortrose in 1913 with its 1906 Lochgorm boiler, Drummond chimney and lock-up valves on dome.   *(Photo: L.G.R. Photographs)*

Fig 89   102 as LMS 15014 in black at Inverness, showing the vacuum ejector pipe moved to the left side at the 1906 reboilering.   *(Photo: F. Moore (L.P.C.))*

appears to have remained at Fort Augustus until the Highland withdrew from the line in April 1907 (Fig 90). In 1912 it was to be seen at Georgemas Junction working the Thurso branch, then in 1919 it was at Burghead and in 1923 at Dingwall for the Strathpeffer branch. Afterwards, as LMS 15017, it was at Inverness as spare engine with perhaps a spell or two on the Fort George branch.

15 started at Fortrose on the Black Isle branch which was opened in February 1894 before going for its short spell of duty as 52 at Fort Augustus. In 1919 it was at Forres and in 1923-24 station shunter at Dingwall. As LMS 15016 it was later on the Lybster branch.

Withdrawal

51B was the first to go, in May 1924 without carrying its LMS number and by the end of 1927 only 15013 and 15014 remained in use, no doubt by virtue of having newer boilers. Both were withdrawn as late as 1934 and were still lying at Kilmarnock Works in mid-1935.

It is strange that the Highland acquired quite fortuitously its most numerous and arguably most successful branch engines which thus ended their days on the London Midland and Scottish Railway instead of on the Ferrocarriles Uruguayenses del Este.

The only mileage figures available are those worked by 15013 and 15014 after receiving their new boilers, namely:

| 15013 | 198,982 | (1919-1934) |
| 15014 | 754,221 | (1906-1934) |

The achievement by 15014 of running an average of over 25,000 miles per annum is an excellent testimonial both to its high availability and to the good service offered on the Aberfeldy and Black Isle branches where most of its work was performed.

Fig 90   54 (ex-14) at Fort Augustus in August 1906. Jones chimney as fitted to the last three of the class. Unlined livery with number plate on bunker.   *(Photo: A.G. Ellis Collection)*

Summary of Class

HR No. 1893	12/1922	LMS No	Name	Maker	Works No	Built	Withdrawn
101	101	15013	—	Dübs & Co	2778	1891★	7/1934
102	102	15014	*Munlochy* (1910)	”	2779	1891★	11/1934
11	51B	(15015) not carried)	—	”	3077	10/1893	5/1924
14	54B	15017	*Portessie* (1901)	”	3078	”	1/1928
15	52B	15016	*Fortrose* (1901)	”	3079	”	5/1927

★ 101 and 102 were not taken into HR stock until 10/1893
The names were removed later. See above.

2.19 Big Goods Class 4-6-0
Jones 5 ft 3½ in Engines

This celebrated class signified the start of a new era for the Highland. The first 4-6-0s to be built for service in Britain, the Big Goods were much larger than anything seen on the line and for a time they were the most powerful engines in the country. The need for them was beyond question. The 2-4-0 goods engines had struggled gallantly over the Perth road but with increasing traffic they were becoming ever more outclassed, while their condition was fast deteriorating. Double-heading was commonplace and there was an urgent call for an engine which could take a substantially greater unassisted load.

In meeting the problem Jones displayed a confidence in himself by proposing to build fifteen straight off which was equalled only by the immense faith which the Board had in him. The Highland had gone through precarious times in the 1880s and, while matters were certainly improving at the start of the following decade, the Company was in no position to make a major investment on this scale without obtaining an ample return. In the event the confidence of all in the Big Goods was totally justified. They did everything that was expected of them and no modification of any consequence over their life span of some 45 years was ever considered necessary.

Jones was fortunate in having as his Chief Draughtsman David Anderson Hendrie whose father had been the contractor for the running shed and workshops in 1863. The young man was in the drawing office at Inverness until 1889 when he went south to work first for Sharp, Stewart and then for Dübs, but he then returned to Inverness in 1893, having seen 4-6-0 engines being designed and built in good numbers for railways abroad, and there can be no doubt that he did much to influence Jones to adopt something similar for the Highland. It is to Jones's credit that he accepted that this was the right step to take and that, after twenty years of building his main line engines with the massive double framing and the Crewe fore-end, he gave these up, although there was still a suggestion of the latter in the wing plates leading down in a short sweep from the smokebox front to the cylinders. The purpose of the wing-plates was to keep the boiler from expanding forward, so directing all expansion to the rear end along the expansion brackets on the outer firebox side. The abandonment of double frames, with a saving of both weight and cost, was probably prompted by improve-ments not only in the quality of steel but also in the Highland permanent way, the latter factor also favouring the big engine decision. At the same time he retained some of his best known features, the shape of the cab, the louvred chimney and the tall brass lock-up safety valves set transversely.

The boiler barrel was 13 ft 9 in long with an outside diameter of 4 ft 9 in, being constructed in three telescopic rings and carrying 211 tubes of 2 in diameter. These were originally of brass but were replaced by steel tubes at or before the provision of new fireboxes in 1901-5. Pressure was at first 170 lbs but was later raised to 175 lbs. The cylinders, inclined at 1 in 24, were 20 in by 26 in. It has been stated that a number of the class had them lined up to 19 in but no confirmation of this can be found. Steam distri-bution was as usual by Allan's straight link motion. The centre pair of driving wheels were flangeless but in some cases thin flanges were fitted much later, perhaps when a number of the engines came to be used regularly on the Skye line. The tender was of increased capacity compared with earlier classes (Fig 91).

A feature of the design was the ease with which even major components could be removed for repair or replacement. For example bolts were used wherever possible instead of rivets, room was provided for fitters to work on normally inaccessible parts and there was a thoughtful and logical sequence of dismantling such components as brake gear, motion and axle boxes. To Jones and his draughtsmen ease of repair had become of paramount importance, and as with all the Jones classes, the Big Goods were designed with an eye to the shops as well as to the road.

The speed with which they were built deserves comment. The Board authorised their construction on 3rd January 1894 and at their next meeting accepted the tender of Sharp, Stewart & Co. (Limited) of the Atlas Locomotive Works, to give them their full title, the firm now being in Glasgow. According to the firm's books the first five were completed in July but the Highland, as we shall see later, did not accept them until September because of difficulty with steaming which was eventually traced to the type of blast pipe. However all fifteen were in service before the end of 1894 and took numbers 103 to 117. Being goods engines they carried no names. They cost

Fig 91   106 at Perth almost new in livery similar to Stroudley yellow. The snow plough brackets and
Westinghouse pump have not yet been fitted.   (Photo: J.F. McEwan Collection)

£2,795 each, a reasonable price which suggests, as does the quick delivery, that Sharp, Stewart were short of orders following their move from Manchester and were anxious to create a good impression.

Dimensions

Cylinders (2 outside)	20″ × 26″
Boiler	
Maximum outside diameter	4′ 9″
Length of barrel	13′ 9″
Pitch	7′ 4″
Length of firebox casing	7′ 9″
Heating surface	
Tubes	1,559 sq ft
Firebox	113.5 sq ft
Total	1,672.5 sq ft
Grate area	22.6 sq ft
Boiler pressure	175 lbs
Diameter of wheels	
Bogie	3′ 2½″
Coupled	5′ 3½″
Tender	3′ 9½″
Tractive effort (85%)	24,362 lbs
Length over buffers	58′ 4½″
Wheelbase	
Engine	6′ 6″ + 5′ 3″ + 5′ 6″ + 7′ 9″
Tender	6′ 6″ + 6′ 6″
Total	48′ 5½″

Weights	
Adhesion	42 tons
Engine	56 tons
Tender	38 tons 7 cwts
Total	94 tons 7 cwts
Water capacity	3,000 gallons
Coal capacity	5 tons

LMS Renumbering

The whole class passed into the ownership of the LMS in 1923 and were renumbered 17916 to 17930.

Tenders

Originally each tender had a tool box at the back but all were removed in Highland days. The platform thus left was used for an extension of the tank to the back of the frames in the case of 105, 110, 113 and 116. Water capacity was increased from 3,000 to 3,100 gallons and the weight increased by a ton or so.

The LMS assigned tender numbers 1823 to 1837 in the same order as the engines.

Livery

There is little doubt that the first few of the class, at least up to 108 were painted yellow of a shade similar to that used by Stroudley. The others were in Jones light green livery with the white, black and red lining and a darker green border. Running board edges and footsteps would be in red brown and cylinder covers in lined green. In due course all received Drummond's olive green with 'H . R' on the tender. With this style the running board edges, cab steps and cylinder covers were usually claret at first but this soon gave way to olive green. 104, 107, 109, 112, 113 and 117 had Drummond's double white and black lining for a time but all were unlined for most of their days. 103, 104, 109 and 111 later (c1921) received the Cumming number plate, replacing the Jones pattern. 110 and 113 were still green as late as 1928.

Shortly after grouping all except 110 (17923) and 113 (17926) were repainted in the LMS first goods style with number in 18 in gold numerals on the tender, 'L M S' in gold in a red panel on the cab side and smokebox number plates. The two exceptions, 110 and 113, retained the Highland livery until they received the second LMS style in 1928/29 and thus were never given smokebox number plates. Nos 17920/1/2 remained in the LMS first style until they were withdrawn, 17920 being in service thus until as late as October 1937 and so retaining its smokebox number plate until the end (Fig 97). The runner-up was 17929 which was in the first style until the end of 1932.

The second style, with 'L M S' on the tender and the number on the cab side, was first applied, probably at Lochgorm, in 1928-29 to 17917/8/9/24/6 /8/30, all of which received red lining and 10 in numerals. The lining was now carried over the round cab corners in a manner which, in contrast to the other Jones classes, had not been used on the Big Goods in Highland days. Although the general policy was now to remove smokebox number plates, these seven retained them for some years. Three of them remained in this style until withdrawn, 17918, 17919 (minus number plate for only its last year 1934) and 17928. In 6/1934 17926 lost its number plate and received 12 in numerals but surprisingly kept the lining.

From mid-1929 (with the exception noted) the lining was omitted at repainting, numerals were in the large 14 in style and the remaining number plates taken off. Engines so repainted were 17916 (1929), 17917 (1934), 17923 (1929), 17924 (8/1931), 17925 (c.1930), 17927 (1929), 17929 (12/1932) and 17930 (3/1933). It seems probable that heavy maintenance of the class was transferred from Lochgorm to St Rollox about 1929.

Detail Alterations

The class never required any major alterations, a fact which testifies to the excellence of the design. Over the years boilers and fireboxes were of course renewed, as were the cylinders in most if not all of the class. Rather unfortunately the LMS, as we shall see, had different views on some of the boiler mountings.

Nevertheless the first two months were critical because when the first engines arrived in July 1894 great trouble was experienced in making them steam satisfactorily and the Highland wisely refused to accept them until the failing was rectified. Sharp, Stewart took up the matter immediately, tracing the problem to the blast pipe. Various patterns were tried until the right type was found and from then on no further difficulties of this nature were encountered.

During and soon after the First World War ten of the Big Goods were sent for repair to contractors and other railways' works, namely:

103	Robert Stephenson, Darlington	1916
	Hawthorn, Leslie	11/1921
106	Yorkshire Engine Co	1917
107	Hawthorn, Leslie	1916
	Yorkshire Engine Co	1920
108	Yorkshire Engine Co	1916/17
109	Yorkshire Engine Co	1916
112	Gateshead Works NER	1916
	Hawthorn, Leslie	1921
113	(?)Inverurie Works GNSR	1916/17
115	Yorkshire Engine Co	1916
116	Yorkshire Engine Co	1920
117	Yorkshire Engine Co	1919

Between 1910 and 1913 the whole class was reboilered and before and after these dates fireboxes were renewed. In these Drummond boilers, which were supplied by the North British Locomotive Co, the number of tubes was reduced from 211 to 203, and in consequence the tube heating surface was reduced from 1,559 sq ft to 1,500.

The Big Goods boiler was classified N73 by the LMS.

For some reason Drummond removed the smokebox wings from at least six of the class, 103, 107, 109, 112, 113 and 117 (Fig 92). These were later restored, generally at the time of reboilering. The Jones louvred chimney also underwent some changes. Following repair by Hawthorn, Leslie in 1921 103 had the chimney shortened — (Fig 93) — while 104 and 105 were given flared tops, the former possibly at reboilering and certainly by 1922, the latter by 1922 (Fig 94). 110 received a Drummond flared chimney in 1916, but the Jones louvred one had been refitted by 1921.

When practically new, 106 and 108 were given brackets mounted on the smokebox for attaching the large snow plough and they received also a lamp bracket on the chimney, as the plough would conceal a lamp on the smokebox. Both engines kept these fittings although 108 (17921) lost the bracket on the chimney shortly before it was withdrawn (Figs 95 and 96).

Below are dates of boiler and firebox renewals:

Engine No	New boiler and firebox	New fireboxes
103 (17916)	1/1913	1902, 1921, 1929
104 (17917)	3/1912	1901, 3/1927
105 (17918)	5/1912	1904, 1926
106 (17919)	4/1910	1905, 1919*, 1926
107 (17920)	10/1912*	1903, 1921, 1927
108 (17921)	6/1911	1902, 1925
109 (17922)	7/1911	1902, 1917*, 1922
110 (17923)	5/1910	1904, 1921, 1928
111 (17924)	4/1911	1904, 1927
112 (17925)	4/1913	1902, 1920, 8/1928
113 (17926)	6/1910	1903, 1920, 7/1928
114 (17927)	7/1911	1904, 1918*, 1928
115 (17928)	11/1912	1905, 1926
116 (17929)	7/1911	1903, 1917*, 1927
117 (17930)	6/1913	1902, 1926

* denotes a steel firebox. The rest were copper.

The whole class had vacuum brake from the start, and shortly after building 106 and 116 were fitted additionally with Westinghouse brake equipment using the small type of pump (Fig 95). 106 (17919) retained this to the end, but 116 (17929) lost it in 1932 when it acquired the frames of 17918. Latterly its pump had been disconnected and unusable.

17921 (108) had boiler repairs in 1928 which resulted in the provision of a rather flatter dome and extra wash-out plugs. Also about the same time it had the vacuum ejector exhaust pipe relocated to run externally along the left side of the boiler above the handrail (Fig 96). A further three had this pipe similarly resited about 1929, 17923/5/7, also rather earlier 115 (17928).

From 1929 the LMS fitted ten of the class with new Caledonian type flared chimneys of Dugald Drummond design, and at the same time removed the smokebox wings. Those concerned were 17916 (1929), 17917 (1/1934), 17920 (3/1932), 17923 (1929), 17924 (8/1931), 17925 (c.1930), 17926 (6/1934), 17927 (1929), 17929 (12/1932) and 17930 (3/1933). This coincided in most cases with certain of the livery changes already mentioned. At the same time Caledonian type smokebox doors were fitted to these engines except 17925 which however was fitted later (c1935), and 17920 which had its Highland door, complete with number plate, to the end. The Caledonian chimneys and the removal of the wings did not suit the Big Goods and seemed to dissipate their solid lines, creating at first sight the impression that they were Drummond engines. Those so fitted had a sharper exhaust (Figs 97 and 98).

The whole class received Ross pop safety valves placed transversely, nearly all about 1928-29 but the lock-ups were retained by 17927 until 1932 and by 17923 until late 1934 or early 1935, the year of its withdrawal.

New cylinders appear to have been fitted to several of the engines during and after the period of reboilering, and it is understood that an order was

Fig 92   112 as running with smokebox wings removed. Drummond lined livery. Inverness c1900.

(Photo: Real Photographs)

Fig 93   103 at Perth c1924 with chimney shortened during repair by Hawthorn, Leslie in 1921.

(Photo: W.H. Whitworth)

Fig 94   104 on an Up goods near Luncarty. Drummond flare on louvred chimney. *(Photo: H.L. Salmon)*

Fig 95   106 as LMS 17919 with Westinghouse pump, snow plough fittings and pop valves. 1928 livery with red
              lining. Smokebox number plate retained. Inverness 1930.   *(Photo: W.H. Whitworth)*

Fig 96   108 as LMS 17921 at Forres in the late 1920s. Transverse pop valves, external vacuum ejector pipe,
              flattened dome and fittings for large plough (including extra lamp bracket on chimney).
                                                                                         (Photo: W.H. Whitworth)

Fig 97   107 as LMS 17920 at Dingwall in September 1937, still in 1924 livery with number on tender. Drummond pattern chimney and pop valves. Smokebox wings removed. *(Photo: A.G. Ellis Collection)*

Fig 98   117 as LMS 17930 in its final years with 14in numerals. Inverness June 1936. *(Photo: W.A. Camwell)*

placed with the North British Locomotive Co for four pairs of cylinder castings as late in the day as 1929.

Some interchange of parts and indeed cannibalisation seems to have taken place between individual engines. 17929 came out of the works in December 1932 newly painted, but several features, including the works plate (4024), indicated that the frames were those of 17918 which earlier that year had been noted as carrying that plate. Moreover what were clearly the frames of 17929, complete with Westinghouse pump, were on the dump at St Rollox Works in mid-1933. However records show that boiler 1247 was put on engine 116 (17929) in 1911 and was scrapped with an engine bearing the same number in July 1936. One must conclude that the boiler of 17929 was amalgamated with the frames, wheels etc of 17918 and that the reconstituted engine was given the number 17929. A somewhat similar case may have occurred with 17930 which is believed to have been considered for withdrawal in November 1929 but was reprieved in February 1930. It seems that parts of 17922 were used to repair 17930 but certainly the emerging engine retained its 1913 boiler, 1343.

It has been recorded that 17926 was given green driving wheels in the course of overhaul in 1938, suggesting that it exchanged wheels with the preserved 103. If such an exchange did in fact take place the purpose may have been to provide 17926 with flanged centre driving wheels for the Kyle line. Those of 103 now are certainly flangeless.

It is interesting to note that the original boiler of 110 became in 1910 the tar tank at Lochgorm Works.

There is no record of a frame failure or of a frame replacement throughout the life of the class.

Allocation and Work

When new the engines were allocated between Perth and Inverness sheds, the distribution in 1901 being:

Inverness: 108-112, 114, 115
Perth: 103-107, 113, 116, 117

They were set to work on the principal goods trains on the main south line and were to be the mainstay of this traffic for the next thirty years. Frequently they were on passenger trains also, especially in the tourist season but they were never provided with steam heating equipment which would presumably curtail their activities in this direction, in winter anyway, when this form of heating became generally adopted.

Soon after the class had started work Jones travelled on the footplate of 105 to check performance. Stopping at Forres on a northbound goods he requested that the load be increased to 60 wagons (including brake van) for the rest of the journey to Inverness. On being told that there were also nine wagons for Nairn he asked that these be included as well. No 105

started this load without slipping. Sadly on another occasion Jones suffered an injury when getting down from one of the class, said to be 103. He was badly scalded and seems to have been increasingly disabled, resulting in his seeking periods of leave of absence from the Directors, who were not particularly helpful. Eventually he tendered his resignation to them on 2nd September 1896 while the Lochs were being delivered.

The opening of the Aviemore Direct line in 1898 presented a considerably tougher haulage proposition than the old route via Forres and the Big Goods had further opportunities to prove their worth not only on hill climbing but also on hard braking on the long descents. The 1914-18 war probably saw them worked at their hardest notably with supplies for the fleet and personnel movements.

Although they were initially excluded from the North line pending strengthening of the canal swing bridge at Clachnaharry, they were to be seen there from about 1904 until 1914 on the fish trains from Wick to Inverness during the fishing season. It was not until the mid-1920s that they began to appear regularly north of Inverness, a change of scene hastened by the arrival on the Perth line of standard LMS 0-6-0s from 1927, the Rivers in 1928 and ten Moguls in 1929. In the early 1930s the Big Goods were sharing with the Barneys the Inverness-Helmsdale through goods trains and the Inverness-Tain local goods workings, as well as numerous livestock specials which were such a feature of those days. But at the same time they were frequently and very effectively used to assist heavy trains from Inverness to the Slochd. Then in 1934 they found a new sphere of activity when they were put to work on the Skye line alongside the Superheated Goods, some 25 years their juniors, and proved themselves well suited to this line also, the principal performers being 17917, 17925, 17927 and 17930. One or two had been to Kyle as early as 1928, presumably on trial, but at that time the use of the Superheated Goods only was preferred.

The Big Goods were however still seen on the Perth road in the 1930s, for example on the forenoon stopping goods from Aviemore to Perth and the corresponding Down goods, as well as on a late evening Up goods from Aviemore. On 28th September 1933 17916 worked a passenger train south from Inverness, albeit only the 5.20 pm local to Newtonmore, and this was preceded by the splendid spectacle of 14766 *Clan Chattan* piloting 17929 on a heavy livestock special to Perth. In the following summer, when the motive power situation on the Highland was extremely critical, 17920 still in its 1924 livery, was transferred to Aviemore for a goods working to Forres and back and also for assisting on the main line. It was a fascinating sight to see the 1894 4-6-0 double-heading an LMS Class 5 built 40 years later. For example, on 28th September 1934 17920 piloted Class 5 5028, then almost brand-new, on the 11.00 am Inverness to Glasgow between Aviemore and Dalnaspidal and the running was very sprightly on the level stretches as far as Kingussie. 17920 was still at Aviemore in 1936 but later moved back to Inverness and was on goods work on the East line in August 1937 and then later in the month was heading south again, assisting Class 5 5169 on a livestock train to Perth. Early in September it was at Dingwall but that must have been just about its swan-song for it was withdrawn a month or two later.

However as late as the summer of 1939 one could still travel on a passenger train behind a Big Goods. On 15th August 17926 was turned out to assist Class 5 5461 on the 3.45 pm from Inverness to Glasgow, the veteran being detached at the Slochd, having combined hard slogging on the climbs with some swift bursts on the easy sections. Six months later the last four survivors had been withdrawn from service.

Withdrawals

In 1929 a start was made in withdrawing the class but it was eleven years before the last one went. The first to go was 17922 in the autumn of 1929 but it was not cut up at the time as it was used as a source of spare parts, possibly for 17930 — see above — and also for 17916 which came to be scheduled for preservation.

Four were still active when the Second World War arrived but they did not last long, which was perhaps surprising as once again the Highland line was going to be desperate for power. The last survivor, 17925, slipped away in February 1940. So passed a class which left its mark on British locomotive development. Dependable, powerful and uncomplicated, the Big Goods were perhaps the enginemen's favourite class, although that distinction was also claimed for the Castles and the little Skye Bogies.

Mileage figures are available for some of the class but cover only the period of the new boilers, for example:

Engine No	Period covered	Mileage
17917	1912-1939	715,497
17919	1910-1930*	588,748
17920	1912-1937	711,883
17923	1910-1935	823,271
17924	1911-1934	709,766
17926	1910-1939	845,855
17928	1912-1933	606,369

* mileage for 1930-34 not stated

From the above it seems that each of the class must have run over one million miles. Indeed, extrapolating the figures for 17926 to cover its whole 45-year life, this engine would have covered some 1½ million miles, most of them involving hard pulling or heavy braking.

Preservation of 17916 as HR 103

Little effort was made to keep anything for posterity in the 1930s and it was therefore especially gratifying to learn that the LMS had decided to keep both a Big Goods and the Caledonian 4-2-2 14010 (CR 123), certainly two worthy candidates for preservation. The decision was all the more surprising because at the time most of the Big Goods were still in service.

Appropriately the first of the class, 17916, was selected and after withdrawal in 1934 it was again fitted with a Highland louvred chimney. This particular one had come from 17919 (106), one of the two snow plough engines, and thus had a lamp bracket which strictly was now incorrect. 17916 had the Highland livery restored and became 103 again, when it sported the Drummond olive green with double-white and black lining, the Cumming number plate and 'H . R' on the tender. It is doubtful whether the engine ever carried this livery in service but it was certainly a careful copy of how several of the class had once looked. After being repainted 103 was sent up to an exhibition at Inverness in 1935 but unfortunately both it and 123 were then tucked away at the back of the erecting shop in St Rollox Works and could be seen only by those who ventured into this hallowed spot, legally or otherwise. During the war they were moved out into the yard and began to deteriorate rapidly, indeed narrowly missing being cut up for scrap. However they were eventually taken inside about 1946 and repainted, 103 now appearing in a lighter green, still Drummond-lined but with several inaccuracies such as the lining of the front splasher which should have followed the arc of the wheel. The tender was still lettered 'H . R'.

In 1958 James Ness, the Regional General Manager, decided to have the two engines restored to running order together with the GNS *Gordon Highlander* and the NB *Glen Douglas*. In the course of the refurbishment the smokebox wings were restored and the Ross safety valves enclosed in tall brass columns resembling those of the lock-ups. It was again repainted, this time in olive yellow with the Jones lining and red-brown running board, edges etc, and with the same number plate. 'H.R' was obliterated from the tender. The appearance is certainly striking, if not perhaps to everybody's taste. In any event one must be thankful for the efforts made to restore this and the other engines which have given so much pleasure to so many people (Fig 99).

103 was first used to work on a number of special trains to Glasgow in connection with the Scottish

Fig 99   103, restored for preservation and after a period of main line service, being hoisted onto a low loader at Govan Goods Station in June 1966 en route to Glasgow Museum of Transport. *(Photo: J.L. Stevenson)*

Industries Exhibition in the Kelvin Hall, generally in company with one of the other engines. It was subsequently used on a number of Rail Tours covering much of Scotland. 103 performed well and one particularly remembers a return trip from Greenock Princes Pier when the veteran had no trouble in climbing the long 1 in 70 gradient. The engine was maintained for much of the time at Dawsholm shed but in October 1964 was transferred to Parkhead. Earlier in that year it was thinly disguised as a French engine for the filming in England of *Those Magnificent Men in their Flying Machines*. It carried the number '23' on the right hand cab side and 'NORD' on the tender. On the left hand side the Highland number plate remained.

The Highland line had several visits from 103 with Rail Tours, the last being in the summer of 1965 when it ran a number of excursions between Inverness and Forres to commemorate the formation of the Highland Railway on 29th June 1865. At the close of these the old warrior left Inverness (No 3 platform) for perhaps the last time on 30th August 1965 hauling the two ex-Caledonian coaches to Perth. On 6th July 1966 it was hauled to Govan Goods station and lifted — the engine to one low-loader and the tender to another — en route to the Glasgow Museum of Transport

situated in the former tramway works at Coplaw Hill (Fig 99). A move took place early in 1988 to the Kelvin Hall at Partick where 103 is again splendidly exhibited not only as Britain's first 4-6-0 but to show posterity what manner of locomotives used to run on the Highland Railway and in particular to perpetuate the genius of the designer, David Jones.

Postscript

To those of us lucky enough to have seen the Big Goods at work on the Highland they have a special place in our memories and affection, forming with the Lochs a bridge between the days of the redoubtable Jones right through to the 1939-45 war which was to change so much. They belonged to the Inverness-Perth road more than to the other lines to which they later gravitated and a memory will always remain of a fine day — not the commonest of things — at Druimuachdar in the summer of 1931. Crossing the line by a sleeper crossing just north of the summit one could hear the steady unhurried beat of a train approaching the summit from the south, having shed its banker at Dalnaspidal. Looking along the straight double line as it humped over the top, little could be seen of the engine exhaust but slowly the chimney of a Big Goods came into view followed by the smokebox

135

and buffer beam. 17917 was in no great hurry but breasting the summit on would go the blower, the regulator was closed and once more, perhaps for the 6,000th time, she had surmounted The Hill. Now sliding past quietly with a wave from the Perth crew, the train rattled by behind her, consisting mainly of coal from the Lothians in private owners' wagons followed by a Highland 6-wheel brake van starting to pitch on the short rail lengths, and all was soon lost among the hills of the pass. An everyday occurrence of course but one which memory will always treasure.

Summary of Class

HR No.	LMS No	Maker	Works No	Built	Withdrawn
103	17916	Sharp Stewart	4022	9/1894	10/1934
104	17917	,,	4023	,,	10/1939
105	17918	,,	4024	,,	5/1933
106	17919	,,	4025	,,	12/1934
107	17920	,,	4026	,,	10/1937
108	17921	,,	4027	10/1894	11/1930
109	17922	,,	4028	,,	9/1929
110	17923	,,	4029	,,	11/1935
111	17924	,,	4030	,,	9/1934
112	17925	,,	4031	,,	2/1940
113	17926	,,	4032	,,	10/1939
114	17927	,,	4033	,,	9/1936
115	17928	,,	4034	11/1894	5/1933
116	17929	,,	4035	,,	6/1936
117	17930	,,	4036	,,	11/1939

The LMS Power Classification was 4; but from 1928 4F.

2.20 Special Tank Class 2-4-0T
Kitson 4 ft 0 in Engine

The Duke of Sutherland's Railway, the section of the North line between Golspie and Helmsdale, was built on the initiative of, and entirely financed by the third Duke. This was completed in September 1870 with the exception of the link to Inverness as a gap of two miles existed between Golspie and Dunrobin, the Duke's seat, while at the north end the final ¾-mile still had to be built from West Helmsdale (Gartymore) to Helmsdale. The Duke had been eager to provide a service to the public as soon as practicable and had already taken steps to acquire a locomotive of his own. He also hired from the Highland a coach, brake van and four wagons which were taken by road from Golspie to Dunrobin, hauled by traction engines. The engine however seems to have been brought by sea to Helmsdale. The stage was then set for an impressive opening on 1st November 1870 of the isolated section of line. The Highland Working Timetable for May 1871 shows two trains operating in each direction daily, leaving Dunrobin at 8.15 am and 3.00 pm, returning from West Helmsdale at 10.00 am and 4.45 pm. All trains called at Brora and took

45 minutes for the journey of 15¼ miles. These fascinating operations continued until the link-up took place in June 1871 and through services commenced between Inverness and Helmsdale, worked by the Highland.

The Duke's engine was a 2-4-0 well tank, built and probably also designed by Kitson of Leeds, bearing the name *Dunrobin*. It had inside frames, horizontal outside cylinders, Stephenson valve gear, a dome in the middle of the boiler barrel and Naylor safety valves on the raised firebox. The boiler was in three parallel rings with an outside diameter of 2 ft 6¾ in. The stove-pipe chimney had an extension of about a foot added soon after delivery to throw smoke and steam clear of the cab. This certainly did not improve the engine's appearance. The cab had an arched roof and side windows but its rear face lacked side protection. While in the Duke's ownership it had only a hand brake with wooden blocks (Fig 100).

The third Duke died in October 1892 and his successor had a replacement engine built by Sharp, Stewart to Jones design in 1895, this being an 0-4-4T

Fig 100   *Dunrobin* built by Kitson & Co in 1870 for the third Duke of Sutherland, standing newly arrived in front of the statue at Dunrobin of the second Duke. Dark green livery. The unsightly chimney extension can be seen.   *(Photo: J.L. Stevenson Collection)*

which is described in Book 2. Thereupon in September of that year he sold the original *Dunrobin* to the Highland who rebuilt it extensively, this including fitting the vacuum brake. It received HR number 118 in November 1895.

Dimensions

Cylinders (2 outside)	$10'' \times 18''$
Boiler	
Outside diameter	$2' 6\frac{3}{4}''$
Length of barrel	$9' 8''$
Pitch	$5' 4''$
Length of firebox casing	$2' 10''$
Heating surface	
Tubes (brass 75 of $1\frac{3}{4}''$)	341 sq ft
Firebox	38 sq ft
Total	379 sq ft
Grate area	6.25 sq ft
Boiler pressure	140 lbs
Diameter of wheels	
Leading	$3' 0''$
Coupled	$4' 0''$
Tractive effort (85%)	4,463 lbs
Length over buffers	$25' 0''$
Wheelbase	$6' 0'' + 5' 9''$
Weights (full)	
Adhesion	16 tons
Total	21 tons
Water capacity	400 gallons
Coal capacity	½ ton

Renumbering

The engine was put on the duplicate list in 1913 as 118A. Although it survived until after the grouping, it was withdrawn in 1923 without being acquired by the LMS.

Livery

As new the engine was probably dark green with the lower cab panel, bunker etc lined with an outer green border, the lining being black with thin yellow edges and concave corners. The name *Dunrobin* was on a plate on the lower panel.

After rebuilding in May 1896, which was still a few months before Drummond's arrival, one might have expected a repainting in Jones livery. But there is no evidence of that and the earliest photographs of the engine on the Highland show Drummond's olive green with black and double white lining, the new name *Gordon Castle* painted on the tank, probably red-brown cylinder covers and steps and a Jones pattern number plate on the bunker. Later the unlined olive green was applied, with 'H . R' on the tank and towards the end the number plate was removed and the number was painted between the Company's initials on the tank in the manner

Fig 101   *Dunrobin* after sale to the Highland in 1895, as rebuilt in 1896 becoming HR 118 *Gordon Castle*. At Burghead c1900 fitted with wooden cab side sheets. Drummond lined olive green livery probably with red-brown cylinders and steps.
(*Photo: J.F. McEwan Collection*)

'H 118 R', probably because the side windows occupied most of the upper cab sides where the number might otherwise have been painted.

Name

In the Duke's ownership the engine, as we have seen, was appropriately named *Dunrobin* after his castle overlooking the sea between Golspie and Brora. The transfer of the nameplate to the Duke's new engine meant that the Highland had acquired a passenger engine without a name. However at rebuilding in 1896 it was given the name *Gordon Castle* to accord with its new surroundings, the Fochabers branch near the residence of the Duke of Richmond and Gordon. The name was however removed in 1900 as it was required for 143, one of the Castles built that year. It has been stated by H.A. Vallance that during its later working on the Invergordon harbour lines the name *Invergordon* was carried but this cannot be confirmed. It may just have been referred to as 'The Invergordon Engine'.

Rebuilding

The Board agreed to the purchase of the Duke's engine at their meeting on 4th September 1895 on Jones recommendation and on the face of it £300 seemed reasonable. In any event as His Grace was present as a director they might have found it embarrassing to turn the offer down! However, heavy repairs were found to be necessary and the engine was sent to Sharp, Stewart of Glasgow who carried them out at a cost of £1,364 so that overall the purchase was an expensive one and certainly a much worse bargain than the purchase a few years before of the brand new Yankee Tanks for £1,500 apiece. At the rebuilding a new and larger boiler was fitted having an outside diameter of 3 ft 3¼ in as against 2 ft 6¾ in of the original, and being pitched 4 in higher. There was a new chimney with a brass or copper flare and a pair of Ramsbottom safety valves over the firebox. New and larger cylinders, 12 in by 18 in, were also provided. The cab was slightly extended to the rear, side tanks replaced the well tanks and the vacuum brake was fitted together with cast iron brake blocks replacing the wooden ones. All in all the work done amounted to a reconstruction (Fig 101).

Most of the dimensions were altered as under:

Cylinders (2 outside)	12″ × 18″
Boiler	
Maximum outside diameter	3′ 3¼″
Length of barrel	9′ 5″
Pitch	5′ 8″
Length of firebox casing	3′ 1″
Heating surface	
Tubes (113 of 1¾″)	503 sq ft
Firebox	49.4 sq ft
Total	552.4 sq ft
Grate area	8.4 sq ft
Tractive effort (85%)	6,426 lbs
Weights (full)	
Adhesion	17 tons
Total	24 tons
Water capacity	560 gallons
Coal capacity	¾ ton

Allocation and Work

The engine first appears in a photograph of the inaugural train on the Duke's railway. It is lavishly decorated and has a crown on the dome. On the footplate is the Duke, while the Prince and Princess of Wales, later King Edward VII and Queen Alexandra, are in the company. Thereafter regular services were operated by the Duke until June 1871, as we have seen. The Duke retained the engine and provided himself with a coach for his own use, the Company allowing him, in recognition of his shareholding and benefactions, to run his private train when he wished on the main line to Inverness. The engine was shedded at Brora but later a shed was built for its successor at Golspie in 1896. When repairs were required which could not be handled by the Duke's staff a visit was paid to Helmsdale shed and at such times the engine usually piloted the regular trains.

Immediately after the completion of the line to the Far North the private train visited both Wick and Thurso. The Duke was the driver and an account of the trip reads like a ducal tour of inspection. In 1879 and doubtless on other occasions the train again visited both towns with a distinguished party from the castle. But most of the private train's journeys were made for the purpose of conveying the castle guests between Inverness and Dunrobin station. Some of them wrote their names on panels in the engine cab which were later tranferred to its successor, the new *Dunrobin* of 1895.

However, study of the Highland timetables reveals the interesting fact that between 1881 and 1885 from July to October the engine was used for the more humdrum task of working a public train once or twice weekly from Golspie to Wick and Thurso. According to the Working Book it carried first and parliamentary class passengers and is shown as to be worked by the 'Dunrobin Engine'. Between 1881 and 1883 the train ran on Saturdays to Wick, 77¼ miles, leaving Golspie at 8.00 am and ariving at 11.05 am, which with 4 ft driving wheels was not at all bad going especially as stops for water would have been necessary. It left Wick at 3.20 pm on the return and reached Golspie at 6.35 pm. In 1884 the train ran on Tuesdays as well as Saturdays, leaving Golspie at 9.30 am and running instead to Thurso where it arrived at 12.15 pm returning at 3.55 pm. In 1885 much the same timings

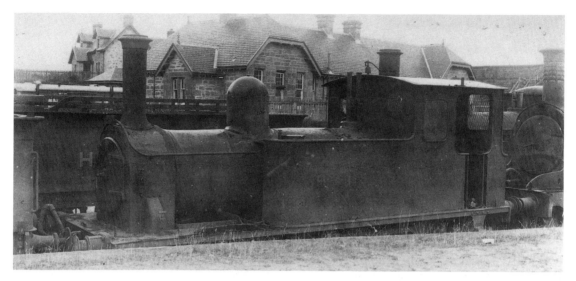

Fig 102　　As 118A nameless laid aside at Culloden Moor in August 1923. Number plate removed and number painted instead on tanks. Unlined olive green.　　　　　　　　　　*(Photo: A.W. Croughton)*

applied but this year the train was on Fridays only. In all cases there were 'Empty Engine' movements from and to Brora where *Dunrobin* was shedded. The train must have been a quaint sight as it made its way along the coast to Helmsdale and over the deserted moors of Sutherland and Caithness, surmounting on its way the 708 ft County March Summit north of Forsinard.

After acquisition by the Highland and assuming the number 118, the engine was sent to work the Fochabers branch but soon afterwards was transferred to Burghead. For the latter work side sheets were fitted across the cab doorway to give protection against storm or sand on the exposed sections. On neither of these lines was it as suitable as the Yankee Tanks or the Drummond 0-4-4Ts. Meantime a need for a small shunting engine had arisen at Invergordon Harbour, and Jones was given authority by the Board to seek tenders from several firms for a 4-wheeled tank engine. Nothing came of this, but in May 1905 the Way and Works Committee was told that a 'pug engine' had been sent to Invergordon, as earlier authorised. This must have been either 118 or a Lochgorm Tank, in this case probably the latter as 118 was recorded on 1st November of that year as being in store at Inverness. But it does seem to have worked at Invergordon, as well as shunting at Inverness between 1905 and 1914-15 when it went on

loan to the GN of S to assist in the handling of Admiralty traffic for which an engine with a light axle load was required to pass from Waterloo Goods to the Harbour at Aberdeen and the work was beyond the power of the 0-4-0 Well Tanks which were now in poor order. 118A, as it had become in 1913, returned to the Highland when the GN of S took delivery of their Manning Wardle 0-4-2Ts in 1915. The fact that the Highland had been able to dispense with 118A at a time of dire power shortage suggests that it was not greatly valued. Possibly it then did further service at Invergordon, but the only definite information on its later activities was that it was at Wick in 1919 for shunting and perhaps as a back-stop for the Lybster branch. Then in 1921 it could be found laid aside in Millburn Sidings at Inverness, prior to which it had done some work on the Harbour Branch.

Withdrawal

In the summer of 1923 the engine had reached journey's end with others in that most fascinating of graveyards, Culloden Moor yard (Fig 102). Soon afterwards it was sold for scrap. So ended a long and colourful career spanning over 50 years. But the Highland cannot be said to have got good value out of the £1,664 which they spent on buying and renovating the Duke's engine.

Summary of Class

No	Name	Maker	Works No	Built	Rebuilt	Withdrawn
118 (11/95) /118A (1913)	*Gordon Castle* (I) (1896) /- (1900)	Kitson, Leeds	1706	8/1870	5/1896	8/1923

2.21 Loch Class 4-4-0
Jones 6 ft 3½ in Engines

The Highland Board must have been greatly impressed by the transformation of goods train operation wrought by the fifteen Big Goods of 1894, and they were prepared to provide something of similar ability for passenger work. The twelve Straths of 1892 had supplemented the eight Clyde Bogies of 1886, while the seventeen Dukes built between 1874 and 1888 were still to the fore, but there was a clear need to provide a passenger engine of greater power than these for the Inverness-Perth line, especially as the opening was approaching of the Aviemore Direct line with its climb from sea level at Inverness to 1,315 ft at the Slochd which was to present new problems of haulage.

Jones therefore put before the directors the final form of his 4-4-0 design and sought authority once more to build fifteen engines of a new class. Dimensionally these differed from the Straths in having 19 in by 24 in cylinders, an increase of 1 in diameter, while the boiler barrel was longer, 10 ft 2 in as against 9 ft 9½ in, with the pressure raised from 160 to 175 lbs. Their tractive effort of 17,070 lbs so achieved was substantially greater than the 14,100 lbs of the Straths. The Board authorised the construction of the engines and at their meeting in February 1896 agreed to accept the offer of Dübs & Co under Order 3392E to deliver them at £2,940 each, including £55 for fitting Smith's piston valves. All had arrived for service by the end of the following September, were given Highland numbers 119 to 133 and were charged to capital. They received the names of inland lochs in the Company's territory.

In the Lochs the Crewe design of fore end was forsaken, as it had been with the Big Goods, and a more modern appearance was presented. Indeed they resembled the Big Goods in general design with the unmistakable Jones boiler mountings, the louvred chimney and tall transverse lock-up safety valves. The boiler itself had 244 tubes of 1¾ in diameter, probably of copper. The grate was slightly inclined, whereas those of Jones earlier 4-4-0s were horizontal. Steam distribution was by the usual Allan motion and 8 in diameter piston valves but the latter, as we shall see, were unsatisfactory and had to be replaced by slide valves. The cylinders were horizontal. There were still compensating levers between the laminated springs of the coupled wheels and another apparent link with the earlier 4-4-0s was

the provision of wing plates from the smokebox front as on the Big Goods which was a small reminder of the Crewe fore-end. The tender was identical with that of the Big Goods and for the first time on the Highland cab doors were fitted from the start. Many of the earlier engines had gradually acquired doors over the years, in most cases of wood, and they must have come to be recognised as highly desirable fitments (Fig 103).

Dimensions

Cylinders (2 outside)	19″ × 24″
Boiler	
Maximum outside diameter	4′ 7″
Length of barrel	10′ 2″
Pitch	7′ 5″
Length of firebox casing	6′ 8½″
Heating surface	
Tubes	1,176 sq ft
Firebox	119 sq ft
Total	1,295 sq ft
Grate area	20.5 sq ft
Boiler pressure	175 lbs★
Diameter of wheels	
Bogie	3′ 3″
Coupled	6′ 3½″
Tender	3′ 9½″
Tractive effort (85%)	17,070 lbs
Length over buffers	54′ 7½″
Wheelbase	
Engine	6′ 6″ + 7′ 0″ + 9′ 0″
Tender	6′ 6″ + 6′ 6″
Total	44′ 9″
Weights (full)	
Adhesion	31 tons 10 cwts
Engine	49 tons
Tender	38 tons 7 cwts
Total	87 tons 7 cwts
Water capacity	3,000 gallons
Coal capacity	5 tons

★ An LMS Diagram Book, apparently dated in the early 1940s, shows the Lochs — by then only three remaining in service — as having 180 lbs of boiler pressure and tractive effort of 17,557 lbs. This must be regarded as very doubtful.

Further Construction

It was a tribute to the design that during the 1914-18 war, when the Highland was in the direst

Fig 103   119 *Loch Insh* at Perth prior to 1903 in original condition. Prince of Wales's feathers and motto on the front splasher. Drummond lined livery.   *(Photo: J.L. Stevenson Collection)*

Fig 104   70 *Loch Ashie*, one of the three 1917 engines. Newly painted in Highland livery and with Cumming style number plates. Westinghouse pump. At Tain, September 1923.   *(Photo: LCGB Ken Nunn Collection)*

straits for motive power, the drawings were brought out again and three more Lochs were supplied by the North British Locomotive Company (Queens Park Works) in 1917 under Order L667. They had actually been ordered in 1915 by the Railway Executive War Committee but delivery was delayed by war conditions. Boilers and fireboxes were in every respect identical to those of the 1896 engines apart from having steel tubes, but Smith, who was then in charge, increased the water capacity of the tender by lengthening the tank at the rear over the space originally occupied by a toolbox in the original design, allowing a further 100 gallons, to 3,100. The Jones louvred chimney and smokebox wings were perpetuated, which was perhaps strange as by 1917 at least one original Loch had acquired a Drummond non-louvred chimney. However the new engines could be distinguished on the left side by the presence of the vacuum ejector exhaust pipe which ran externally along the boiler above the handrail while on the right side they carried Westinghouse pumps of the large type which had been retrieved from Big Bens 60, 61 and 62 respectively (Fig 104).

These three Lochs were numbered 70, 71 and 72. Their dimensions, where differing from those of the earlier engines, were as under (the differences in boiler dimensions quoted being due to variations in the mode of calculation):

Heating surface

Tubes	1,175 sq ft
Firebox	116 sq ft
Total	1,291 sq ft

Weights

Adhesion	32 tons 14 cwts
Engine	50 tons 11 cwts
Tender	37 tons 3½ cwts
Total	87 tons 14½ cwts
Water capacity	3,100 gallons

Understandably the cost of these three engines, namely £4,541 apiece, greatly exceeded the £2,940 for each of their fifteen 1896 sisters.

LMS Renumbering

All 18 members of the class survived to be taken over by the LMS and were renumbered 14379 to 14396, the last three numbers being given to the 1917 engines. Two of them went on to enter British Railways stock in 1948 but neither carried a BR number. HR 125 *Loch Tay* was the last survivor. When withdrawn in April 1950, still as LMS 14385, it had divided its life equally between Highland and LMS/BR ownership.

Names

The lochs which provided the names are of course all in the counties served by the Highland Railway and in seven cases are visible from it. Names of sea lochs, such as Loch Carron, were not used. Loch Ashie, a small and rather featureless sheet of water, was perhaps selected through being the source of Inverness's valuable soft water.

In the early days a hyphen was used for a short time, thus *Loch-Insh* and *Loch-Ericht*. In rendering Loch Laoghal the Gaelic spelling was preferred to the more usual phonetic version 'Loyal', as used on the later Small Ben. Unfortunately this was wrongly spelt as *Loch Laochal* when red livery was applied (probably at Kilmarnock) and the error was perpetuated into the black livery. 14379 *Loch Insh* became nameless, most likely at a visit to St Rollox in November 1942, and it was still thus in the summer of 1945 but the name had been restored by March 1946, presumably by scraping off the black paint at Aviemore shed.

The locations of the eighteen lochs are as follows, all related to the nearest point on the Highland line:

Loch Insh:	At Kincraig, six miles south of Aviemore.
Loch Ness:	The largest loch in the Great Glen, 24 miles long extending from Fort Augustus to Dores, six miles south-west of Inverness.
Loch Ericht:	Another long straight stretch of water, running south west from Dalwhinnie for 15 miles.
Loch Moy:	On the east side of the line at Moy station, 15 miles south of Inverness.
Lochandorb:	Seven miles north of Grantown.
Loch Laggan:	13 miles south-west of Newtonmore and now extended south to Moy dam near Tulloch station on the West Highland line.
Loch Tay:	Six miles south-west of Aberfeldy.
Loch Tummel:	Three miles west of Killiecrankie.
Loch Garry:	About a mile south-west of Dalnaspidal.
Loch Luichart:	Beside the Kyle line at Lochluichart station. The level of the loch has been raised as part of a hydro-electric scheme, necessitating the relocation of the line at a higher level for about a mile and the provision of a new station. The new section was opened in 1954.
Loch Maree:	A particularly beautiful loch in West Ross, 10 miles north-west of Achnasheen.
Loch Fannich:	Three miles north of Achanalt (on the Kyle line). A large and remote loch.
Loch Shin:	Stretching north-west from Lairg, a length of 15 miles.

Loch Naver:	At Altnaharra in Sutherland, 20 miles north of Lairg.
Loch Laoghal: (pron. 'loyal')	In Sutherland, five miles south of Tongue and 25 miles north of Lairg.
Loch Ashie:	On high ground six miles south-west of Inverness.
Loch Garve:	On the north side of the Kyle line, east of Garve station.
Loch Ruthven: (pron. 'riven')	Near Loch Ashie, 11 miles south-west of Inverness.

Livery

The original fifteen engines when built had the then current light green livery and carried the Jones number plate, but soon afterwards 119, 120, 123, 125, 128-131 received the Drummond olive green with lining, although 128 and 131 appear to have been rather lighter than olive, except for the border outside the lining. On these there were variations also in the tender lettering, 120, 125, 126, 128 and 131 having 'THE HIGHLAND RAILWAY' in full, while 'H . R' was borne by the others. Then beginning in 1903 the Lochs were painted in Drummond's olive green, now unlined, with 'H . R' on the tender, an exception being 119 which had 'HIGHLAND RAILWAY' by 1915 and until 1919. Earlier this engine had been distinguished by having the Prince of Wales's feathers and 'ICH DIEN' painted on the splashers below the name shortly after it had been delivered in commemoration of hauling a train in September 1896 conveying the Prince from Perth to Grantown-on-Spey. It carried this embellishment until about 1903. The three 1917 engines were in unlined olive green with Cumming's style of number plate having the number on a red background, and the same type of plate was fitted to 122, 124 and 133 in 1919, 1921 and 1920 respectively. During the 1914-18 war 121, 128 and 131 had their number plates removed and the number was painted high on the cabside in the Smith style, 121 and 131 having the number also on the smokebox door. Later 121 and 128 recovered their plates (Fig 105).

In some instances the olive green was replaced by a much lighter shade of green, unlined, 122 so appearing after overhaul by Hawthorn, Leslie in 1919, at which time its buffer beams also were painted green. This was one of the last engines to receive Highland livery, in March 1923. When Lochs were unlined, so having the wheel outline no longer traced on the cab side, the number plate was sometimes moved from the location of the wheel centre to the centre of the lower cab side. This was done either at repainting or afterwards and at least nine of the 1896 engines were so treated, 119-122, 124, 127, 130, 132 and 133. The three 1917 engines had the plates in the higher position from the start.

With the exception of 14394 (70), all the Lochs were repainted after grouping in LMS lined red with

Fig 105   131 *Loch Shin* at Perth in the Smith livery of 1914-5 with number painted high on cab side. Number plates taken off.   *(Photo: Real Photographs)*

the usual 18 in gold numerals on the tender and the LMS emblem on the cab side. Apart from 70, the last to become red was probably 127 which was still green in July 1926. As on the other named Highland classes, the names were painted in letters with serifs unlike the plain shaded block letters used by the Highland. Only two significant differences appeared in the 1924 style of lining and lettering as applied to the Lochs. 14387 and 14392 had the tender numerals spaced rather wider than normal, while the former had its name *Loch Garry* related to the arc of the splasher rather than to that of the rim of the driving wheel. It was also painted further forward, as it had been latterly in Highland livery. On 14392 the name *Loch Naver* was written in a straight line and did not reappear in the normal curved style until its second repainting black in 1936. The red paint must have been of excellent quality because 14390 retained it until withdrawal in February 1937 while 14380 was red for a few months longer, receiving its coat of black as late as mid-1937. Two early withdrawals, 14387 and 14396, also kept the red livery until the end. All the red-painted engines (ie all except 14394) were fitted with LMS smokebox number plates which were removed when or soon after black livery was applied, this coinciding in a number of cases with the fitting of a Caledonian type of smokebox door. 14379/81/90-2 received the red livery with the Caledonian boiler (see next section), whereas 14382/3/5/6 were red before reboilering.

From 1928 onwards 14379-86/8/9/91-5 received the black livery with red lining and a variety of styles of numerals. In the case of 14383/5/6 the change to black livery corresponded with rebuilding and they blossomed forth with 14 in numerals, as did 14384 (1929), 14391 (1935) and 14392 (1932-3). On 14391 these replaced the 10 in numerals which were the first style on 14379/81/2/8/9/91/3-5. After 1930 12 in shaded numerals were generally used and these appeared — in all cases except 14380 replacing other sizes — on 14379 (1938), 14380 (1937) 14381 (1932), 14382 (1935), 14384 (1935), 14385 (1937), 14386 (1936) and 14392 (1936). The last survivors, 14379/85/92, were latterly unlined and the first two — also, it is believed, 14382 — finished up with the late 1930s style of 10 in shaded numerals.

Detail Alterations and Rebuilding

As already mentioned, the Lochs were built with 8 in diameter Smith piston valves of outside admission type. They were the first class of engine in Scotland to have piston valves but these proved to be unsatisfactory in service with broken rings a frequent occurrence. Drummond reported to the Locomotive Committee in January 1899 that he had altered one engine — believed to be 131 — giving it Richardson's balanced slide valves, and he was given authority to convert a further three at a cost of £120 apiece. Later in the year he was allowed to proceed further with the conversions, aiming to have the whole class fitted with slide valves of this type in time for the following summer's traffic. Much later, in 1921, 126 was given ordinary slide valves.

In common with the other classes concerned, the fitting of steam heating was a long drawn out affair, starting with the equipping of 125 in 4/1910 but still being incomplete in early LMS days when 123 was recorded as not so fitted. Other known dates are: 120 (2/1912), 121 (12/1916), 122 (11/1919), 127 (2/1923), 128 (12/1916), 132 (11/1919) and 133 (7/1917).

One or two chimney changes took place. 119 lost the Jones louvred chimney as early as 1903 when Drummond fitted one of the pattern which he had designed for the Small Bens, a change which rather spoiled its appearance. The same engine underwent a further change in 1919 when a hybrid chimney was provided, having a louvred barrel and a Drummond flared top, while a similar hybrid chimney was fitted to 120 a year or so later (Fig 106). 130 also had changes, receiving a plain chimney with a flared top about 1916 as well as a steel firebox at or about the same time. Previously it had run with an experimental feed water heater between October and November 1913.

Thirteen of the Lochs were sent south to locomotive works for repair during and soon after the First World War, the cost of the work being on average about £2,000 per engine. Those concerned were:

120	Yorkshire Engine Co	1919
122	Hawthorn, Leslie	1919
124	Hawthorn, Leslie	1921
125	Yorkshire Engine Co	1916
126	Yorkshire Engine Co	1916
	Yorkshire Engine Co	1921
127	Yorkshire Engine Co	1917
128	Yorkshire Engine Co	1918
129	Gateshead Works (NER)	1916
	Yorkshire Engine Co	1920
132	Hawthorn, Leslie	1918
133	Hawthorn, Leslie	1921
70	Beardmore	1920
71	Hawthorn, Leslie	1920
72	Hawthorn, Leslie	1921

The most important work was that done by Hawthorn, Leslie on 124 and 133 both of which were given new boilers, although that on the latter was numbered 452 by the LMS consistent with con-struction in 1896! Both engines emerged with a shortened Jones chimney, together with longitudinal pop safety valves replacing the transverse lock-ups (Fig 107). They also received large flattened domes and Cumming style number plates. Among work

Fig 106   120 *Loch Ness* with Drummond flare on the chimney piloting 14767 *Clan Mackinnon* on a Down train
at Aviemore in 1924.   *(Photo: J.L. Stevenson Collection)*

Fig 107   133 *Loch Laochal* (name mis-spelt) as LMS 14393 at Aviemore c1927. Hawthorn, Leslie 1921 boiler
with pop valves, flattened dome and shortened chimney.   *(Photo: W.H. Whitworth)*

done on the other engines overhauled outside was the fitting of new fireboxes to 120, 125, 127, 128, 129 and 132 also probably to 126. Other known dates of firebox renewals are 119 (7/1914), 121 (7/1915), 122 (6/1915), 123 (7/1919) and 130 (6/1916). The three 1917 engines, 70-72, had their fireboxes renewed in 1928, 1926 and 1928 respectively. Those fitted in the years 1915-18 would have been steel.

When the LMS took over in 1923 the Lochs were thus pretty well in their original condition and, apart from 124 and 133, all had their old boilers, classified N.41 by the LMS. The need was recognised to extend the lives of these useful and well-built engines economically and fortunately a Caledonian design of boiler, that fitted to the McIntosh 0-6-0s, LMS 17550-17645, was found to be suitable, its classification being N.51. Accordingly ten of the 1896 engines were so rebuilt. Most of the rebuilding is believed to have been done at Kilmarnock but one at least was dealt with at St Rollox while three, 14381, 14390 and 14391, were almost certainly rebuilt at Lochgorm and at least two of the boilers were built there. The rebuilding was spread over the years 1924 to 1928, the individual dates being shown in the summary of the class (Fig 108).

The dimensions of the new boilers are shown below with those of the original boilers in brackets:

Boiler

Maximum outside diameter	4' 9¼" (4' 7")
Length of barrel	10' 3½" (10' 2")
Pitch	8' 2" (7' 5")
Length of firebox casing	6' 5" (6' 8½")

Heating surface

Tubes (275 of 1¾" diam)	1,332.9 sq ft (1,176)
Firebox	118.8 sq ft (119)
Total	1,451.7 sq ft (1,295)
Grate area	20 sq ft (20.5)

Rebuilding increased the weight of the engines from 49 tons to 49 tons 19 cwts.

It can be deduced from these figures that this rebuilding, like that carried out by the LMS on other Highland classes, was intended to prolong life rather than to improve performance. The appearance of the engines was however completely altered, mainly because the new boiler was pitched 9 in higher and the Caledonian chimney and dome were shorter than the originals. The result gave the engines a more modern appearance and was quite pleasing and well proportioned, although marred by the fact that, except on 14381 and 14390, the dome was higher than the chimney. Gone were the smokebox wings and the tall transverse safety valves, the new boilers having pop valves in line. Pickersgill style one-piece chimneys were fitted to all except 14381 which at first

Fig 108   119 *Loch Insh* as LMS 14379 at Aviemore in 1929. Rebuilt with Caledonian class N 51 boiler but retaining Highland smokebox door.   *(Photo: A.G. Ellis Collection)*

Fig 109   121 *Loch Ericht* as LMS 14381 rebuilt in 1924 as running with a built-up chimney until 1932. Newly
painted in lined black livery with 10in numerals and retaining the smokebox number plate. Aviemore
1929.   *(Photo: A.G. Ellis Collection)*

had a built-up one of McIntosh design (Fig 109),
replaced however by the Pickersgill pattern when a
second new boiler was fitted in 10/1932. The vacuum
ejector exhaust pipe was visible running along the left
side of the boiler above the handrail which itself
showed a variation in that on those engines rebuilt
prior to 1927, 14379/81/2/90/1, it was carried on a
wider arc round the smokebox front, whereas on the
others a narrower arc located it below the level of the
smokebox top (compare Figs 108 and 110). The handrail on 14381 was altered to the narrower arc in
10/1932.

The Highland design of smokebox door was
retained on rebuilding by 14379/81/2/90/1/2, whereas
14383/5/6 were given doors of Caledonian pattern and
14380 received a modified door with shorter hinges.
Later the Caledonian type was fitted to 14379 (1/38),
14381 (10/32), 14382 (1/35), 14391 (5/35) and 14392
(c1932). Fig 108 shows the Highland door with the
longer hinges and securing levers while in Fig 111
14385 has a Caledonian door with its wheel. This
shows also the flatter dome which the engine acquired
with a boiler change in December 1943. Whistles
were another source of variations. 14380/3/5/6/92
carried a Caledonian whistle from rebuilding but
14390 retained its Highland whistle throughout. The
other four rebuilds had Highland whistles at first but
there were subsequent changes. 14379 received a
Caledonian whistle in 1/1938 but had reverted to a

Highland one by 7/1945 while 14381/2/91 were given
Caledonian whistles in 9/1928, 10/1932, 1/1935 and
5/1935 respectively.

The N.51 boilers fitted to the Lochs on rebuilding
appear to have been new but this cannot be confirmed
in every case. Many changes took place later as
engines went through the works and boilers were
moved around. The exact rebuilding date of 14380
has proved difficult to establish. Most authorities
state this to be in the latter half of 1928 but this cannot
be so as the engine was turned out in red livery on
rebuilding. Moreover a statement dated apparently in
1927 shows 14380 as rebuilt but 14392 as unrebuilt.
The latter received its first N.51 boiler in March 1927
and it seems therefore fair to conclude that 14380 was
rebuilt at the beginning of that year.

14383 had a short life as a rebuild, being withdrawn
in October 1934, whereupon its boiler was fitted to
14382 whose boiler then went the rounds of six
McIntosh 3F 0-6-0s. 14381 was favoured by being
given a second new boiler in 10/1932 only, as we shall
see, to perish in the Aviemore accident of March
1940. 14390 had a 1924 Lochgorm-built boiler when
it was withdrawn in 1937 and this also reappeared on
various 3F 0-6-0s. 14391 took a retrograde step when
it lost a 1925 boiler to 17559 in 1935 and received a
much older one dated 1909 off 17551. But 14392
came off even worse in May 1941 when it was given
an ancient Sharp Stewart boiler of 1900 with

Fig 110   132 *Loch Naver* as LMS 14392 at Dingwall in August 1945 with N51 boiler of 1900 having Ramsbottom safety valves. Extended tender body.   *(Photo: J.L. Stevenson Collection)*

Fig 111   125 *Loch Tay* as LMS 14385 at Forres in July 1945. Caledonian smokebox door and large flattened dome.   *(Photo: J.L. Stevenson)*

Ramsbottom safety valves which latterly lost their casing (Fig 110). The boiler had previously been on 17570.

Most of the other eight Lochs which were not rebuilt underwent some changes under the LMS. These are summarised as under:

14384 New firebox and Caledonian smokebox door 1929. Smokebox wings removed probably at the same time but certainly by 8/1931. New smokebox door and Caledonian McIntosh chimney 5/1935 (Fig 112).

14388 Caledonian McIntosh chimney on new smokebox (minus wings) also new firebox with transverse pop safety valves 1929 (Fig 113).

14389 Transverse pop safety valves 1929.

14394 New firebox and transverse pop safety valves 1928.

14395 New firebox and transverse pop safety valves 1926. Unlouvred chimney with flared top 1930 (Fig 114).

14396 New firebox and transverse pop safety valves 1928 also Caledonian smokebox door. Smokebox wings removed.

Two changes had been made to engines prior to being rebuilt. 14383 received transverse pop safety valves probably when repainted red and certainly before rebuilding in 1928, while 14386, as HR 126, had acquired an external vacuum ejector exhaust pipe by 1917, as on the engines delivered in that year, and retained this until it was rebuilt.

The rebuilding achieved its aim of extending the life of the engines by up to twenty years. By the mid-1920s the 1896 boilers were more or less worn out and the engines concerned would otherwise have had a very limited life.

Tenders

As already stated, the 1896 tender body stopped short at the rear end in order to accommodate a tool box, a common feature of the time (Fig 103). But the bodies of the 1917 build extended over the full length of the frames so enabling water capacity to be increased by 100 gallons and most of the older tenders were later lengthened to make them similar, for example those behind, 14381 (121), 14382 (122), 14385 (125), 14388 (128), 14389 (129), 14390 (130), 14392 (132) and 14393 (133) (Fig 107). In other cases the toolboxes were taken off without extension of the tank (Fig 115). But there were exchanges of tenders between engines and 14381 reverted to having the original type of tender when painted red in 1924.

In 1927 the LMS allocated numbers 1779 to 1796 to the Loch tenders in the same sequence as the engine numbers.

Three of the Loch tenders found a new use after withdrawal from service. According to a list dated 9th October 1942 emanating from Derby, 1786 was then in use as a water-softening tender at Coalville shed while 1782 and 1791 were being converted for a similar purpose at Nottingham. These had been behind 14386, 14382 and 14391 respectively but the last-named must have required replating as the engine, presumably with its tender, was used for target practice at Shoeburyness in 1941-2, as described later.

Allocation and Work

The Lochs were at once put to work the principal passenger trains between Inverness and Perth. They were however partially displaced from these duties soon after the Castles arrived, from 1900 onwards. But the Lochs were still to be seen on the South line for nearly another half-century although usually as pilots. Indeed this was among their last duties, and as late as March 1946 a sparkling run north from Perth behind a brand new Class 5 4924 was splendidly enhanced at Aviemore by the spectacle of a shining *Loch Insh*, 50 years senior to the Class 5, backing down to assist to the Slochd.

Until the mid-1930s three Lochs were normally stationed at the south end, at Perth or Blair Atholl, working local passenger and goods between these points and on occasional banking duty. In 1919 these were 122, 123 and 127, the last named finishing its days at Perth as LMS 14387. They also sometimes were on the Aberfeldy branch. By the 1930s 14382/4/92 were at Blair Atholl, 14392 going to Inverness in mid-1936, 14384 being withdrawn in the late summer of 1938 and 14382, old 122, finally landing at Inverness in May 1939. The arrival of five LMS 2-6-2Ts at Perth and Blair Atholl had rendered the Lochs redundant there although in the event these modern engines stayed only for a year or two and were replaced by Caledonian 4-4-0s which did most of the banking almost until the end of steam, providing scant shelter for the crews on the long descent.

Aviemore became another stronghold of the class, with one sometimes at Kingussie until its closure in the 1920s. 119, 120, 126, 128 and 132 were at Aviemore in 1919, and four or five remained there until about 1934, usually 14379/81/5/6/93, Castles eventually displacing all except 14379 and 14381. The Lochs were mainly employed on piloting to Slochd, Dalnaspidal and Dava as well as on ballast and livestock workings, but 14381 *Loch Ericht*, the pick of the bunch, was a common sight in the late 1920s on the Inverness (via Carr Bridge) portion of the midday express from Perth returning on the 5.20 pm local to Newtonmore. It may well have been the last Loch to have worked a train over the southern end of the line, heading a northbound goods from Perth to Aviemore on 31st August 1939. Soon afterwards the engine was

Fig 112   124 *Loch Laggan* as LMS 14384 with 1921 Hawthorn boiler. As fitted in 1935 with Caledonian pattern chimney and new smokebox without wings.   *(Photo: J.F. McEwan Collection)*

Fig 113   128 *Loch Luichart* at Aviemore in May 1930 as LMS 14388. Caledonian chimney on original boiler with transverse pop safety valves on new firebox. No wings on smokebox.   *(Photo: H.C. Casserley)*

Fig 114

71 *Loch Garve* as LMS 14395 at Tain in September 1933, as fitted with transverse pop valves in 1926 and Drummond pattern chimney in 1930.

(Photo: J.R.H. Cormack)

to meet a tragic end on the evening of 5th March 1940 while piloting Class 5 5015 on a northbound goods. Some twenty wagons and a Highland brake van broke away from the preceding train just short of Slochd crossing, careered downhill and hit the oncoming train about two miles north of Aviemore. The Loch's crew were killed and great destruction was caused. A small monument was later erected to the Aviemore men beside the scene of the accident, built mainly from *Loch Ericht's* brick arch.

Earlier, in 1925 when newly rebuilt, 14381 worked from Helmsdale shed on a daily turn to Inverness and back. The Inverness-Tain stopping trains were another sphere of Loch activity, 14390 in its well polished red livery being regularly at Tain shed for the last five years of its life. 14394 also appeared on these workings and had an unhappy experience on 21st August 1930 when it was marooned on a defective Tain turntable for some six hours until it was rescued by fitters from Inverness. This engine also worked fairly often on the Kyle line in the late 1920s, but like the other two 1917 engines, 14395/6, never seems to have been recorded working south, all three being stationed throughout at Inverness or one of its sub sheds. One of the few noteworthy appearances of the trio was that of 14395 heading the 'Further North Express' from Inverness to Wick in July 1931, a Friday afternoon summer train which was replaced by a thrice-weekly summer service in 1933 named 'The John o' Groat'.

Forres shed also provided local turns for the Lochs in their latter days when 14380 and 14391 took over from Straths, these including an occasional trip over the Dava line to Aviemore, and indeed Forres was the final home of the last of the class, 14385 which could be seen on such workings as the 8.15 pm Inverness to Keith.

The Lochs were to be found also on those branches where tender engines were permitted. For example

130 was at Thurso in 1916 and 14395 was there in 1927. 14389 and 14395 each had a spell at Fort George in 1930 as had 14391 in 1937. The presence of 14387 at Aberfeldy has already been mentioned and 14382 was at work there in 1931, while 14386 was the Fortrose branch engine in June 1936.

They were popular engines with their crews and well known to the travelling public. Like all the Highland engines they were good steamers and a sound straightforward design, while their 6 ft 3½ in driving wheels made them quite swift runners. Over their life span of 54 years the Lochs had a notable record of good service.

Smith in 1915 produced a rather ungainly outline design for what he termed a 'Superheated Loch' to work the North line mail trains, a task for which the Big Bens were proving inadequate. On the direction of the Locomotive Committee three firms were to be asked to prepare drawings for the engines which would have had 6 ft 0 in driving wheels and 20 in by 26 in cylinders. Nothing resulted directly and no doubt that particular approach was dropped with his hasty departure from Inverness in September of that year. However in the following month the Board asked that Hawthorn, Leslie should provide a design for two engines for the work in question, these eventually materialising as *Snaigow* and *Durn*, which will be described in Book 2. The design of the new engines was far removed from that of the Lochs.

Withdrawals

These started in 1930 with the departure of 14387 from Perth and of 14388 from Aviemore but it was another twenty years before the class became extinct, although the first withdrawal of a rebuilt engine, 14383, took place as early as 1934. The last unrebuilt Loch 14384, departed from Blair Atholl shed in the late summer of 1938. Three survived the Second World War during which they rendered yeoman

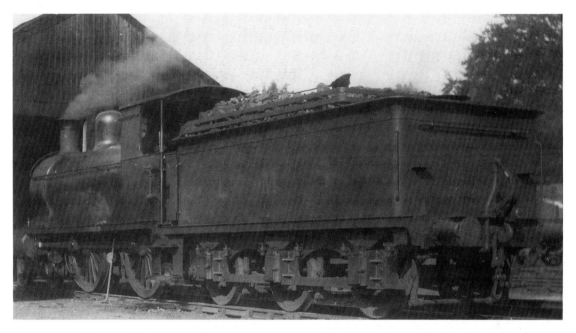

Fig 115   Original length tender tank showing space formerly occupied by tool box. LMS 14384 ex-HR 124 *Loch Laggan* at Blair Atholl in September 1937.   *(Photo: J.L. Stevenson)*

service in assisting heavy traffic, 14379 at Aviemore from where it made innumerable runs up to the Slochd, 14385 at Forres where, apart from local workings, it assisted trains to Dava, and 14392 which spent most of these days at Dingwall shed, mainly banking trains of naval supplies as they struggled up to Ravens Rock on their way to Kyle of Lochalsh but also working trips to Invergordon Harbour.

Two survived to come into British Railways stock in 1948, although not renumbered. 14379 had only three months to go and was withdrawn in March 1948 from Aviemore shed where it had spent at least thirty years, but 14385 plodded on at Forres until April 1950.

Wartime operations led to strange ends for two of the class. 14382 was sent after withdrawal to the Cairnryan Military Railway near Stranraer and was used to supply steam for a year or so, while 14391 went even further afield ending up as a target for bombing practice at Shoeburyness in 1941-2. The engine was cut up at Bow at the end of 1942 but the tender survived as earlier described.

Total mileages of the original fifteen Lochs are unknown, but they are available for the 1917 engines, namely:

14394	495,377
14395	496,527
14396	407,961

These figures represent average annual mileages of around 25,000.

Sadly ill-health had overtaken David Jones before the Lochs came out. He had been granted three months leave of absence in 1895, rather grudgingly extended for a further two by the Board. He did return to work in 1896 but tendered his resignation in September of that year. His efforts were handsomely and deservedly praised by the directors who were very conscious of the splendid service which he had rendered to the Company over 41 years, 27 of them as Locomotive Superintendent. They gave him a not ungenerous retiring allowance of £239 per annum which with his superannuation provided him with a salary of £500 until his death in London on 2nd November 1906.

Summary of Class

HR No	LMS No	Name	Maker	Works No	Built	Rebuilt with N51 boiler	Withdrawn
119	14379	Loch Insh (Note 1)	Dübs & Co	3392	7/1896	11/1925	3/1948
120	14380	Loch Ness	,,	3393	,,	-/1927 (Note 2)	11/1941
121	14381	Loch Ericht	,,	3394	8/1896	4/1924	3/1940
122	14382	Loch Moy	,,	3395	,,	6/1926	12/1940
123	14383	Loch an Dorb (Note 3)	,,	3396	,,	10/1928	9/1934
124	14384	Loch Laggan	,,	3397	,,	—	8/1938
125	14385	Loch Tay	,,	3398	,,	9/1928	4/1950
126	14386	Loch Tummel	,,	3399	,,	6/1928	8/1938
127	14387	Loch Garry	,,	3400	,,	—	12/1930
128	14388	Loch Luichart	,,	3401	,,	—	12/1930
129	14389	Loch Maree	,,	3402	9/1896	—	2/1931
130	14390	Loch Fannich	,,	3403	,,	8/1925	1/1937
131	14391	Loch Shin	,,	3404	,,	9/1924	7/1941
132	14392	Loch Naver	,,	3405	,,	3/1927	4/1947
133	14393	Loch Laoghal (Note 4)	,,	3406	,,	—	11/1934
70	14394	Loch Ashie	North British Locomotive Co (Q.P.)	21456	3/1917	—	9/1936
71	14395	Loch Garve	,,	21457	,,	—	11/1935
72	14396	Loch Ruthven	,,	21458	,,	—	9/1934

Note 1. No 14379 ran without the name c1942-45.
Note 2. There is some doubt as to the exact rebuilding date of this engine. See text.
Note 3. Early photographs show the name rendered as *Loch andorb*. This was changed to *Loch an Dorb* certainly by 1920.
Note 4. *Loch Laoghal* was wrongly painted as *Loch Laochal* from about 1925.

3. APPENDICES

3.1 Loading of Trains

The following information is taken from the 1901 Highland Railway Appendix to the Working Timetable. It is intended to include similar details for 1922 in Book 2.

The undernoted points are relevant:

(i) The Up direction on the various sections of route is:

Inverness to Perth
Inverness to Aviemore via Forres
Wick to Inverness
Keith to Forres
Kyle of Lochalsh to Dingwall

(ii) Certain of the engines shown in the classifications had in fact been laid aside by 1901.

(iii) It will be seen that Lochgorm Tank 49 and Jones Tank 50 are shown as "Tank Branch Engines", whereas the others of these classes are designated "Shunting Engines". At this time 49 was working the Fort George branch while 50 was at Perth and, being fitted with larger tanks, was available to work the Aberfeldy branch.

1. Classification of Engines

(a) Passenger Engines

Special Class 140-145 (Castles)

First Class   1-17 (Small Bens)
119-133 (Lochs)

Second Class 31, 60-69, 71-75, 84 (Dukes)
76-83 (Clyde Bogies)
89-100 (Straths)

Third Class   28, 35, 46, 47, 55 (Glenbarrys)
29, 30 (Raigmore II)

(b) Goods Engines

Special Class 103-117 (Big Goods)

First Class   134-139 (Barney 0-6-0)

Second Class 18-27 (Small Goods)
32, 33, 34, 48, 70, 85-88
(Skye Bogies)
36-45 (Medium Goods)

Tank Branch 49 (Lochgorm Tank)
Engines   50 (Jones 4-4-0 Tank)
51, 52, 54, 101, 102
(Yankee Tanks)
53 (Strathpeffer Tank)
118 (Special Tank)

Shunting   56, 57 (Lochgorm Tanks)
Engines   58, 59 (Jones 4-4-0 Tanks)

Passenger Engines, 119-133 and 140-145 (Lochs and Castles) also Special Engines 103-117 are confined to the working of traffic between Inverness and Perth via Forres or Carr Bridge.

2. Loads of Passenger Trains

The loads are shown as PAIRS OF WHEELS and are calculated on the average composition of passenger trains:-

Section of route	Special Class		First Class		Second Class	
	Up	Down	Up	Down	Up	Down
Inverness and Aviemore (direct)	33	36	24	30	21	24
Aviemore and Kingussie	50	50	42	42	36	36
Kingussie and Blair Atholl	40	33	30	27	24	21
Blair Atholl and Perth	50	46	40	42	40	38
Inverness and Forres	50	50	46	46	42	42
Forres and Grantown	33	40	24	34	21	27
Grantown and Aviemore	50	50	44	44	38	38
Wick and Golspie			30	30	24	24
Golspie and Invershin			30	30	27	27
Invershin and Dingwall			40	40	36	36
Dingwall and Inverness			46	46	42	42

	First Class		Second Class		Third Class	
	Up	Down	Up	Down	Up	Down
Keith and Forres	33	33	27	27	24	24
Kyle of Lochalsh and Dingwall	30	30	27	27	21	21

3. Loads of Goods Trains

The loads are expressed in terms of loaded goods wagons and the following equivalents apply:

Two 10-ton wagons fully loaded	= Three loaded goods wagons
Three 8-ton wagons fully loaded	= Four loaded goods wagons
Four 7-ton wagons fully loaded	= Five loaded goods wagons
Three wagons loaded with cattle or dead meat	= Four loaded goods wagons
Loaded 6-wheel wagon or oil tank	= Two loaded goods wagons
Brake Van	= One loaded goods wagon
Three empty wagons	= Two loaded goods wagons

	Special Class		First Class		Second Class	
Section of Route	Up	Down	Up	Down	Up	Down
Inverness and Aviemore	24	28	24	28	18	22
Aviemore and Newtonmore	50	50	50	50	42	42
Newtonmore and Dalnaspidal	35	40	35	40	27	32
Dalnaspidal and Blair Atholl	40	28	40	28	35	20
Blair Atholl and Dunkeld	50	40	50	40	42	30
Dunkeld and Perth	40	40	40	40	30	30
Inverness and Forres	50	50	50	50	42	42
Forres and Grantown	28	40	28	40	20	30
Grantown and Aviemore	50	50	50	50	42	42

	First Class Goods		Second Class Goods		Third Class Passenger	
	Up	Down	Up	Down	Up	Down
Keith and Mulben	50	50	40	40	40	40
Mulben and Orton	50	30	40	18	40	16
Orton and Elgin	50	40	40	28	40	26
Elgin and Alves	46	50	34	40	30	40
Alves and Forres	50	50	40	34	40	30

	Down	Up	Down	Up	Down	Up
Inverness and Dingwall	50	50	40	40	36	36
Dingwall and Invershin	48	46	35	35	33	33
Invershin and Rogart	30	32	18	20	16	16
Rogart and Golspie	46	46	35	35	33	33
Golspie and Brora	28	32	18	20	16	16
Brora and Helmsdale	46	46	30	30	28	28
Helmsdale and Georgemas	28	28	20	20	18	18
Georgemas and Wick	48	46	35	35	33	33
Dingwall and Kyle of Lochalsh	25	25	19	19	—	—

When Passenger Engines of first or second class work goods trains the load is to be as for a Goods Engine of second class.

3.2 Turntables

These were provided at the normal locations, namely at termini (including those of some of the longer branches), at main junctions and at the terminating points of shorter distance workings. Surprisingly turntables were never provided at Dalnaspidal or Slochd where they would have been valuable to turn assisting engines.

The following is a list of turntables and their lengths at four stages covering the years 1881 until the end of the LMS. Following this is a list of the total wheelbase of the principal classes.

Location	Years			
	1881	1901	1920	1948
Wick	44′ 10″	46′ 3″	55′ 0″	55′ 0″
Thurso	44′ 3″	44′ 9″	51′ 11″	52′ 0″
Lybster	—	—	46′ 3″	—
Georgemas	44′ 0″	46′ 3″	46′ 3″	48′ 6″
Helmsdale	45′ 0″	50′ 4″	55′ 0″	55′ 0″
Golspie	18′ 0″	18′ 0″	21′ 0″	21′ 0″
Lairg	—	50′ 0″	50′ 0″	50′ 0″
Tain	17′ 5″	50′ 0″	50′ 0″	60′ 0″
Dingwall	42′ 0″	43′ 6″	43′ 6″	—
Strome Ferry	42′ 0″	43′ 7″	—	—
Kyle of Lochalsh	—	50′ 0″	50′ 0″	54′ 0″
Muir of Ord	—	50′ 0″	50′ 0″	55′ 0″
Fortrose	—	50′ 0″	50′ 0″	50′ 0″
Inverness	45′ 0″	55′ 2″	63′ 4″	63′ 4″
Forres	44′ 8″	50′ 3″	48′ 6″	50′ 0″
Keith	39′ 9″	50′ 4″	50′ 4″	55′ 0″
Portessie	—	45′ 0″	45′ 0″	—
Grantown	44′ 10″	46′ 7″	48′ 0″	—
Daviot	—	55′ 0″	—	—
	(See Note)			
Aviemore	—	55′ 0″	55′ 0″	55′ 0″
Kingussie	—	50′ 0″	50′ 0″	—
Newtonmore	40′ 0″	46′ 6″	—	—
Dalwhinnie	18′ 0″	18′ 6″	—	—
Blair Atholl	42′ 0″	46′ 8″	55′ 3″	55′ 3″
Ballinluig	—	26′ 0″	—	—
Aberfeldy	—	26′ 0″	—	—
Dunkeld	—	17′ 3″	—	—
Perth	45′ 0″	53′ 7″	54′ 9″	54′ 0″

Note: The turntable at Daviot was transferred to Wick in 1902.

Wheelbase of Principal Highland Classes

2-4-0	Small Goods	35′ 3″
	Medium Goods	35′ 6″
	Glenbarry	35′ 9″
	Raigmore II	34′ 3″
4-4-0	Duke	41′ 6″
	Skye Bogie	42′ 9″
	Clyde Bogie	44′ 0″
	Strath	44′ 0″
	Loch	44′ 9″
	Small Ben	44′ 1½″ (47′ 7½″ with 8-wheel tender)
	Big Ben	43′ 11½″ (47′ 6″ with 8-wheel tender)
	Snaigow	46′ 5½″
0-6-0	Barney	38′ 2½″
4-6-0	Big Goods	48′ 5½″
	Castle I and II	52′ 5½″ (8-wheel tender)
	Castle III	50′ 10″ (6-wheel tender)
	River	49′ 4½″
	Superheated Goods	46′ 6″
	Clan	50′ 0″
0-6-4T	Banking Tank	27′ 3″
0-4-4T	Passenger Tank	18′ 3″
4-4-0T	Yankee Tank	20′ 3″

3.3 Engine Water

The Highland Railway was generous in providing water supplies en route. From Inverness to Wick, 161 miles, water could be obtained at 15 intermediate points, although at three of these in a northbound direction only, while from Inverness to Perth, 118 miles, there were 13 intermediate supplies. The most surprising feature was that over the 35 miles of the Inverness to Aviemore Direct line water was obtainable at each of the five intermediate stations as well as at Aviemore. The full list of watering points is as under:

All motive power depots and principal yards also at the following stations:-

Georgemas	Culloden Moor
Aultnabreac	Daviot (Up only)
Forsinard	Moy*
Kildonan (Down only)	Tomatin
Helmsdale	Carr Bridge
Golspie (Down only)	Aviemore†
The Mound	Kingussie
Rogart	Dalwhinnie
Lairg	Dalnaspidal

Bonar Bridge	Blair Atholl†
Tain	Pitlochry (Down only)
Invergordon	Ballinluig
Dingwall	Dunkeld
Muir of Ord	Nairn
Beauly (Down only)*	Forres
Garve	Elgin
Achnasheen	Keith
Achnashellach (Up only)	Dunphail
Strathcarron (Down only)*	Dava
Strome Ferry Goods	Grantown
Fortrose	
Munlochy	
Strathpeffer	
Portessie	
Fochabers	
Lybster	

*Removed by 1916
† At Aviemore and at Blair Atholl (Down side only) twin columns were provided to enable engines of double-headed trains to be watered simultaneously.

3.4 H.R. Locomotive Class Letters
1901 and later

Drummond introduced a system of letter classification for the various classes in 1901. New classes introduced during his superintendency were added to it, but the system was apparently discontinued after Drummond left Inverness. Letters A to H were allocated to passenger tender engines, I to N to goods tender engines, and from O to U were tank engines. The four classes which came out subsequently under Drummond were given letters U to X. There were two occupants of classification U, the first of these, *Needlefield*, having been sold in 1904.

The basis of the system was clearly power, with the larger engines leading the groupings, but this was upset by the addition of later builds. In these respects it resembled the North British system.

There is little indication of what purpose the letters served. They were not the basis of the train loading tables nor were they used by the staff in referring to the engines, but they may have been used for workshop and/or accountancy records.

Class Letter	Class Name	Class Letter	Class Name
A	Castle	N	Small Goods
B	Loch	O	Jones Tank
C	Small Ben	P	Yankee Tank
D	Strath	R	Lochgorm Tank
E	Clyde Bogie	S	Strathpeffer Tank
F	Duke	T	Special Tank
G	Glenbarry	U	Needlefield Tank
H	Raigmore II	U (later)	Big Ben
I	Big Goods	V	Shunting Tank
K	Barney	W	Passenger Tank
L	Skye Bogie	X	Banking Tank
M	Medium Goods		

3.5 Acknowledgement of Photographs

Most sincere thanks are due to the photographers whose work has illuminated so many obscure points relating to the construction, rebuilding and liveries of Highland engines. Grateful acknowledgement is made especially to the undernoted who provided the photographs reproduced in this book. In doing this difficulties in some cases arise with the acquisition and disposal of collections but, as far as possible, the original photographer is quoted, failing which the source of the photograph when acquired in the first place by the authors of this book.

W.A. Camwell Fig 98.

H.C. Casserley Fig 113.

J.R.H. Cormack Fig 114.

A.W. Croughton Figs 28, 38, 71, 72, 82 and 102.

A.G. Ellis Collection Frontispiece, Figs 10, 27, 31, 37, 42, 43, 48, 50, 59, 65, 90, 97, 108 and 109.

Major S. Forbes Figs 41 and 57.

LCGB Ken Nunn Collection Figs 26, 49, 70, 84 and 104.

Locomotive and General Railway Photographs Figs 17, 74, 80 and 88.

D.C. McBean Fig 79.

James F. McEwan Collection Figs 14, 18, 19, 21, 32, 44, 69, 85, 91, 101 and 112.

B.D. Matthews Collection Figs 56, 75 and 86.

F. Moore (Locomotive Publishing Company) Figs 22, 24, 29, 33, 36, 47, 55, 60, 62 and 89.

Real Photographs Figs 4, 13, 16, 34, 35, 46, 54, 61, 68, 78, 92 and 105.

Dr. R. Struan Robertson Collection Fig 5.

John B. Russell Fig 9

Henry L. Salmon Fig 94.

E.E. Smith Fig 2.

W.O. Steel per R.J. Essery Figs 8, 23, 25, 30, 39.

Hamish Stevenson Fig 51.

J.L. Stevenson Collection Figs 1, 3, 7, 15, 40, 45, 52, 53, 63, 66, 67, 73, 77, 83, 99, 100, 103, 106, 110, 111 and 115.

Wallace, Tain Figs 11 and 12.

W.H. Whitworth Figs 58, 64, 76, 81, 87, 93, 95, 96 and 107.

The colour plate of the Highland Railway crest is taken from a shield kindly lent by Dr. R. Struan Robertson.

The Railway Correspondence and Travel Society was founded in 1928. Its objects are to help members in every way in the study of their hobby. A monthly journal, *The Railway Observer,* is sent to each member. In addition, there are indoor meetings at many centres throughout the country, railtours and numerous visits to centres of railway interest.

Full details of the Society and how to become a member will gladly be supplied by G. Hooper, 160 Hillend Crescent, Clarkston, Renfrewshire G76 7XY.

LOCOMOTIVES OF THE LMSR

The Society has undertaken to publish a complete history of all locomotives owned by the LMSR and their work. Details of origin, dimensions, construction, rebuilding and withdrawal dates of each engine, detail variations, classification, engine diagrams, allocations and work will all be described with illustrations.

Correspondence on this book or the LMS series should be addressed to the Hon Editor of the series, Mr W. Greenwood, 7 Bracken Hill, Osbaldwick, York YO1 3QE. Additional information will be particularly welcome.

Correspondence on, ideas for, and volunteers of help on publications are keenly sought by the Hon Chairman — Publications, Mr A.R. Wood, 21 Winthorpe Road, Lincoln, LN6 3PG.

Further copies of our books may be obtained from the Hon Assistant Publications Officer, Mr N.J. Claydon, 'Hazelhurst'', Tiverton Road, Bampton, Devon, EX16 9LJ.